PROPAGATION OF PLANTS

Propagation of PLANTS

V.K. SHARMA

INDUS
PUBLISHING COMPANY

INDUS PUBLISHING COMPANY
FS-5, Tagore Garden, New Delhi-110027
Tel.: 25151333, 25935289
mail@indusbooks.com
www.indusbooks.com

ISBN 81-7387-172-8

Published by M.L. Gidwani, Indus Publishing Company
FS-5, Tagore Garden, New Delhi 110 027, and printed at
B.B.N. Printers, Najafgarh Road Indl. Area, New Delhi

Preface

It is a common saying that as you sow so shall you mow. Nursery growers are producing the plants of normal quality in bulk for sale in the market to gain economic benefit but they do not bother for the quality. The growers are getting them planted in their fields as such with the result that there are no quality plants in the field and farmers are getting low yields of inferior quality. They get the plant material of the choice of the nursery grower and then spend lot of money on the cultivation and management of plants in the field, the average yield or the performance of plant is rather poor with net result that they get less income from the crop.

Nursery production is an art which can be learnt with experience and some knowledge about the physiological and other activities of the plant. Every grower cannot become a nursery grower as this art needs lot of money, expertise, skill and patience. In order to raise quality plants, grower should have a background of the material and the aim of production of nursery.

Production of nursery of annual plants may not be problem as they are generally raised from the seed, which can be had from the local market or from a reliable source. For perennial plants like the fruit trees, avenue trees, landscaping trees and other plants of economic importance, quality plants have to be raised that need quality mother plants or the material from a reliable source. Thus, a nursery grower has a responsibility to produce plants that are high yielding and have good quality. For the survival of business, he has to put in hard labour and his expertise.

Right from the collection of seed or the material needed for propagation of plant to its uprooting, through management and various methods of plant multiplication for almost all the common crops have been described in details in different chapters in this book. List of equipments and accessories required for an average nursery has also been given in a separate chapter. In the present book efforts have been made to incorporate the available technical know-how in a very simple way so that a common nursery grower may understand and follow the practices. Along with this, I have tried to include my own experience in this field for the benefit of the growers with the hope that the nursery growers will make use of this information for their benefit.

Shimla V.K. SHARMA

Contents

Part One

General

1

Introduction

Generally fruit growers, vegetable growers, floriculturists, foresters and other plant growers are largely dependent upon the nursery plants available in the local market or nearby market place where these plants are raised without much care about their quality and purity. The main aim of a nursery grower is to earn money and as such the raised plant material is mostly of average quality. On the other hand, common grower is also not very much conscious about the quality. Both of them produce in bulk, former the plants while the latter raises the produce and both of them do not bother till there is a slump in their income.

Now some of the growers and producers have gained awareness and have become conscious about the quality of plants and the produce, which has opened the field of nursery management for profit and quality. This avocation will bring more money and fame to the nursery grower. With the introduction of new species and varieties of higher yielding capabilities with better quality fruits, seeds, vegetables or any other part of the plant, which can be sold, growers have become aware and they need plants of paramount quality.

Nursery management, which includes the raising and sale of nursery plants of different kinds, is an art and a skill, which cannot be acquired by everyone. It needs experience, patience, foresightedness and technical know-how about this art. Nursery growers have to devote much of their time, labour, money and energy for the successful implementation of their plans at low cost to produce plants of high quality in bulk and at reasonably cheaper rates in comparison to other growers.

Nursery growers have to manage the sale or disposal of their plant material at the earliest possible. Retaining the unsold raised nursery plants, after the normal season of their planting is over, becomes unmanageable and these have to be sold either next year or are to be destroyed which makes the enterprise uneconomical.

An efficient nursery grower must be able to plan out and dispose off the material meant for sale at a reasonable rate before others are planning to sell. For this, he has to be vigilant and technically sound.

2

Multiplication of Plants

Multiplication of plants is a complex process by which a single plant may give rise to one or many plants which may be like the parent plant or different from that. It depends upon the nature of the species and skill of the grower to have many plants out of the parent material.

It is a natural phenomenon of the plant kingdom and other living beings to produce the progeny of the same characters, which has been designed by the nature for the continuation of the species. It is the man, who has taken the advantage of this natural liberty to get more number of plants and to make every seed or other means of propagation a success.

Multiplication of plants is done through their seeds or other parts, which are able to give rise to another plant. Seed when sown in the soil, on germination gives rise to a plant that again produces seeds. Other plant parts in use for multiplication are tubers, stems, bulbs, leaves and roots. On getting suitable environmental and soil conditions, these parts swell, send their roots downward and the stem portion upward towards the sunlight. These are known as radicle and plumule, respectively. In this way, we may classify this as Reproductive or Vegetative propagation, which is also known as Sexual and Asexual propagation, respectively.

Sexual Reproduction

This method of reproduction is possible in plants, which produce flowers. Flowers have male and female parts and they may be borne on a single plant or on different plants like the papaya. Even female and male flowers may be on the same stem in different plants. Plant may be unisexual (single sex), i.e., male or female, or hermaphrodite (bisexual), i.e. both the sexes occur on the same plant or in the same flower.

When male and female parts of the flower, i.e. pollen and stigma, etc. are mature, there is pollination, which is followed by their union/fusion known as fertilization. Successful pollination and fertilization results in the formation of an ovule, which later matures into a seed. There may be a single seed as in the case of mango, peach, plum, cherry, coconut, avocado, almond, etc., or many as in apple, custard apple, guava, pear, pea, cucumber, salvia, etc. These seeds when placed under suitable conditions for their germination, give rise to a new plant. A single seed may give rise to a single plant or many plants, depending upon the species, but generally, a single seed gives rise to a single plant. Other plants multiplied by seeds are cereals, pulse crops, grain crops, many vegetable and ornamental plants, grasses, etc.

The details about the seed, its quality, germination and other information are discussed under appropriate headings.

Asexual Propagation

In this case, flowers are not involved at all and it is only the other parts, commonly known as vegetative parts of the plant like leaves, stem or root cuttings and their modifications which are used for the purpose of their multiplication. It is the ability of a particular part to give rise to an identical plant when placed under suitable conditions of their development and multiplication. Every active part of the plant, i.e. the growing apex can be used for multiplication and this is the technique of raising plants under tissue culture. By genetic manipulations, some changes can be made in the plant characters while they are being multiplied under tissue culture technique.

Common parts used are stem cuttings: hard, semi-hard or soft-wood cuttings of apple, pear, cherry, quince; root cuttings of apple; leaves of ruscus plant; stem tubers of potato; rhizomes of banana, ginger; bulbs of onion and leek; suckers of mint; crowns of pineapple; runners of strawberry; corms of gladiolus, etc. Other plants propagated by vegetative parts are raspberry, Globe artichoke, carnation, chrysanthemum, geranium, poinsettia, iris, peony, phlox, turmeric, coconut, etc.

These parts when mature, on placing under congenial conditions for their multiplication, give rise to new plants. All these parts do have eyes on them, which are technically the buds, i.e. vegetative buds. They develop, swell and burst open; the dormant leaves embedded in them come to the open and they start straightening and increasing in size. New leaves start the manufacture of food for themselves and later the same is stored for future use. On the other hand, near the bud, from the node, the radicle/roots develop which go downwards into the soil. As a result of both these activities, a new plant comes into being. Depending upon the number of buds and nodes on a particular part of the plant kept for development, the number of plants can be had may be estimated. The success of the technique of separating each plantlet into a separate plant of commercial value is the ability of the grower. The young plants so raised are known as saplings. These saplings are usually identical to their parents in almost all characters.

This method is ideally suited and generally used for propagation of horticultural plants of commercial value which include apple, mango, litchi, gladiolus, iris, rose, potato, ginger, arum, mint, strawberry, geranium, lily, etc. In this method the maintenance of plant characters is much easier and the characters are retained for a long time. Further, more number of plants can be multiplied in a shorter time.

There is another category of plants that can be multiplied both by seeds and vegetative parts. These include apple, peach, pecan, citrus, tung, Dogwood, flowering peach, flowering cherry, crab apple, juniper, potato, etc. Though they can be propagated by seeds and vegetative means they are preferred to be multiplied by vegetative means.

General characters of plants raised by asexual propagation

1. Small in size.
2. Bearing starts at early age.

3. Identical to their parents in all characters.
4. Comparatively of less age.
5. Uniform growth pattern.
6. Uniform in size.
7. Easy for cultural operations.
8. Easy to harvest.
9. Uniformity and regularity in ripening.
10. Uniform quality of the produce.
11. Less tolerant to insects, pests and diseases.
12. Only method available for multiplication since they may not produce flowers under natural conditions of their growth or the seeds may be rudimentary.
13. Less hardy to weather conditions.
14. Easy to manage.
15. Regulation of cropping is possible.

In order to improve the quality of plants, they may be budded or grafted with some other suitable variety of known characteristics. It is also practiced where the seeds are not available and the seedlings are raised by some other means. In some cases, where the scion does not root but provides a good canopy, is grafted or budded on the seedling stock. In such cases, these methods are useful. They are discussed in detail elsewhere.

3

Types of Nurseries

It is a place or piece of land where plants are raised either from the seed or other parts of the plant, which are easy to propagate. Here, all the operations, right from soil preparation to packing of plants are done and as such its success depends upon able administration, good management, practical experience in this field and good knowledge of the enterprise.

Why to Raise Nursery Plants?

In general, plants reproduce to maintain their identity or the species, which is the law of nature, but nursery growers are propagating or multiplying the plant material either for their own use or for selling to other people for earning money. Other uses may be:

1. For production of food material like fruits, vegetables, cereals. etc.
2. For fibres like jute, flax, cotton, etc.
3. For fuel and timber.
4. For fodder for animals.
5. For medicines and drugs.
6. For beautification and landscaping.
7. For covering the soil to check soil erosion.
8. For improving the ecological conditions.

Some of the plants are multipurpose in nature, i.e. they can provide more than one use for human beings, e.g. fruit trees can provide fruit and nuts as food, wood for fire, fuel and timber, and the seeds for reproduction of the species.

Advantages of Nursery Raising

This enterprise has many advantages both in terms of money and other aspects. It depends upon the ability of the grower and the producer to harness the maximum benefits. Some of the major advantages are given here.

1. Purity

Nursery growers raise the plants at their own place to make sure about the purity of the variety or species. Valuable and precious plant material, cross-bred or imported, is safe in the hands of a self-nursery grower. This can not be entrusted to beginners or unreliable growers since it needs strict supervision and employment of certain techniques, but the purity of the species or a variety is maintainable.

2. Surety

For raising genuine plant material, this is the only way of doing so since the grower himself is the owner of nursery. He can have a thorough check over all the activities in order to be sure about the quality of produce. He knows what he is raising and how much produce he will get under average conditions of growth and climate.

3. Quality

Apart from purity and surety of the germ-plasm, nursery grower has full control over the quality of the plant material being raised, since he is to meet the requirements of various categories and classes. Further, to compete in the market, new and high quality plants are essential.

4. Economy

Plants raised by a nursery grower are always cheaper than those purchased from other nurseries. This applies for bulk production as raising of few plants is costly since it requires special provision for seed, manure, soil and technical know-how. When the number of plants needed is small, it is economical to buy them from a reliable source rather than going in for their raising himself. Bulk production is always cheaper since the expenditure incurred on various items of production is spread/distributed over a long period.

5. Easy availability

When a commercial grower is to go for large-scale production of crops, trees or other kinds of material, he is bound to raise the plant material himself since he can save money on carriage, transport and care of plant material during transport. He can uproot and replant the material at his will and ease. Loss during transportation is avoided.

6. Timely availability

Number and type of plants needed at a particular time can be met only when grower himself is involved in this trade. He does not have to bother for booking or reservation of plant material in advance.

7. Freedom from diseases and insects

Since the plants are raised under strict supervision of the nursery grower, the grower has control over the treatments to be applied for the check and control of diseases and insects. Plants, which are healthy during their early period of growth, are usually more vigorous since they establish very rapidly.

8. Utilization of resources

Proper utilization of land and farm resources is also possible. The land in between the two trees, i.e. outside their basins, small terraces, places near the water-site, etc. can be put under nursery production. Some of the farm resources like hand tools, implements, stores and waste products like manures and dropped plant parts can be used for addition of fertility of the soil.

9. Other benefits

Apart from these advantages, the nursery production business provides work to unemployed labour since this business needs lot of manpower to carry out different cultural operations like preparation of seed-beds, nursery-beds, grafting, budding, weeding and hoeing, earthing up, irrigation, desuckering, digging, packing and packaging of plants.

Scope

There is no end to the scope of nursery production. Till the human being has life and soil is able to produce, we need food and other materials for our survival. We get all the necessary food material like carbohydrates, fats, proteins, mineral matter, vitamins, amino acids and other essential ingredients necessary for maintenance and building up of our body. Further, these essential elements are supplied along with the most useful fibre that is helpful in the movement of undigested food in the body of animals and human beings. Supply of food material and other ingredients is in balanced and proportionate manner, which comes in highly palatable manner and does not need the recommendation of a medical physician or other professional. Mother Nature provides these through plant laboratory. Thus, the production of nursery plants will never cease to be a fashion. Only the quality nursery producers who can compete in the market with quality product will survive.

It has been observed and found by various surveys that multiplication of plants in nursery of any kind like fruits, vegetables, ornamental plants and other kinds is always more paying than raising of plants in the field. Nursery production though needs less space yet it demands a highly efficient management of the available resources.

Financial benefits gained by a nursery grower will depend upon his management abilities, skill and techniques of selling his plants in the market. A nursery grower can earn a profit of about Rs. 50,000 per annum from an acre or about Rs. 1,25,000 from one hectare of land of moderate fertility and roadside location.

Classification of Nurseries

Nurseries may be classified according to their size of production or the kind of materials raised.

Depending upon the number of plants raised, it can be of two kinds:

a) Commercial Nurseries

Here, the number of plants raised is quite high. Kind and variety of the materials multiplied are according to the demands of the customers and market. Only few nurseries are of this kind in our country. These nurseries have huge infrastructure to raise and maintain the plants. They usually specialize in the production of some specialized plant materials. These nurseries supply all sorts of plant materials like plants, seeds, tubers, corms, bulbs, bud-sticks, etc. They may have different departments to look after individual type of material. They do have their own mother-trees or parent plant materials. Generally, they do not tell the growers about the parentage of the material or the source of collection of their germ-plasm. One may buy the material either on the spot or by ordering through some reliable media. Generally, there is reliability of the plant material since their aim is satisfaction of the customer.

b) Small-scale Nurseries

In these nurseries, the nursery plants are either raised for own use or for limited sale to meet the local needs. Number of plants raised is limited and so there is no leftover. These are generally specialized nurseries since they produce either fruit plants, vegetable seedlings or seedlings of ornamental flowering plants and forest plants. These nurseries usually raise different varieties of plants, which are suitable for a particular area because of limited scope, which is based on investment. This business is usually a minor or supplementary business with the main trade. Here, the grower usually raises nursery plants for his own use but he is able to sell some portion of it since the number of plants raised is slightly more than the requirement. Investment by the nursery grower is limited and so is the profit. These are popular among the local growers. Their number is plenty.

In a nursery, all types of plants, annuals to perennials, deciduous or evergreen, trees or bushes, etc. are multiplied and raised.

According to the kind of material raised, the nurseries can be of following types:

1. Fruit plant nurseries

Fruit trees can be grouped under various heads according to their habit of growth, food value, climate and time of availability but generally, the nurseries are classified on the basis of the climate since

Fig. 1. Guava nursery.

they can not grow plants requiring different types of climate at one place. Plants of temperate and cold region can only be raised and multiplied under cool conditions hence they are restricted to cool places which are generally the hills while the tropical and subtropical plants are raised under warm climate due to their success in these areas. Hence there are two main classes:

a) Temperate fruit plant nurseries: Trees and seedlings of temperate fruits like apple, pear, peach, plum, apricot, cherry, walnut, pecan nut, chestnut, persimmon, Kiwi fruit, hazelnut, almond, etc., are of this climate.

b) Tropical and subtropical nurseries: Here, trees of mango, litchi, loquat, olive, Indian Gooseberry, citrus, date palm, coconut, banana, papaya, custard apple, pomegranate, ber, sapota, mangostein, guava, etc., are raised.

In these nurseries, cultural and other operations right from seed sowing to the digging and packing of propagated trees are done. It involves the use of propagation techniques, care of the propagated plants, i.e., after they have been budded, grafted or layered, packing and packaging of the trees. Usually, a plant, which is generally referred to a tree after grafting or budding, remains in the nursery for almost a year but may remain there for few years if the growth in the initial stages is poor or the budding or grafting had been unsuccessful.

Temperate plants and trees are uprooted and packed in gunny

bags while the tropical and subtropical trees are uprooted with earth-balls, quite intact and then packed properly so that their roots are not damaged during transport and they reach their destination with compact earth-balls. They may need some watering during transit and transport.

Many a times people buy the seedling plants or grow them *in situ* where they are budded or grafted by a grafter but now-a-days availability of seedling plants is not there.

2. Vegetable nurseries

Seedlings of various vegetables can be raised at any place but it should be preferred that seedlings needed for temperate climate should be from the cold areas while for the tropical and subtropical areas, they should be from the warm areas. In case of seedlings being raised under different/adverse conditions, seedlings grown under greenhouse, plastic house or poly-tunnels are preferred for their multiplication.

These can be transported very easily since they are usually light in weight, small in size and easy to carry. They need lot of care from uprooting to transplanting. Generally cauliflower, cabbage, capsicum, sweet pepper, brinjal, tomato, kale, Brussel's sprout, Chinese sarson, endive, onion, leek etc., are raised. These plants remain in the nursery beds for about one and half months or so. They are uprooted when they have attained the height of about 8 to 10 cm and are with 3 to 4 leaves as they can withstand the shock of being uprooted and they can establish easily on transplantation at a well prepared place. They establish in the new field quite easily provided they are planted with due care by using the right technique.

They should not be allowed to remain in the nursery for a longer period than required, as they do not get congenial conditions for their growth and development.

3. Flowering/ornamental plants nurseries

Though all the angiospermic plants do flower but under this category, annuals, perennials, cacti and foliage plants, which either bear flowers that are for beautification or their foliage is beautiful, are propagated in the nursery. They may be multiplied by their seeds or other vegetative parts. Generally, the plants that are raised from seeds remain in the nursery beds for about 4 weeks but others may remain there for about 3-4 months depending upon the plant part used and the conditions in which used. These plants are raised under great care with some precautions since the seeds of these plants are costly.

Flowering plants include cosmos, larkspur, gerbera, carnation, stock, petunia, primula, salvia, rose, chrysanthemum, begonia, cyclamen, coleus, pansy, antirrhinum, calendula, aster, candytuft, dianthus, fuchsia, geranium, monstera, euonymus, etc.

There is another category of plants of this character which are used either as avenue trees or for landscaping. They include some bushes also. Common plants are Acacia, Bottle brush, Silver oak, Magnolia, Rhododendron, Ashok, Thuja, Gulmohar, Simbal, Kachnar, etc. These plants are usually grown in the nursery for about 6 months or so. Seeds or cuttings of these plants are sown in well-prepared beds where they are allowed to have 3 to 4 leaves and by that time they gain the height of about 10 cm or more. These young plants are uprooted with care and planted in the nursery beds at a wider spacing to provide sufficient place for their growth for another three months or more. When the thickness of the main stem is about 1 cm at 40-50 cm height they are uprooted with care, transported, and then transplanted elsewhere. Sometimes these plants are retained in the nursery till they gain the height of 1 m.

Procurement of quality seed, maintenance of varietal characters and low germination rate are some of the problems, which need attention of the nursery grower, but they can be overcome by acquiring the desired technical know-how and experience. These plants need more care and attention at all stages.

4. Forest plant nurseries

Like the fruit trees, these species are of two kinds, i.e. meant for temperate climate, and subtropical climate. They can be deciduous or evergreen in nature. They include trees of economic and environmental importance. Major species are pines, oaks, cedar, rhododendron, teak, eucalyptus, poplar, acacias, casuarinas, etc.

They are seasonal so far as their plantings are concerned. Generally, the deciduous trees are ready for transplanting during winter while the evergreens are planted with the onset of rainy season. The beginning of these two seasons vary in different parts of the country, and so is their time of transplanting.

Some of the seeds are sown direct in the soil but for ease of care and carriage of seedlings, they are planted in polybags of various sizes and gauges but the soil mixture for them is almost of the same nature as for soil plantation.

Time taken by a seed to become a plant depends upon the time required for the seed to germinate: seeds needing after-ripening or some period to complete their dormancy will need a longer time than others. Some of the species of forest trees have their seeds with hard coats, which have to be broken by giving some mechanical or chemical treatments to hasten their germination. In general, the time taken for a seed to become plant of the size fit for transplanting is almost little over 6 months.

These trees are generally raised for planting in the forests or the areas which are under social forestry or environmental protection programmes. These are in great demand these days as the area to be planted under such programmes is vast.

5. Miscellaneous nurseries

These include plants of high economic value like rare, medicinal, herbal, drug, fibre, etc. Some of them are raised for extraction of essential oils and other chemicals, which are used for cosmetic, pharmaceutical and household use. Some of the common seedlings of this category are geranium, rose, lavender, calendula, belladonna, berberis, mint, marigold, discorea and many other herbal plants.

The time spent by a plant in the nursery may vary from 3 months to 6 months but care should be taken that they should establish themselves quickly on transplanting.

Private persons or government bodies may run nurseries. It has been observed that privately established nurseries are better due to timely care and attention by private nursery growers. In some states, the nurseries aided by government are also run. Kisan Nurseries are one of them where the farmers for the department of forests grow forest species. Nurseries are governed by certain rules and regulations in some of the states, as such these nurseries are often inspected by the concerned Plant Protection authorities of the state.

4

Site and Its Selection

Site is the basic requirement of a nursery. One may go for raising plants in pots, polybags or in the soil but some place has to be fixed for their placement since they can not be kept in the sky. Site is a place upon which one can grow or keep the plants. Thus, it has to suit in many respects.

Qualities of a Good Site

While selecting a suitable site, nursery grower must look for the following qualities.

1. Nearness to road

Nursery site should be near to the main road as far as possible, or at least there should be a pucca path, preferably motorable road till the site. This is necessary for the speedy movement of labour, inputs and seedlings to other distant places. Since the growers are expected to visit the nursery for purchase of plant material, it should be easily accessible. It will be an added benefit for sale.

2. Near a habitat

As far as possible, a nursery should be located near a colony since the nursery grower is a human being who needs company, being a social animal. Moreover, some labour has also to be arranged for various operations to be carried out at the nursery from time to time. Further, man needs protection from wild animals and birds for protecting the nursery and other material. There can be problems of medical aid, schooling of children and communication with other people when the nursery is located in an isolated place. An isolated family cannot reap good profits due to lack of communication with others. It is only possible when they live in a social way, i.e. in a society.

3. Suitable climate

Limited number of plants can be looked after properly under controlled atmosphere, say in a greenhouse, poly-tunnel or poly-house but large scale production is possible only under normal field conditions. Mild climatic variations in a suitable area can be overcome, but abrupt changes or absolutely different climate cannot yield good plants. Growth and development of plants are generally conditioned by the prevailing climatic conditions surrounding them. A suitably selected site keeping in view the climate is essential for economic raising of plants, otherwise a grower may have to spend a lot on the maintenance of desired conditions for the germination and aftercare of the seedlings and young plants. Creating congenial climatic conditions in an artificial manner is a difficult task, which needs lot of technical know-how and money.

4. Neither shady nor exposed area

Since the nursery is meant for young and tender plants that need proper care and management during their early stages of growth and development, they should not be raised under a shady place or on highly exposed surface. Both these conditions are injurious for the normal health of a seedling. Seedlings and plants grown under too much shade become lanky in growth with their stems being weak and the leaves may become etiolated and the plant may become weak in constitution. Shady areas invite pathogens that attack the tender and weak parts of the plants more readily causing them damage. Damping off is a common serious problem of this nature in vegetables and flowering plants. On the other hand, over-exposed surfaces or areas needing lot of water or humidity to keep the root zone moist where roots can develop and grow, becomes difficult to manage. Partially shaded areas are considered quite suitable.

5. Sufficient sunlight

Sun is not merely a source of light but is also necessary for the proper growth and development of plants. Light is an essential factor for the manufacture of food material by the plant. The light from the sun is absorbed and the leaf manufactures the basic food, i.e. carbohydrates from carbon dioxide and water from the atmosphere and plant respectively, but without sunlight, it is not possible since sunlight is the major starting factor for production of carbohydrates.

Further, sunlight helps in raising the temperature, dries the excessive humidity from the soil surface, keeps the transpiration current within the plant at a suitable rate, provides turgidity to the cells, tissues and plant, etc. Sun also has a germicidal effect; it can kill the spores of fungus and bacteria. Some of the remains of the insects and eggs are made ineffective by the sun due to its high temperature.

A site providing moderate sunlight that too in the morning is always considered most suitable.

6. Avoid windy and hail-prone areas

Some of the pockets in every type of climate may have windy areas where the speed of wind or air current is high, resulting in the loss of water from the plant surface through transpiration and by evaporation from the soil surface. Both these processes force the water to draw it from the storehouses within and outside the plant. Further, speedy air currents may blow up the weak plants along with their roots, and may cause bending of grown up plants. Swaying of plants has a bad effect on their growth. It may cause lodging which may harbour the attack of fungal diseases and rats.

In valley areas, there is frequent flow of high-speed wind, which may be hot or cold. In desert and dry areas, there are winds, which are warm during the day but cool during the night. It usually happens in dry areas of Ladakh, Kinnaur, Lahaul-Spiti, Rajasthan and Maharashtra. The abrupt change in the temperature causes variations in the temperature of the neighbouring zones. It hampers the normal growth of plants.

Winds always have higher rate of evaporation. The higher rate of absorption of atmospheric humidity puts direct pressure on the plant to absorb and lose more water and then indirectly affects the humidity in the soil, which causes wilting of the plant. Plants when cannot withstand temporary wilting, go into permanent wilting from which they can not return back to their normal position and as such they dry up and die.

Speed of the wind is another havoc for the nursery and the nursery grower. Wind in high velocity causes evaporation of water from the soil and the water reservoir, transpiration from the plants, soil erosion, uprooting of tender plants, forcing the plants to grow lopsided, and loss of fertility. Thunderstorms are the most damaging ones to the nursery.

Hails are injurious to the health of plants, both young and grown up; younger ones are most affected. Hails damage the leaves and twigs of the plants; extreme conditions may cause complete defoliation of the plant. Injury caused by hails is not repairable and the resultant plant remains stunted. It is the speed of hailing and the size of hails which plays the damaging role. Bigger the size and higher the speed, more is the loss. Young seedlings with their plumule leaves are almost killed.

Frost is also injurious for young plants. The low temperature may cause freezing of solute/water in the cells since water occupies more space on becoming ice than normal water and this results in demand for more space which is not there. Cell walls being elastic can expand to a certain limit but cannot cope with more space so they rupture causing bleeding of cell sap. Grown up plants can adjust or adapt to frost upto a particular point but young plants are not able to adapt and hence they die.

7. Away from forests

As far as possible, the site selected for a nursery should be away from the forest. Some of the diseases, insects and pests of the forest plants are liable to attack and damage the young plants in the nursery. On the other hand, bushes, weeds and trees in the nearby forest areas may serve as alternative hosts during the period of their (pathogens) critical survival. Control of diseases and insects and pests demands extra labour, energy and money.

Moreover, wild animals and wild birds that cause excessive damage to the plants usually visit places adjoining to forests. They pick and uproot the plants for their seeds, bulbs, corms and other succulent parts to meet their food requirements. Apart from this, they do have damaging approach to the human beings also.

Generally, areas near the forests or the areas surrounded by large and spreading trees provide excessive shade, which is not good for food manufacture by the leaves of the young plants growing under their shade. Further, excessive shade may hamper the plants by the attack of insects and diseases due to high percentage of humidity of the place.

8. Good irrigational facilities

Great care should be taken to have regular and permanent source or continuous supply of water for irrigating the young seedlings. Apart from quantity of water, it is the quality of water, which plays a vital role in the maintenance of normal growth and development of the young plants. In general, requirement of water is about 3-4 times more in a nursery than in an ordinary field. It should be advisable to have a permanent source of water from where regular supply can be had.

The quality of water may be analyzed by a chemist to rate its suitability for irrigational and other uses at the site.

9. Flat land

Fairly flat land with moderate slope is of great value since water can be drained off with ease, whenever necessary. Undulated site needs lot of money and labour to get in a workable condition. In the hills and valley areas, small terraces are suitable but levelling should not be practised in this area as the topography of the soil is disturbed during terracing. It also affects the fertility status of the soil, as the soil which is usually fertile goes deep, while the sub-soil which is less fertile may come to the top. Site having a gentle slope should be used for nursery production. In such sites, irrigation and drainage of water is easy and the loss of fertility is minimum.

Another word of caution is the necessity to see that the area is not waterlogged. Rain water should not remain stagnant but should go away at a normal speed

10. Soil characters

Nature of the soil which is judged by its physical, chemical and biological characters, is of vital importance and is a decisive factor for the adoption of soil for a particular type of nursery production. Forest and fruit plants can be raised in an ordinary soil while vegetables and flowering plants need heavy and good soil.

Soil may be examined physically and chemically for its texture, structure, water-holding capacity, slope and fertility by an experienced farmer himself or by a scientist who is expert in this field. It is better to get the soil analyzed prior to the start of nursery business.

Too clayey or too sandy soil is not fit for nursery raising and it has to be modulated either with the addition of sand or clay as the case may be and an additional quality of organic matter. All this requires extra money, labour and time. Clay-loam or sandy-loam soil is considered most suitable since it has particles of moderate size, which have good water-holding capacity and provide good drainage of water and then movement of air is also possible which keeps the soil fauna in active state.

Soils with ample water-holding capacity are preferred as they pose fewer problems during dry spells, otherwise frequent irrigation is required to keep the soil moist for proper development of the roots. Soils having granular and crumb structure are highly suitable for nursery production because they are moderately friable and easily manageable.

Soil pH is also of prime importance. It is an indicator of the chemical reaction of the soil solute and so is necessary for the assessment of soil suitability for different crops. Its value less than 5.0 denotes the soil to be highly acidic which is not conducive for plant growth while the pH value above 7.0 or 7.5 is also not beneficial, as at this level, assimilation and absorption of mineral matter or nutrients from the soil solution is not possible. Soils having pH value of 7.0 are generally considered as buffers or neutral and such soils do not exist in our areas. Plants absorb most of the soil solutes when they are with slightly acidic reaction. Plants can grow in a slightly acidic condition and as such the soils having pH value ranging from 5.5 to 6.5 are considered suitable for nursery production.

Slope of the land has a marked effect on the site. General slope of 2° is enough. Lands with steep slopes have to be terraced or levelled before putting under use. Terracing may need money while levelling may cause the land to become infertile or at least less fertile due to disturbance of the topography. This also disturbs the soil pattern, i.e. the particles at the top are usually bigger in size that have more pores rather than having good porous space. This condition is neither good for soil fertility nor for moisture retention, so such soils are usually poor. Even after terracing, the sides of the terrace have to be built either pucca or planted with suitable grasses or bushes to get it settled. This helps in checking the soil erosion. Terraced soils need more organic matter and other fertilizers to make them suitable for nursery production.

Where the nursery plants are to be dug with their roots along with intact earth-balls, nursery grower must see that the soil is deep enough to provide soil for at least 2-3 years on the same site. This is particularly necessary for the nursery production of evergreen trees like citrus, mango, loquat and litchi plants since they are uprooted along with their earth-balls.

Fertility of the soil is another factor, which makes the nursery business a good success. A soil with moderate to high fertility is considered good for nursery production whereas less fertile or infertile soil is of no economic use for the nursery grower. Young seedlings need more nutrients, which have to be supplemented by extra supply of fertilizers and manures. Fertility status of the soil is also related to its pH value and water-holding capacity. Soils highly rich in fertility have low pH value and high water-holding capacity and are darker in colour and finer in texture and structure. These are not very conducive for nursery production.

11. Means of transport

Nursery business is interdependent with other activities. For raising seedlings and trees, inputs like seeds, bulbs, tubers, corms, bud-sticks, fertilizers, plant nutrients, growth hormones, chemicals like insecticides, fungicides and herbicides, hand tools, implements, packing material, labour, etc. have to be brought from other sources. The output of the nursery, i.e. nursery plants has to be sold or sent to the market. All this needs a good transport system, which should be assured. The site must be at a place which is suitably connected by road or rail as the case may be.

In nutshell, the site selected for nursery raising should be moderately flat, having good fertility status with enough irrigational facilities, neither away from a town nor very close to the forests, easily accessible by road or rail and in a suitable climate. Man can control some of the factors while others are beyond his control. He must not go against the nature. Good soil, good water and good shade are must for successful nursery enterprise.

5

Preparation of Site

Selected site has to be prepared in such a way that the seed or other plant parts can be planted and then the young seedling plants are able to grow there vigorously for a period of not less than a month or so depending upon the kind of nursery plants being raised.

The site should be cleared of bushes and weeds, levelled and made suitable for planting seedling and holding the plants for a fairly long time. After selecting the site, first thing is to mark its boundary. Marking of the total area is usually done with the help of a person from Revenue Department so that no litigation is involved. But the grower himself can do demarcation within one's own area. It is better to get the area fenced either before clearing of bushes and trees or after getting them removed.

Fencing

The main objectives of fencing are to protect plant material, demarcate the boundary and to have control over the land and plants. Fencing may be done in the following ways:

1. Wire fencing

Simple or barbed iron wire is used. Depending upon the need, its kind may be selected. Places near to the forests, and likely to be visited by strangers, wild animals and stray animals are usually fenced by barbed wire while other places may be fenced by ordinary iron wire.

The wires are fixed on poles, which may be of wood or iron, which are strong enough to resist bending when pushed. Among the wooden poles, bamboo poles are the best as they last longer due to their thick, hard and impermeable surface, which does not allow it to rot with water and soil. Wooden poles are painted with waterproof paint to lengthen their life span. Lower ends of these poles are usually painted with coal tar to protect them from the attack of white ants. This also helps in non-absorption of water by them. The height of a pole is generally 1.5 metres which includes a portion of about 30 cm plus 20 cm painted with coal tar and fixed in the soil and the rest, a metre or more, is above the ground level.

Angle irons are also used in place of wooden poles. Angle iron of two and half centimetres width is suitable for this purpose since with this thickness they do not bend easily and resist the pressure from outside. One can hold the wires in a perfectly tight or stretched condition for a fairly long period. Generally, their lower ends, which are to be fixed in the earth, are not painted with coal tar, but if painted, this will increase their durability. Instead of coal tar, ordinary paint can also be used. Where money is not the main consideration and durable fence is required, angle iron poles should be employed as they can last for about 20 years, if their maintenance is carried on in a normal way. With wooden poles, when they are to be replaced, the iron wire gets entangled and damaged during the replacement and as such the cost of wooden pole wiring is more than that of angle iron in the long run.

Poles at a distance of about 3 metres are fixed in a row depending upon the total area to be fenced. Number of poles required should be worked out earlier. Normally, 3-4 wires at a distance of about 30 cm from one another, leaving a distance of about 20 cm at the bottom, are fixed on the poles. To keep the wires tightened and for better security and protection purposes, two more wires are stretched diagonally from the top of one pole to the base of the other pole. They are fixed on the same spots where the horizontal wires have already been fixed.

On bamboo or other wooden poles, wires are fixed with the help of nails of 6 cm length while on angle irons, they are fixed with the help of specially prepared hooks of iron made out of simple wire. This is usually of aluminum as it is rustproof. Wires are fixed after stretching them straight with the help of pliers. They may be tightened annually to keep them in the right position. These wires and poles may be painted with silver paint every year. This gives a better look and protection against rusting.

Poles, wooden or iron, are fixed in the earth deep enough to hold them straight and rigid. They may be fixed by pressing the earth and small stones or brick pieces round their bases. Base may also be made of concrete and cement mixture, which serves as a permanent structure. Tops of the wooden poles may be covered with slanting or wedge-shaped tin pieces to protect them from decay by rain water.

2. Planting of trees and bushes

Fast growing and spreading trees or bushes, preferably with thorns or spines, are planted close in a row near to the boundary, particularly within the boundary of the area. These plantings are made at least a year or so before the start of nursery business since the nursery plants do need some shade and protection, and further, these trees and bushes need sufficient time to get them established. Poplar, Eucalyptus, Zizyphus, Citrus, Acacia, Grevillca, Mulberry, Bottle brush, Bauhinia, etc., are some of the trees which can be planted. In some cases, Jatti khatti (Citrus spp.), a rootstock for citrus is also planted. Duranta, Hibiscus, Tecoma, Bougainvillea, Spirea, Henna, etc. are some bushes recommended for plantation on or along the boundary.

On establishment, these trees and bushes do not allow the soil to wash away by rain or swept away by speedy wind currents. Apart from serving as a mark of boundary, they work as windbreaks. In some cases, they can provide fuel-wood to the owner and fodder to animals. Their maintenance is not difficult as they need some training in the beginning and pruning at a later stage. Tops of the trees should not be allowed to grow very vigorously.

This type of fence is almost permanent in nature but needs regular look-after, particularly in terms of irrigation, training and pruning. Close planting is always desirous to harness the maximum utility.

3. Brick or stonewall

For the construction of a permanent fence or boundary wall, to enclave the area, bricks or stones may also be used. This is highly expensive but has to be erected when there is danger of frequent visits by wild animals, pilferage, stealing, etc. Width and height of the wall will depend upon the need. Sometimes, pieces of glass or barbed wire on small angle iron pieces are also fixed on the walls to make the fence safer. In some cases, round or rectangular holes are provided in the walls for the passage of air current which is necessary during summer in plains as the air near the walls become warmer than the adjoining places. Moreover, this type of modified construction can save some money.

Minimum width of the wall should be 15 cm while height should be a metre or more. Thin and low walls do not serve the purpose of fence but can work as a mark of boundary.

4. Live or electric fence

Electric current of mild voltage is allowed to pass through a steel wire, which is placed around the boundary. Mild electric current to the living being helps in repulsion. This repulsion forces them to avoid crossing. The electric shock provided by the electric current is to be maintained properly, particularly, during the rainy season or when the soil is too wet. This type of fence is not in common use in this country due to its complexity and high expenses.

In India, fence of live trees or bushes is generally used which also serves as a windbreak when fully established. Fuel and fodder can also be had from these trees and bushes. The quantity of fuel-wood or fodder available from these trees and bushes depends upon the species used and the frequency of removal of pruned wood and other surplus leaves which serve as fodder. Further, trees when become old enough to be removed or replaced, their wood can be used for different purposes like wood for furniture, timber or other purposes. Their leaves and twigs that drop on the soil during their life span are useful since they provide organic matter on their decay. They can also be used as mulch, if collected properly. They also provide partial shade. Passage of air is possible at all stages but at a slow speed. It does not need extra money, care and fertilizers for their maintenance and upkeep. Selection of trees or bushes should be appropriate to climate and soil.

Clearing

A new site may have trees, bushes or weeds since it is usually a neglected piece of land, which has not been used for production for a season or two or may be more. The site may be carved out of an area not in use in the past. First of all, trees are lopped and cut near to the base; their roots are dug to a certain comfortable limit. Bushes, shrubs and weeds with thick stems are also cut to the ground level. Later they are removed from the site.

In general practice, the leftover vegetation is burnt. This does not allow the regeneration of these plants since their roots also get burnt. Burning adds mineral matter to the soil but it should be avoided. As a matter of fact, all the stubbles may be removed; leaves and twigs put in a pit to convert them into manure, which can be used for manuring of crops at a later stage. This will not hamper in the ecological balance, as this process is eco-friendly. Wood can be used for different purposes while the stubbles may be used as fuel-wood for burning.

For digging stubbles, furrow turning plough, spade and pick axe may be used.

Levelling

In case the land is not a level one but is undulating, it may be levelled by using a plank, *karaha* or scraper, If need be, the upper surface may be dug with a furrow turning plough.

In hills and valley areas, the land is usually with steep slope and the land available for cultivation or for nursery raising is limited. Here terraces or small fields have to be made. Great care should be taken to see that the topography of the land is not disturbed. As per slope, terraces may be made.

In plains, after running a furrow turning plough, running a disc harrow may follow planking. Plank is used to level the soil and it may be run across if needed. It is advisable to have a gentle slope of natural level so that rain water does not remain in the field for a long time but it should drain off very quickly and easily.

Levelling is done for two purposes: (1) for irrigation, i.e. to get the water reach to each plant when they are irrigated, and (2) for the drainage of water during rains for removal of excessive water from the field/beds. It is only possible on gentle slope. Undulated lands pose problems of water stagnation, which causes the decay of roots due to more humidity and lack of air in the root zone of plants. An added benefit is pulverisation of soil since working the soil with a furrow turning plough and disc harrow or spade helps in making a crumb structure which increases the pore space in the soil and this in turn helps to provide good water-holding capacity and conservation of organic matter and mineral matter which remains adsorbed to the fine soil particles.

6

Plant Growing Containers

Plants may either be multiplied by their seeds which is a result of the reproduction process or by other means of vegetative propagation like the bulbs, corms, tubers, etc. but they need a place to grow, i.e. they need some physical support and some nutrient-supplying media. Thus, the best growing place is soil though they can be grown in other places also. Soil is not only a physical basis but also is a place for the combination of chemical and biological activities since the mineral matter and soil fauna adhere to the soil particles to occupy the pore space.

Sometimes, seeds are sown in specially prepared containers, which have a soil mixture, known as pot mixture or some other artificial media. Here the seeds are sown so that the seed may germinate easily and quickly and the young plants may remain there for two months to tide over adverse climatic and other conditions. The tender or precious plants can be grown in such pots or containers for their best growth and care.

Flower Pots

These are simple pots, which are usually round in shape with a small hole in or near the bottom. The shape, size and position of the hole vary. Generally, these pots are narrower at the base and the diameter gradually increases as the height increases. These are sold by the diameter of the upper rim which may be from 10 cm to 30 cm. Usually height of the pot is equal to its diameter of the rim.

Fig. 2. Plant in earthen pot.

Fig. 3. Plants in plastic bucket can grow for 3 years.

In market, square and rectangular pots are also available. Square pots are usually cuboids in shape while the rectangular pots have less height. Their length increases as the height decreases. They are used for growing small plants or for raising seedlings of rare plants. Position of the hole is usually in the centre of the base but it can be on the side also. The hole on the side is much better than that in the centre since it restricts the flow of water and causes it to move out at a slow speed.

Traditionally these are termed or known as earthen pots but they can be of glass, ceramic, plastic, fiberglass or cement and concrete mix. Plastic buckets of various sizes are also used for raising seedlings for 1 to 2 years due to their ease in carriage being with handles. Pots made of earth are given the desired shape and size and then put in a kiln to make them strong, where they get the red colour due to burning of the adhesive on the soil particles. These containers may last for 2-3 years depending upon their care and maintenance.

The advantage of these pots is due to their size and weight, which enables the growers to shift them as and when necessary. Small pots are lighter in weight as compared to large ones as they contain less soil/media. Thus, small pots are easily manageable.

For raising seedlings, flat earthen pots are also available in which the young seedlings are grown for about a week or more after germination and later they are shifted to other places for their further development and growth.

Sometimes the seeds are sown *in situ* in these pots; in that case, large pots should be used depending upon the total life of the plant. In such cases, the soil or the soil mixture in the pot has to be changed every year.

Life of earthen pot is shorter as compared to other types of pots and as such they need great care during handling. Ceramic and fibre-glass pots are costlier and they also need better management and care. Plastic containers may last for 3 seasons or so depending upon their use and care and the thickness of the plastic used for their manufacture. They should not be over-exposed to extreme and highly fluctuating temperatures and to sunlight, which results in short life span.

Plants that are to be sold with pots are usually planted in light containers, and for commercial use the earthen pots are used. Plastic pots can be used with advantage. They are generally used for home-gardens and for keeping in drawing rooms.

Polybags

Polybags of transparent polythene of various sizes are used for *in situ* plantation of seeds. Stem cuttings are also planted in these bags. These are cylindrical in shape with the sealed base. Their size, thickness and weight when filled are as follows:

Size (cm)	*Thickness (gauge)*	*Weight (kg)*
10 × 20	150	1.45
15 × 25	200	3.63
20 × 30	250	7.27

These bags are light in weight and easy to handle but can be damaged by frequent shifting or their movement under rough conditions. These are used when seeds are to be sown in soil and the seedlings emerged are to be planted at a distant place after being transported or carried by manual labour. It is also beneficial for the plants that are to move with their earth-balls intact. Polythene is an excellent source to resist against damages during transportation. They do have the advantage of being looked-after easily with little care. They are also easy to carry when empty.

These bags must have 3 or 4 holes for drainage of excessive water since they are sealed at the bottom. Too much water in the polybag will damage the root system. One drawback with these bags is that they cannot be weeded by mechanical means. Only hand weeding is possible, that too with great care. Another disadvantage with these polybags is their non-reusability, as they can be used only once.

Polybags when filled with earth or soil are placed in rows on the earth in a block so that sprinkler can water them easily. Regular watering has to be made, otherwise the plant may dry up. Heavy watering is to be avoided in all cases.

During transplanting, a vertical cut is made on the side of the polybag and is placed in a well-prepared bed or pit.

Boxes or Crates

These may be wooden or of moulded plastic but should be strong enough to hold sufficient quantity of soil in them. Sometimes trays made of tin, aluminum, iron or even concrete mix are also used but they are quite costlier. These can be reused but need proper care and attention. Wooden trays/crates can be repaired and reused thrice depending upon the conditions under which they are maintained. For commercial purposes, the concrete trays or wooden boxes of big size are worth usable but the soil has to be changed after every digging. Young plants can be kept for few weeks. For permanent raising of plants, these can be built near the road side or near the sides of the field. For nursery production, their utility is limited to only seed sowing and then uprooting the tender seedlings after 3-4 weeks. Just after that, whole or at least half of that soil must be replaced.

Plastic trays or crates are best suited for sowing of seeds since they are light in weight, durable and easily manageable. Soil has to be changed every season.

Fig. 4. Tomato nursery in wooden box.

All the trays or crates, of whatever material, should have a hole on the side near the bottom to drain off the excessive water. If it is a big hole, a piece of stone may be kept to narrow the passage but it should not completely block the drainage of water.

These crates can be filled with many types of media like soil, soil mixture, pot mixture, sawdust, vermiculite, etc. Normally, they are filled upto 15 cm. Their shape is usually rectangular, size being 20-25 cm height, 30-60 cm length and 30 cm width with a strong flat base.

Seeds are sown in lines and seedlings are uprooted when they attain height of about 8-10 cm depending upon the kind and species. Seedlings should not be grown for a long period as there is less space for development of their roots in the soil and further, there will be great competition over the soil surface for the growth of young seedlings.

Bamboo Baskets

Baskets made by joining and weaving the strips of bamboo are used for raising plants of high commercial value that need special care during their early growing period. In some places, instead of bamboo, mulberry or willow shoots are used. Since they are prepared from the locally available material, some other material, which may bend and resist water decay, can be used. In the early days of commercial nursery production, nursery growers were using this type of material but now it has become a fancy for growing of ornamental plants. They can be made to hang from the wall or roof by specially prepared hooks.

An improvised technique is the use of iron wires or metal strips or iron netting which is given the shape of a basket, usually semi-circular, the base being semi-circular and the top being flat. The size is quite variable. For seed sowing and raising of seedlings, they are usually 15 cm high and about 60 cm in diameter at the top. For hanging, the baskets are usually of 25-30 cm in diameter with a depth of about 10 cm or so.

The baskets are usually lined with moss and then soil mixture is filled at least 3 cm below the level of the rim. Hoeing and weeding and irrigation are possible by manual labour only. Since these baskets have less quantity of soil mixture, frequent irrigation and fertilizing are essential but have the advantage of their easy movement.

Germinating Dishes

For testing the ability of seed to germinate and germination percentage, these specially prepared dishes are used. They are circular plates of glass with their height of about 2-3 cm and diameter being 10 cm both at the base and at the top. Some projections or raised portions inside on the base are there, over which the filter paper is placed. Seeds are placed over the filter paper. Water is added which goes to the bottom layer after wetting the filter paper. The layer of the water remains touching the filter paper. The seeds start to germinate on getting air and water. Too much moisture is avoided. In place of germinating dishes, ordinary petri plates or dishes can also be used.

Seeds which have sprouted, i.e. their radicles and plumules have come out, are to be placed in some other containers where they may get the desired conditions for their growth and development.

Seedlings are generally raised in the soil but precious and difficult to germinate seeds may be sown in trays depending upon the quality and period of their stay in the pots. For bulk production of seedlings soil is the best media and place while for small scale production of seedlings and *in situ* plantation, earthen pots may be preferred. For the movement of plants with their earth-balls, polybags are ideal. Choice should be made on the basis of the material to be raised, quantity to be raised and money to be spent.

7

Growing Media

A plant seed germinates on getting congenial conditions like water, air and temperature but it needs a place where these conditions can be provided in a proper manner. So the first and the foremost need is place, which may be a soil, soil mixture or some other artificial media. Plants are also grown in water tanks—hydroponics—where a wire netting is provided on the top of culture solution from which the roots of plants can pass through and get the plant nutrients from the solution while the top of the plant remains outside the solution in the air. Proper air circulation and maintenance of the culture solution in its right concentration is a must. Here, the seeds will not germinate but a seedling can grow. This method is very costly, laborious and needs utmost care and technical know-how and is beyond the scope of an ordinary and commercial nursery grower.

Soil

Best media for planting of seeds and other vegetative parts of the plant is the soil. It is available in plenty and is easily replaceable. Soil has resulted, after centuries of weathering of rocks, in the form of soil particles on which the organic matter has put up its layer. Ordinary ground soil, fine in texture is passed through a sieve to get rid of stones, pebbles and other unwanted material. Passing through a sieve of a particular measurement ensures uniform size of the particles and deletion of some remains of insects and diseases that can be seen visually.

The soil is upper crust of earth that has fine particles of minerals and organic matter and it may be a piece of land that is selected by keeping on eye over the remains of insects and other unwanted material. This remains of insects and diseases are removed. This may be mixed with sand or clay as the case may be but should have the structure and texture of clay-loam soil. Other qualities of soil must be considered with advantage.

Preparation of Land

After clearing and levelling the land for the nursery as described in the preceding chapter, a furrow turning plough followed by disc harrow or an ordinary cultivator may be run to get the roots and stubbles of the older plantation uprooted. Apart from uprooting the stubbles, this process will bring out the remains of diseases, insects and pests from the lower surface of the soil to the top. Remains of insects and other living beings are eaten away or destroyed by birds and sunrays and some of them may die due to unfavourable conditions for their survival, i.e. aerobic conditions. Spores and other forms of diseases, bacteria, etc., are inactivated due to their exposure to sunlight and air. This serves as disinfection of soil particles.

Two to three days later, a plank may be run to level the land which should be followed by another ploughing in the other direction or across to have the complete exposure of the soil to sun. If needed, 2-3 ploughings with an ordinary plough or cultivator may be made to get the complete breakage of clods.

In the hills, it is difficult to get ploughing with a machine, i.e. tractor, so ordinary bullock driven ploughing may be resorted to. Due to slopes in most of the cases, there are small terraces where even ploughing by bullocks is not possible due to small size of the fields and undulated lands. In such cases, land has to be tilled or worked with a pickaxe, spade, *khilna* or *khurpa*. Generally, in small pieces of land the movement of bullocks is not possible and only manual labour has to be employed, hence land preparation becomes costlier as compared to the plains. This is true for the hilly areas of Jammu & Kashmir, Himachal Pradesh, Uttaranchal, Nagaland and Mizoram and parts of the hilly areas in Maharashtra, Gujarat, Karnataka, etc., where small pieces of land or undulated land is available for cultivation.

In all the cases, the land has to be levelled fairly with the use of any machine or implement suited to the area. Big boulders and stones should be removed from the site. Other unwanted material may also be removed so as to have a flat land, which is free of bushes and weeds.

Preparation of Soil

For economical and successful nursery production, the basic material is the soil and as such the soil should be in a fair state of its fertility with congenial conditions for the germination of seeds, development of young seedlings and growth of young plants. Soil is the mother that receives the seed and provides us the plant.

As already mentioned, land with gentle slope and moderate fertility, having pH range between 5.5 and 6.5 and with good water holding-capacity is best suited for nursery production. Of course, it has to be free from insects, pests and diseases. Such qualities are usually found in clay-loam soils.

Purpose of Preparation

The soil is prepared for following purposes:

1. For keeping the polybags
2. For greenhouse
3. For seedbeds
4. For nursery beds.

Whatever the purpose may be, soil has to be flat and solid.

For keeping the polybags

A level piece of land is required. It does not need any preparation except that it is hard, flat, free from any obstacles, with efficient drainage facilities and safe. This piece of land can be a single field or small terraces depending upon the slope of the land. It is better to have partial shade. Paths may be made as per need. Since the polybags are kept in blocks and lines, paths of reasonable width of half a metre may be kept for movement of labour, inter-culture and sprinkling.

For greenhouse

Land prepared for keeping the polybags can be used for construction of greenhouse or a poly-house. There are two main objectives in a greenhouse, one is to keep the pots, polybags or other containers and the other is to grow plants in the soil.

For keeping the pots and other containers, there is no need of working the land deeply. One should ensure about the slope of the land to have proper sanitation, and to provide good conditions for the development and growth of the young and grown-up seedlings.

For growing plants in a greenhouse, the soil particles should be fine with a slight acidic reaction but the soil conditions should be quite suitable for quick germination (bursting of the seed-coat after swelling up due to absorption of water) and then development of the roots. Generally, small plots or beds with concrete sides are made to grow the plants. Detailed procedure is given under the heading of preparation for seedbed.

In a commercial greenhouse, plants are raised in containers, so the land may be flat and plastered with mud or cement by keeping slope for drainage of water.

For seedbeds

Seedbeds are the well-prepared beds with sufficient fertility where seed is sown for having seedlings on their successful germination.

As a common practice, these beds are 1 metre wide and 3 to 10 metres long, having a path of half metre width on either side. The path serves as an irrigation channel, a passage and a drain for removal of excessive water from the bed. The path is also used for hoeing and weeding of the plants and for other cultural practices.

The length of the bed is never more than 10 metres since it becomes unmanageable due to its length and slope of the land. Lengthy beds need large quantity of seed and extensive care for its maintenance while slope of the land goes on changing after 10 m or so. Since the nursery bed has to be irrigated freely, the length has to be rational so that water is neither wasted nor remain unutilised by the plants. Length of the bed will depend upon the soil conditions, slope and need of the grower. In terraced area, 3-4 metres length is reasonable and same is the case for lands having steep slopes. The length may be reduced according to need and availability of the land but width should not be increased. A man can weed out only from a distance of half metre while sitting in the path. The seedbed may be divided into small beds with their length being a metre and as such the small seedbeds are 1 × 1 metre that are easily workable and manageable. Soil in between the two small beds may be raised slightly for demarcation.

The seedbeds may either be raised (under high rainfall conditions) or sunken (under drought or summer conditions) than the normal soil level. Raised beds facilitate the drainage of water while sunken beds retain the moisture for a long time as the water from the adjoining soil of normal level seeps into the sunken beds. In other cases, raised beds can be made during rainy season while sunken beds can be prepared during summer or other dry months. Great care should be taken that the young plants should neither be submerged in water nor they should be left to dry up due to lack of moisture.

After demarcation of seedbeds and paths, the path or channel is first prepared. A spade or a *khurpa* may be used to raise or lower the beds. Sides of the beds may be pressed hard but should be kept slanting.

Required quantity of well-rotten farm yard manure or compost along with needed quantities of Super Phosphate and Muriate of Potash are added to the soil and mixed thoroughly. Farm yard manure and compost must be well rotten and in that case, the colour will be dark brown. If there is danger of white ants or other soil-borne insects, suitable insecticide like Gamaxene, Aldrin, BHC or any other soil insecticide may be mixed with the soil surface. Mixing should be thorough; generally, 20-25 g of the insecticide is added to an area of 1 × 1 metre. Spreading them over the soil and then mixing with a spade and a plough mixes manures. Small beds can be worked out with manual labour only and as such spade, *kassi, khilna* or *khurpa* is best suited. Manures are mixed 4-5 cm deep at least two months before seeding. Insecticides are mixed a day or two prior to seeding.

Small beds of 1 × 1 m dimension are carved out of the length of the seedbed for easy working. A small raised band of 5 cm height is made to separate the beds. The topsoil is pulverised and should have ample moisture before or at the time of seeding. Great care should be taken that these beds are flat as far as possible. Well prepared soil will facilitate the early germination and growth of the plants due to its having sufficient water-holding capacity and good fertility.

For increasing the conservation of moisture in the soil, irrigation may be given once or twice to the seedbed during their preparation right from mixing of manures to pulverization.

For nursery beds

The method of preparation of nursery beds is almost identical to that for seedbeds as described earlier but only the size of the bed is kept much bigger than the seedbed since spacing in between the plants is kept more. Flat land is preferred and is prepared as usual. In these nursery beds, young seedlings are planted for providing them strength and hardening so that they may be transplanted in the field without any setback.

Generally, young seedlings of 3 to 4 weeks age with 3 to 4 leaves and height of 10 cm or more are transplanted in these beds. They are allowed to grow for about a season. Those needing grafting, budding or any other operation are raised till their stems attain the diameter equal to pencil thickness or one cm. At this time, they are usually 30-45 cm tall.

In nursery beds, the plants get better conditions for their development and growth due to wider spacing, better aeration and other better growing conditions. Normally these plants are kept in these beds for one or two seasons.

Pot Mixture

A mixture made for filling pots or containers for growing of plants is known as a pot mixture. It is also known as soil mixture or soil mix. A mixture is prepared by mixing various ingredients in different proportions but they have the basic material as soil, which is fine in texture. The ingredients are necessary for the development of plant right from the start of placement of seeds in them to the end of the plant.

In general, pot mixtures are usually used for sowing of small seeds that need care, and planting of cuttings and other vegetative parts of the plants, which can give rise to individual plants on their sprouting.

Commonly, one part of soil, one part of peat, moss leaf mould and one part of sand are mixed together to form a mixture. Every ingredient has to be finely ground and of almost uniform size.

Another mixture is prepared by using the following formula

Ingredients	*Quantity*
1. Mineral matter	45%
2. Organic matter	5%
3. Moisture	25%
4. Air	25%

In another preparation, clay and sand are mixed in the ratio of 3:1 and then one third of this quantity is added to one part of well-rotten farm yard manure (FYM) or compost. To make it simpler, use the following mixture:

Clay	3 parts
Sand	1 part
FYM	1 part

To make a good mixture, soil particles are crushed and passed through a sieve of 0.1 mm mesh. Farm yard manure is also ground with a wooden mallet to have the desired size of particles. Too fine particles should be avoided. Mixing should be thorough and it is better to mix all the ingredients in an heap and then the pots may be filled with the mixture.

Sand

For testing the germination percentage of seeds under field and laboratory conditions, sand may be used as a media. It is washed in water once or twice depending upon the source. In case it is needed for study of nutritional aspects affecting the seedlings, pure sand is washed in acid and then 3-4 times in pure water till it has no chemical reaction.

For sowing of seed and growing seedlings for few days (2-3 days) sand as such or washed in water is an excellent medium.

Since sand cannot provide any nutrition to the plant and cannot retain moisture, it is used for a specific period of 2-3 days after the germination of seed or sprouting of the vegetative parts of the plant. Difficult to propagate parts of the plants can be grown under this type of media, but great care has to be taken at a later stage by supplying nutrition through artificial media.

In general, more watering and good amount of nutrients is necessary for raising plants in sand. Once the stored quantity of food material in the cotyledons of the seed, cutting or other vegetative part of the plant is exhausted or finished, either the young plant should meet its own requirement by making food through photosynthesis or the young plant should be provided nutrition by artificial means, i.e. solutes.

Sawdust

Sawdust is a waste product from the sawmills and that is used for sowing of seeds and growing of plants for nutritional studies. Its use is like that of sand but being of organic nature, it has the ability of attracting pathogens. Sawdust can not be washed like that of sand and hence may retain some of the impurities. It takes long time to decay fully but starts decaying after a month or so. Sawdust can absorb maximum amount of water and as such becomes wet very quickly and may suffocate the embryo of seed that results in cessation of germination and hence no plant seedling occurs. Further, when moisture is plenty in the sawdust, conditions are quite congenial for the spread of diseases.

Vermiculite

This material is artificially prepared from mica, which can absorb water and can lose water when dried. It can be washed chemically for its reuse. It is readily available in the market. It does not provide any nourishment to the young seedling since it is not a growing media. It is used for specific purposes and for a short duration. It is not popular among commercial growers due to the requirement of nutritional solutions, which are difficult to prepare by a common man and moreover this method is more costly and laborious.

The above mentioned three media—sand, sawdust and vermiculite can be used for testing the germination of seeds but if the seedlings are to be raised in these media, one has to provide the nourishing material by timely and regular calibration of the nutrient solutions which is highly risky and needs technical know-how and as such can not be used for commercial purposes.

Jiffy

Now-a-days specially prepared growing media packed in self-biodegradable netting is available. It is generally a circular block of 3 to 4 cm diameter and ½ to 1 cm thickness enclosed in a net, which is not visible at the first glance. Square blocks are also available. This is usually olive green to brown in colour and has a good capacity to absorb moisture (Fig. 5).

The seed is placed in the centre of this flat disc or block where it is slightly sunken and water is given to it. On receiving the humidity, the disc swells up and the seed is covered over by the sides of the block of Jiffy. These discs have sufficient and suitable plant food material for the young seedling to grow for about 2-3 weeks. Individual blocks can be transplanted in a pot or in the field without

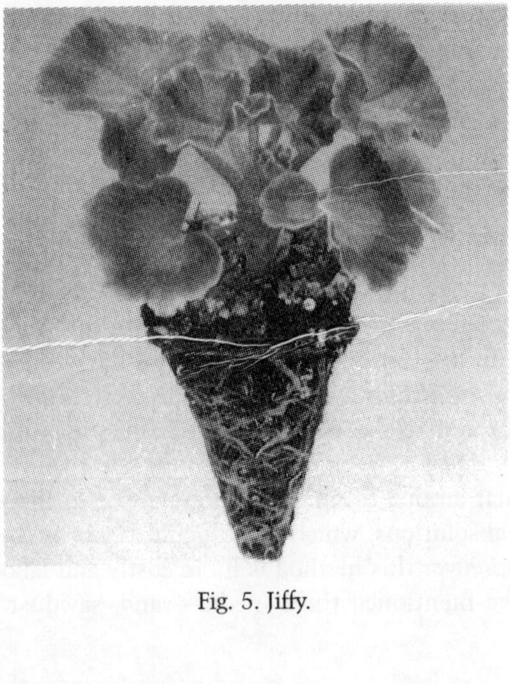

Fig. 5. Jiffy.

making any cut. On transplanting, the roots can come out of the netting without being damaged, so the growth of the young plant goes unrestricted.

This product is available in foreign countries and is yet to be made available in our country but is highly suitable for valuable and small seeds, which need care and attention during the early stage of their development.

The reserve or stored food material of the seed is utilized on the emergence of radical and plumule and after that for want of food material, the young seedlings are forced to die. This media has to be used with great care and utmost precautions.

8

Greenhouse

Plants, under natural conditions grow and bear flowers, fruits and seeds in their own specific manner but there are some hurdles like unfavourable weather conditions, attack of insect-pests and diseases etc., which restrict their development and growth. Therefore, there is need to protect the plants from such adverse conditions, so as to allow them to grow vigorously. This led to the invention of a shelter where the plants can grow or pass over their critical period of growth under most favourable conditions. The shelter so prepared is known as *Greenhouse,* which is generally a structure, covered with a transparent material to utilize the solar radiant energy and to provide suitable environmental conditions for the optimum growth of plants.

Types of Greenhouses

A greenhouse is a place where plants can grow under controlled conditions so as to grow, develop and produce at the will of the grower. In the beginning, these houses or structures were fully covered with a thatched roof or a covering that could be lifted with ease. But later on, they were being covered with slates and further, with glass and as such they came to be known as glasshouses. Now, many types of materials are available to cover them, hence different other names are given to them, depending upon the type of covering used.

A glasshouse is with a roof and sides of glass of different sizes. Instead of glass, fibreglass, which is stronger, durable and does not break into pieces, is used and so the name of such a house is fibre

Fig. 6. Greenhouse in the hills.

glasshouse. This is hardier than the glasshouse but is costlier than that, though the chances of its breakage are much less. Plastic house or plastic greenhouse has a cover of a transparent alkathene or polythene, which is strong enough to withstand the varying temperatures of summer and winter, hails, strong winds, etc. These are also known as poly-houses, poly-tubes or poly-tunnels. But, in general, greenhouse is the commonly accepted and popular name (Fig. 6).

Structure of greenhouse

Types of material used for making a structure of the greenhouse also vary. Two things are necessary for a greenhouse, i.e. the framc or structure and the cover. To support the cover and structures on the sides, pillars are needed. The structure of pillars or support may vary with the type of frame and size of a greenhouse. Small and semi-circular greenhouses, i.e. poly-tunnels may not need pillars or support in the centre but heavy or large greenhouses which may have heavy structure of iron or wood, do need strong support to have the roof and sides intact.

Fig. 7. A shelter house locally prepared.

Frames may be wooden or of iron or aluminum for a greenhouse of glass cover. Pieces of glasses are fixed tightly in the frames by putting some fixing material along the sides of the glass. In case of poly-house, the sides and roof are covered with a polythene sheet, which is placed deep in the soil to hold it. In some cases the sheet is put in between the two tubes/frames.

Pillars of cement and concrete mixture are also built to support the roof of a greenhouse of glass or fibreglass. Number of pillars required will depend upon the size of a greenhouse but six pillars are necessary at the minimum level. The height of these pillars

Fig. 8. A greenhouse structure.

varies but generally the highest pillar may be 3 metre tall. Pillars can be round, square or rectangular but in practice, the side pillars are usually square in shape while the central ones may be round to avoid unnecessary clash in the greenhouse. When wooden pillars are used, they are usually square in shape, of the width of 8-10 cm. Iron or metallic pillars are also used but they are usually of round but hollow pipes of the diameter of 5-10 cm. Pillars of cement and concrete mix are usually white-washed or painted with a white paint while the wooden and metallic structures are painted with paint. If more money is available, these structures may be painted with a silver paint. Doors and windows may also be painted with white or silver paint. Some people paint the wooden frames with green paint that is also good but white or silver paint provides a good sanitary look (Fig. 8).

Depending upon the material to be kept, the specific period of keeping it in the greenhouse and the type of material for construction and coverage, the size and shape of the greenhouse varies. Heavy greenhouse with pillars of cement and concrete mix with a fibreglass top or cover may last for 2 decades or more while others may last for 5 years. On the other hand, plastic-houses or poly-tunnels do last for 2-3 years only provided they are maintained in the best manner.

Shape of the greenhouse is generally pentagonal from the front and back. For about 2 metres, they do have the straight walls and then it tapers towards the top to form a triangle, which is needed for the easy run off of rain water and snow. Wind may pass over it. Leaves, etc., if they fall on the roof, do not stay there for a long period and are blown off by the wind.

Equipments for Greenhouse

Common greenhouses are just shelters for the plants with the aim of protecting the plants or other plant material from extreme variations in the temperature like snowfall in hills, drought in plains and excessive rains. These greenhouses have only benches to keep the plant pots or trays in order. They do have a hard floor preferably a cemented one and there is good provision for the drainage of water. For control of temperature and circulation of air, the doors and windows are opened for free passage of air current.

Equipments and fittings needed in a greenhouse will depend upon the type of material to be raised or kept. Simple greenhouses are the structures which can house the plants under shade. They are not provided with sophisticated equipments. Generally, during a warm weather, plants are either watered frequently or a pond of water is created artificially in the centre to keep the humidity under check. Doors may be opened or closed to provide necessary ventilation, air passage and to raise the temperature.

Misting, cooling, heating, balancing the air supply with its quantity and quality, artificial lighting, controlling temperature and humidity are some of the operations that are governed by different automatic equipments fixed in a greenhouse.

An ideal greenhouse must have a good system for control of temperature, humidity, nutritional requirement and pathogens. Heating, cooling and ventilation are must which may be controlled manually or automatically. For an efficient control and good working, lot of money is needed to provide controlled electronic gadgets. Further, some expenditure has also to be incurred on the upkeep and maintenance of these equipments.

Some of the greenhouses, where the plants from the tissue-culture laboratory are kept for hardening, need good care and management. Humidifiers, misting chamber, thermostatic control of temperature and light, and provision of artificial shutters/blinds for darkness are some of the common accessories needed in a greenhouse of average range.

Qualities of Greenhouse

Generally, greenhouses have equipments for the maintenance of temperature and humidity and are equipped with heating, cooling and ventilating equipments and for maintenance of gas levels within the greenhouse. These are meant for scientific purposes and for a good commercial use. An ordinary greenhouse is the one where plants can be kept or stored to protect them from hot winds, hails, icy winds and for maintaining isolation distances for the purpose of producing pure seed. A greenhouse may be partitioned to suit the need and for economic utilities. Shelves and stands are usually provided for efficient working and easy management. Above all, a greenhouse must have a satisfactory sanitation system where the water spilt over the floor should be drained off at the earliest. No pathogen should be allowed to develop. Thus, phyto-sanitary precautions are a must in a good greenhouse to have healthy, disease-free and vigorous plants.

Advantages of Greenhouse

Greenhouses are gaining popularity day-by-day in every country due to the following advantages:

1. Protection from severe winter

Young and tender plants cannot survive under severe cold, particularly in the temperate region where the temperature falls many degrees below the freezing point. They get injured in the open due to freezing of their cell sap. These plants can be kept in the greenhouse to protect them from severe winter temperature where they can get ambient conditions for their growth.

2. Protection from adverse climatic conditions

Hails, hot winds, winter frost, etc. are the common vagaries of nature that drastically affect the growth and development of young and tender plants in the field. Hails during spring and late summer, hot and dry winds during summer months and frost in early winters hamper the growth of both the young and old plants. They can be protected against all such calamities if kept in a greenhouse.

3. Protection against pathogens

Number of diseases, insects and pests attack the plant material in the open since they (pathogens) multiply frequently under field conditions and it becomes difficult to control them. Further, it becomes a costly affair to protect the plants under field conditions. Control in greenhouse is easy and cheap. Depending upon the plant material being raised and the presence of different equipments in a greenhouse, the attack of these calamities can be minimised. Generally, plant material raised in greenhouse is checked thoroughly before being entered in a greenhouse. If the plants are raised right from their seedling stage, there is very little possibility of the intrusion of pathogens in the greenhouse, but, if the pathogens have entered, they can be controlled very easily provided they are detected in the early stage. In case it has taken the epidemic form, whole of the plant material has to be treated. Early detection of pathogens can be controlled with much ease and at less cost.

4. Maintenance of purity of plant material

In case of cross-pollinated crops, particularly the Cucurbits, Solanaceous and other plant species, genetic purity of the seed produced is of prime importance. It is easy to maintain the species and varietal characteristics within a greenhouse, which may be almost difficult to maintain under field conditions where isolation distance of at least 200 metres has to be kept in between the two varieties apart from keeping them away from the reach of honeybees and other insects, which help in pollination. Greenhouse is the best alternative where a particular variety can be raised or multiplied in a single separate chamber and thus, the chances of cross-pollination are completely eliminated. The genetic purity can be maintained since it is easy to monitor and observe the characters very closely and if found variable, can be checked.

5. Regulation of temperature

Since most of the greenhouses have the arrangements for control of temperature, the plant material grown can be provided with a desired temperature to modify the physiological processes going on within the plant either to hasten or delay the harvesting date. Regulation of temperature is also beneficial for speedy germination of seeds and pollination.

6. Control of humidity

Humidifier fitted in the greenhouse is designed to maintain the desired level of humidity for plant growth and development. This is particularly essential for the germination of seeds and growth of foliage and cactus plants. Too much humidity invites pathogens, while too little causes more evaporation of water from soil surface and more transpiration of water from the leaf surface.

7. Regulation of light

Light, whether it is sunlight or artificial light through electric bulbs or tubes, is essential for the flowering of small plants. Light controls the vegetative and reproductive phases of the plants in most of the cases. There are only few plants, which are not affected by the light intensity, i.e. they can grow well under short-day and as well as under long-day conditions. Plants sensitive to light duration and intensity are affected the most since daily light frequency, intensity and exposure has a marvelous effect, this may induce early flowering or late flowering. Generally, greenhouses are designed to have the maximum exposure of plants to sunlight but by providing blinds, the effect of light can be reduced. By providing artificial light during the night, more exposure to light is possible. Thus, the vegetative and reproductive phases of the plant can be regulated.

Light intensity affects the temperature and as such exposure to light for more hours may raise the temperature and the effect is increased double-fold.

8. Maintenance of fertility level

All the plant materials grown in the greenhouse can be provided with a uniform and desired level of fertility. Since the fertility in the greenhouse is maintained by supply of macro and micronutrients through a system of liquid fertilization/fertigation, the normal or differential doses can be regulated. Generally, the soil in the greenhouse is uniform in fertility and other ingredients because the soil is either collected or prepared in special ways to have uniform structure and fertility. These plants can be provided with any type of dose as per need. For commercial production, uniformity of fertility is most essential while for experimental purposes differential doses of nutrients may be used. For the study of deficiency or excessive symptoms of various nutrients, it can be successfully conducted in a greenhouse, since fertility calibration is possible.

In case the manures and fertilizers are to be added in solid/powder form, a known quantity can be added to each and individual plant which may not be possible and easy under field conditions in the open.

9. Made-to-order production

Different activities like seeds can be sown, plants can be grown and harvesting of the produce can be done at will without waiting for the suitable climatic conditions to come and other natural conditions of the open field since all these conditions can be created artificially in the greenhouse. Off-season vegetables, (the vegetables out of season for a place where they are not commonly grown in that season) flowers, medicinal plants, herbs and some minor fruits like strawberry, berries, grapes, etc., can be harvested whenever needed. Generally, in a greenhouse, the maturity is almost uniform but it can be regulated as per need of the market. Out-of-season crops are sold at a good premium and as such the cost of production under greenhouse can be covered-up.

10. Home produce is always superior

It is believed that plants grown under own supervision and in close containers are always superior in quality than plants produced from other sources. It is a psychological effect, which provides mental satisfaction to the consumer who is himself a grower. Satisfaction derived from kitchen gardening is always maximum to the consumer and the same is true for the greenhouse. This aspect may not be very important from the commercial point of view since there is no provision of self-touch in that system.

11. Personal care

Plant material which is expensive, not easily available, rare and needs close care and supervision can get due attention and care in a greenhouse. It is easy to supervise and look after the plants in greenhouse rather than those in the open field under natural conditions. Difficult to propagate, small and costly seeds, young seedlings and tender plants can be raised easily in greenhouse.

Maintenance of Greenhouses

Ideal greenhouses need regular maintenance and check-up by a qualified person. Slight negligence may cause severe hazards. Once the contamination has entered, it may be difficult to eliminate so it is better to take the necessary precautions at the entry point.

Following are some of the measures, which one should take in maintaining the greenhouse.

1. Check-point

Plant material and seeds being taken into the greenhouse must be inspected and examined carefully to avoid the entry of pathogens and other unwanted material that may cause trouble in the greenhouse. It is better to keep the plant material under shade for a day or two before they are kept in a greenhouse, it will get them acclimatized.

2. Construction

The greenhouse should have at least double-door system so that no impurity or unwanted material finds its way into the greenhouse. Construction should be good, having no crevices but should have strong and well-filled joints. The owner should inspect it off and on.

3. Cleanliness

For managing a greenhouse, one must pay due care towards the simple rules of hygiene and cleanliness. Removal of scrap, rubbish, soil droppings, decaying leaves and other unwanted plant parts must be carried out regularly. If these are left in a greenhouse, they may attract insect-pests and may harbour diseases. All debris must be removed regularly, so that there is no danger of its being attacked by pathogens.

The debris removed from a greenhouse should be thrown, destroyed or burnt, away from the greenhouse. Material to be used for making compost or farm yard manure may be collected separately and put in a pit. The drain pipe going out of the greenhouse should be taken quite away from the greenhouse.

4. Painting

It is better to paint all the wooden or iron pieces and other structures within and outside the greenhouse, with a white paint. Wooden frames are generally painted with a good sticking paint of white colour while iron frames and structures are painted with a silver paint. Apart from protecting the wood from decay and iron from rusting, this painting provides a better look. Glasses may be cleaned with a tissue paper or a newspaper to ward-off the excessive moisture and dirt from them since dirty glasses block the passage of light from outside. Smoky look should be avoided. Pillars of cement and concrete mix or brick may be white-washed at regular intervals. Doors must be painted and cleaned regularly.

5. Fumigation

Great attention for the control of natural enemies like insect-pests and diseases must be paid. It is better to fumigate the greenhouse before the start of its use and later, when the plant material had been taken out. In between, regular inspection should be made. Different fumigants are available in the market, which should be used. After fumigation, close the doors and ventilators perfectly at least for 12 hours or so. Avoid too strong fumigation since the manual labour is to enter the greenhouse very off and on.

Affected material may either be given suitable treatment or destroyed and burnt to eliminate the cause. If left unattended, they invite pathogens, insects and viruses. There may be bacterial infection.

6. Light

Provision of proper amount of light is a must. Clean glasses will provide maximum light intensity but when light of required intensity for particular period is needed, arrangements have to be made for putting blinds or other stuff to block the entry of light, which should not hamper the temperature.

Electric bulbs, tubes or shutters, if provided, must be checked regularly. If these are workable by automatic mechanical or electronic system, they should be inspected regularly.

7. Ventilation

The movement of air within the greenhouse is to be regulated. In a normal or simple greenhouse, ventilators of double doors are provided for the removal of warm air and they are generally near the roof. Exhaust fans with flippers may be used. They should not allow the air to come through the exhaust fans. Lack of ventilation will raise the temperature and gas level in the greenhouse. These are harmful for natural growth since higher temperature helps in early ripening or maturity while the altered level of gas may cause abnormal growth and its imbalance may lead to alteration in the photosynthesis and respiration rates.

In general, there is photosynthesis in the day in which carbon dioxide is used by plants while they give out oxygen but during the night, the plants respire in which carbon dioxide is given out, oxygen is taken in and there is release of energy that leads to more of carbon dioxide in the environment. Carbon dioxide when in excess leads to serious hazards. There are other gases also, so the ventilation is a must. Here, the ventilation is for the purpose of regulating the level of various gases and temperature.

8. Humidity

Humidity in terms of moisture present in the atmosphere and soil plays an important role in the well-being of plants. Without humidity, a seed cannot germinate since the water/moisture absorbed by the cotyledon of a seed enables it to rupture and the embryo to activate vigorously to get the radicle and plumule. On the other hand, excess of humidity may cause blockage of air passage in the soil, causing the death of the root and in the atmosphere it causes slow down of the transpiration rate, which means stoppage of the movement of the cell sap.

Humid atmosphere within the greenhouse attracts fungal attack and the speedy growth of spiders and mites. Humidity has to be regulated at regular intervals. Thermostatic humidifiers may solve the problem to a large extent but they have to be monitored at regular intervals to check the flow of water to them and then its release. Damping-off is a common hazard in young seedlings of vegetables and flowering plants, which is a result of over-watering in the greenhouse.

9. Feeding

Since the plants are more or less under controlled atmospheric conditions, their nutritional needs have to be taken care of very carefully and seriously. It is certain that the demand of nutrients under field conditions and greenhouse conditions is quite different due to variation in growth and development patterns under the two entirely different situations. Liquid feeding has to be made and for this purpose, due precautions for the preparation of balanced solution of nutrients must be viewed upon seriously. Due care is to be taken regarding the demand of different plants and crops. Regular inspection of the feeding line, its distributors and its joints should be made. Broken or leaking joints and nozzles must be replaced as soon as they seem to be out of order. During the spray, the solution should be stirred so that it does not have anything settled at the bottom.

10. Heating

During winter, when the temperature outside the greenhouse is quite low, there is a normal feature of power failure causing chill within the greenhouse. During heating, regulation of temperature by a thermostatic control is a must. Dependable heating unit or system should be resorted to, particularly in hills where the temperature inside and outside the greenhouse is of great variation. In plains, the temperature variations are severe only during the last quarter of the night.

Usually steam or hot water pipes are used for heating purpose since provision of heaters, electric or others are not suitable. Burning of charcoal, straw or other refuge is done but this practice should not be encouraged since it causes infection in the first instance, then the smoke and finally the burnt material in the form of ash may move or be blown-up hither and thither which causes shabby look, spoilage of leaves and the smoky glasses.

11. Cooling

This is necessary in plains as during the summer months, the temperature in the open may go as high as 50°C or so but in the greenhouse, it may rise even few degrees more. Generally, the plants grow best under the temperature range of 25°-30°C and when the temperature rises further, there is great loss of water from the plants through transpiration. Simply opening of ventilators does not serve the purpose of lowering down the temperature. Some suitable and dependable system of cooling has to be provided in the greenhouse.

Opposite to that of heating during winter, cooling in summer is desirable for luxuriant growth of plants. Slight negligence can raise the temperature to such a level that plants may completely dry-up due to incipient wilting followed by permanent wilting.

12. Drainage

When there is excess of moisture in the trays or growing containers and other structures, it causes root rot, which may invite some other diseases. Mere contact of water for a long time causes softening of the tissues, which results in fungal infection. Proper draining is provided for the removal of excessive water from the pots and the greenhouse. Drainage channels have to be made and covered by a suitable cover for the speedy drainage of water. Drains are to be cleaned periodically. Level of the drains has to be gradual. Moreover, the floor of the greenhouse should also have a gradual slope. Where benches have been made, due care has to be taken for the collection of surplus water from them so that it does not remain there and is passed out. Water when stagnant, is the root cause of spread of fungal diseases, algae and lichens.

Similarly, seepage from the floor of the greenhouse must be checked. Seepage increases the amount of water needed by the greenhouse in the beginning and once it is saturated, causes dampness and reduces the requirement of water by the plants growing in the greenhouses. Seeping down of water may cause the floor to sink down or have uneven level. Thus, it is essential that the floor of the greenhouse should be a cemented one, which does not allow the water to seep down. Drains should also be cemented and checked regularly against their breakage.

13. Repair

A thorough check should be made for the broken glasses, torn or worn out polythene sheets, cracked pillars and floor, breakage of the frame or structure of the greenhouse, benches, pipes for the flow of water and nutrient solutions and other liquids, heating and cooling system, control for temperature, humidity, gaseous exchange, etc. All the equipments fitted or placed in the greenhouse must be in a good working condition. Broken pots or containers must be repaired or replaced. Doors and ventilators must be thoroughly checked.

Suitable Crops for Greenhouse

1. *Off-season vegetables*

Tomato, peas, beans, lettuce, cucumber, onion, brinjal, radish, leek, asparagus, endive, sweet pepper, Brussels's sprout, etc.

2. *Flowering plants*

Azaleas, fuchsias, cannas, begonia, cyclamen, rose, salvia, geranium, narcissus, gladiolus, lilies, chrysanthemum, carnation, orchids, etc.

3. *Cactus and succulent plants*

Different types of cacti and succulent plants like agaves, crassula, euphorbia, sedum, rubber plant, monstera, ferns, etc.

4. *Climbers*

Passion flower, ipomoea, ferns, tradescantia, jesmenium, etc.

5. *Foliage plants*

Asparagus, fern, ruscus etc.

6. *Pot grown fruits*

Apple on M 9 rootstock, pear on quince rootstock, peach and plum on their own rootstock/seedling, orange, mango, grape, fig, strawberry, etc.

7. *Medicinal and herbal plants*

Lemon grass, lavender, scented geranium, etc.

8. *Seedlings*

Seeds of vegetables, flowering plants, medicinal plants, herbs, etc. are sown for getting the seedlings.

9. *Difficult to seed and propagate plants*

Tubers, corms, bulbs, asexually propagated plants raised from the stem cuttings, grafting, budding, etc.

9

Seed

Seeds are the outcome of successful pollination followed by successful fertilization in flowers that leads to zygote, which becomes seed on maturity. In technical or scientific terms, it is the ripened ovule containing an embryo and as such some parts of the flower may remain attached to the seed. They are available in plenty depending upon the species. A single plant may give rise to thousands of seeds, so the nursery growers can easily collect them. In general, the tree or plant sheds its seeds on maturity for further dispersal and they germinate to raise identical plants for maintenance of the species. This is the law of nature.

Seeds are important from many aspects. They are storehouse of food material for the new seedling. They provide food and other ingredients to the living beings, including the mankind, animals, birds and insects. Seeds are the vehicles for the spread of new life from place to place by the elements, animals and people. Seeds are a wonder and possess remarkably complex and effective protective mechanism that insures survival.

Plants raised through seeds are generally alike to their parents since they are usually self-pollinated, i.e. the pollination occurs within the same flower and as such the characters remain almost identical to the parent plant. Many vegetable, cereal and fruit crops are self-pollinated. In cross-pollinated crops, the pollination may occur from the pollen of a different flower of the same variety or of the other variety. When they are of the same variety, the characters exhibited by the seed are identical but when there is a different variety, the characters may be different. Thus, in cross-pollinated crops, great care has to be taken. Nursery growers are advised to collect the seed of a particular variety from a reliable source. In case the seed is to be raised by himself at his own place, maintenance of isolation distance should be there. Maintenance of genetic purity is not an easy task and it has to be learnt from a professional and then followed in letter and spirit.

Uniformity of expression of characters in the offspring is of vital importance for successful and commercial production. As far as possible, the progeny or the seedlings should have genuine but identical characters. It is of prime importance for the seedlings of ornamental plants since the flower colour and other characters can change with slight negligence. One can not assume or assess the colour of flowers to appear in plants in their seedling stage and it is only the grown-up plants that flower at a later stage, showing these characters, thus selection of seed is very important for the success of nursery.

Qualities of Good Seed

The term good seed signifies a good variety, high rate of germination, uniform and correct size, freedom from diseases and the absence of weed and other crop seed. Seed should be capable of germinating satisfactorily and the percentage and speed of germination being of considerable cultural importance.

There are certain characters, which are common to all seeds that must be considered seriously at the time of selecting or procurement of seeds.

1. Purity

Seed sample should be pure and true to type in genetical, varietal and other characteristics. Seeds of other species or varieties should not be in the sample. To get uniform crop of a single variety, it is very essential that the seed sample should be of the particular variety, otherwise the cost of production is liable to increase by demanding extra expenses on weeding and rouging at a later stage.

2. Clean

The seed sample should be free from inert material like stones, pebbles, dust, dirt, broken seeds, their husks and other unwanted material. This material adds weight to the seed sample and decreases its value, since it has to be cleaned before sowing. Nursery growers must see this personally.

3. Physical characteristics

Shape, colour, shine, hardness, specific gravity, weight, etc., are of prime importance in enhancing the value of a seed sample. Every species or variety of crop has definite shape and colour. Misshapen seeds are not preferred, as they have either been affected by the inclement weather or by pathogens or insects. Colour of the seed has a bearing on its quality. Properly mature seeds have dark colour rather than of light colour. Bright shine on the surface of the seed indicates the proper maturity. Fully mature seeds are usually plump, bold, hard and of specific weight while the immature seeds are not so, they lack the shine, are usually shrivelled and light in colour and weight. Weight of the seed is generally expressed as that of 1000 seeds. The size of the seed has also a role to play. Normally, the mature seeds are of normal size, while the immature seeds may be small in size with irregular shape. Mottled colour, misshapen, light in weight, dull in appearance are the qualities of seeds which must be rejected outrightly since they do not germinate and if they germinate, the seedlings are weak and shortlived.

4. Health

Seeds should be healthy, free from the attack of insect-pests and diseases. Samples may be examined visually or through a hand magnifying lens to ascertain the absence of such material in the seed lot. Sometimes, the insects may not be visible to the naked eye but their eggs or pupa may be there which become active on getting suitable conditions for their growth when the seeds are sown in the field or in a pot. Similarly, the spores of bacteria and fungus adhering to the seed-coat may be inactive to view but they become active during the seed germination. Healthy seed will give a healthy look and will yield a healthy plant that is generally tolerant to the attack of various pathogens whereas weak seeds are easily attacked by insects and pests. Moreover the cost of production is increased by spending money and labour on the control of these pathogens at a later stage.

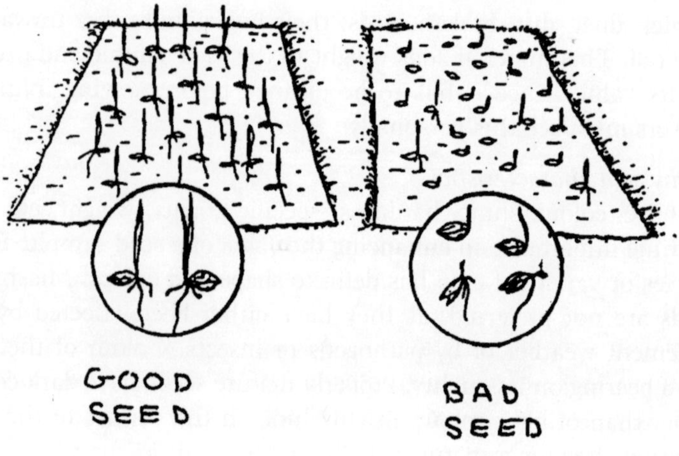

Fig. 9. Germination pattern.

5. Maturity

Fully mature seeds are the best ones to germinate and provide healthy seedlings as immature and over-ripe seeds delay the process of germination and produce weak plants that do not take-up the growth in a uniform way. Immature seeds do not separate easily from the parent material which may be a pod or pulp and in getting them out of the pod, fruit or pulp, their embryo or the point of joint with the pod may be damaged. Thus, immature seeds are not able to germinate.

On the other hand, over-matured seeds do have their testas or seed-coats hardened due to being on the plant or in a fruit for more than the required period. Over-ripening also causes delay and loss in germination. It is a common belief that tree-ripe or plant-ripe fruits yield better seeds. They should be removed as soon as possible so as to avoid the over-maturity. In general practice, seeds that are going to ripe shortly, i.e. in about 3 days or so, are picked and dried in the sun and as such they get fully matured in this period.

6. Moisture content

The moisture content of the seed has a direct bearing on its keeping quality. The moisture content is usually expressed as a percentage of the dry weight. High humidity with the seed is harmful as it leads to the swelling of seeds before their actual germination. On the other hand, dry seeds lose their viability much earlier than the normal seeds. In general practice, seeds are dried under the sun for 2 to 3 days before they are stored. Generally 9-10 per cent moisture humidity in seed sample is considered sufficient for its longevity.

7. *Germination capacity*

In general, every seed must germinate when provided with suitable conditions for the germination but all seeds may not germinate and even some may germinate after the expiry of their normal time of germination. Therefore, seeds are tested for their germination capacity, which is expressed as the percentage of the seeds germinated in a fixed normal period. This period is usually not more than 10 days, but will depend upon the kind of seed. Sometimes, the seeds take about 2-3 months to germinate as in the case of apple, pear, cherry, plum and peach. They should complete their germination in a reasonable time.

Seeds should have at least 80% germination, otherwise due addition of seed quantity is to be compensated which means more addition to expenditure. With low germination percentage, more quantity of seed, space and operations will be required which adds extra cost in the production of nursery plants.

Germination percentage may either be tested in the laboratory or field. Germination percentage tested in the field is generally lower than that of the laboratory since they get all the congenial and controlled atmospheric conditions in the laboratory whereas in the field, there are many vagaries of nature.

Collection of Seeds

Nursery growers who can afford may collect the seeds of various plants themselves. Though it is a time-consuming job but there is surety of the quality and the quantity. For nursery of perennial trees, a nursery grower may have the mother trees in the nurseries or attached orchards for the procurement of seeds, bud sticks and other propagation material. For annual and seasonal crops, seed has to be raised. This may not be possible with all nursery growers due to so many factors. Production of crops is a separate business while nursery growing is another but different avocation. Combination of both may not be possible with most of the commercial nursery growers, since various resources like land, time and conduct of different operations limit them.

Seeds from the healthy plants or trees are collected when they are almost fully ripened. Generally, on ripening, the seed is separated from the fruit or stalk and is dispersed by natural and artificial means like wind, water, animals, birds, etc. Ripe fruits, mature pods and other parts that are healthy may be collected and then the seed may be separated and processed after cleaning or sown as the case may be.

Pods of plants like pea, beans, acacia, salvia, radish, etc., are collected just before they are opening, i.e. splitting up and then spread in the sun over a polythene sheet or tarpaulin. This helps in the automatic opening of pods on the polythene sheet. If required, the pods may be opened manually by putting slight pressure in between the fingers of hand. They may be beaten gently to crush the covering of the pods to get the seeds out of the jacket. Drying in the sun for 2-3 days is usually sufficient for the splitting of pods and separation of seeds. This happens in the natural way. These seeds may be collected and dried for a day or two to get rid of the surplus moisture and the mixture is cleaned to get the seeds sepa-

Fig. 10. Seed extraction, washing in water and collection.

rated from their hulls and other unwanted material and packed in airtight containers or polythene bags for future use.

Fruits of apple, pear, cherry, guava, *Madhuca indica*, egg plant, *Syzygium cumini*, *Azadirachta indica* and many other species are soaked in water for a day or two and then washed in pure water once or twice so that the pulp is separated from the seed. If needed, fruits may be cut into two or four pieces to expose the seeds, but a caution must be followed. The blade of a knife should not damage the seeds. They should not be allowed to remain in the pulp for a long time otherwise they will lose their viability and may not germinate easily.

For other species, particularly the forest trees and social forestry trees, the seeds may be collected from the ground while they are still within their fruits or pods. In this case, only the healthy and disease-free fruits or seeds should be collected. It is possible where the seed is bigger in size and is not readily damaged by remaining on the ground for a day or two. Moreover, the number of seeds borne on a tree is plenty. It is better to get the pods, capsules, cones, etc., harvested or picked from the tree itself and then seeds collected under own supervision. These seeds may be cleaned, dried and stored in a airtight container.

Cleaning the Seeds

Seeds collected from any source must be cleaned thoroughly. They do have some impurities that must be removed before they are being stored or sown in the field. Visual watch and passing them through specified sieves and even simple careful winnowing is most essential. This will make them get rid of the inert material like dust, small stones, crumbs, parts of the plant, etc.

Winnowing the seed mixture helps in the separation of hulls, husks, broken seeds, immature seeds, pieces of the leaves, stalks, pods, etc. since both these categories have different specific gravities. Passing through a sieve helps in gradation of the seed sample and removal of bigger or smaller seeds. During sieving and winnowing, some of the unwanted material can be picked up manually but with mechanical means, it is not possible (Fig. 11).

It is very important to remove seeds of weeds, broken seeds,

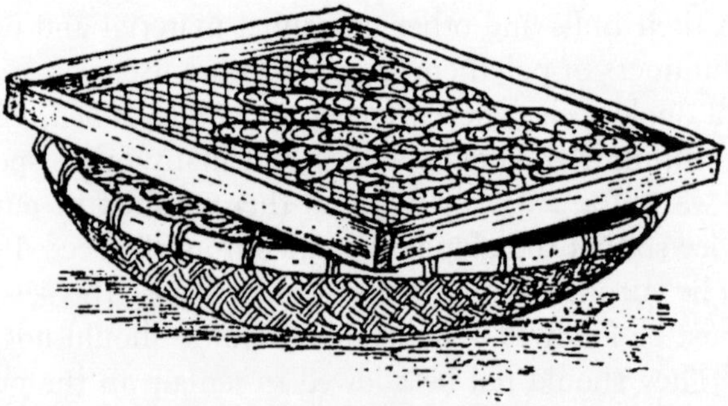

Fig. 11. Draining water from seeds through sieve.

immature and damaged seeds, seeds of other species or varieties and other material.

If the seed sample needs a quick washing with clean water, it may be done very gently and the seeds should not remain in the water for more than five minutes. They may be washed, drained by putting over a sieve and dried under shade and then under the sun.

Storage of Seeds

Generally, seeds after collecting are stored and sown when needed. As a common practice, the seeds that mature in the present season are sown in the second season. For example, apple seeds are collected in September-October and are sown in the month of December or so. In case of citrus, the seeds are collected, washed and sown in a week's time of their collection. Some seeds may be stored for a longer time.

To ward off the attack of pathogens, insects and the effect of unfavourable climatic conditions, seeds are stored to remain safe, viable and intact for a long time. Storage life of the seeds varies from species to species and it may be from a few days to 3-4 years. The storage life of the seed depends upon a number of factors like the kind of species, nature of seed, maturity index of the seed, container in which the seed has been stored and the conditions of storage. In general, the seeds have to be stored from the time of their harvest to the time of sowing. Most of the farmers and nursery growers store the seeds in earthen pots, which are sealed after putting the seeds in them. Some use plastic bottles or containers to store the seeds. These being easily available and cheap are in practice with most people but are not very safe for long term storage.

There are different types of containers for the storage of seeds. Containers may be of different materials, shapes and sizes. The simple way is to store the seeds in paper packets or sachets that are sealed and then kept in a room or in an almirah where they get low temperature and are away from the reach of pathogens, insects and rodents. These paper bags may be printed and the particulars about the seed quality and quantity may be written on them. The date of collection and packaging must be mentioned on them along with the kind of seed. These packages are good for small sample and seeds of small size. Most of the seeds of the vegetable and ornamental plants are packed in paper bags. These paper bags may be lined from inside by a thick waterproof paper which does not allow moisture to get into or get out of the bag. They should have all the requisite information on the cover.

An improvement over the paper bags is the use of polythene bags. These bags are useful for storage of seeds under unfavourable storage conditions of moisture since they are impermeable to moisture, so the movement of moisture is restricted. Polythene may be transparent or opaque, but in general, transparent one is used as the seeds are visible from outside, but opaque is still better as the seeds do not get unnecessary exposure to light which reduces the life of the seed. Since the polythene bags are stored in a room or a box, which is not opened frequently, the seeds contained in them do not get extra quantity of light and so they remain viable for a pretty long time. Label must be put on the bag or a label may be put inside the bag before sealing. For commercial purposes, there are printed bags, which have the complete information about the kind, quality, quantity, date of packing and date of expiry of the seed. The commercial seed producing companies use these types of bags. Bags of small quantity should be preferred as it is easy to handle and manage them.

Seeds are also stored in cardboard boxes of small size. Seeds after packing in a paper bag or a polythene bag are put in these containers that are fully labelled. This provides extra cover to the seed packets so that they are not damaged during transport of these boxes. This packing becomes bit costlier than that of paper or polythene bags. Similarly, the paper or polythene bags may be stored in wooden or tin boxes to provide extra safety against rats and insects but adds to the cost.

Seeds may be packed in wooden or metallic containers. Both have no provision of air circulation during storage. Therefore, the seed remains viable for a long time. Wooden boxes are usually rectangular in shape while the metallic boxes or containers are usually cylindrical. Metallic containers are of tin or aluminium. These are most suited for long distance transport and movement under unsatisfactory transport and weather conditions.

Large samples may be stored in gunny bags and iron-bins or bins. After putting the seeds in bags, they are properly sealed and placed in cool and dry place, which is not visited by rodents and other animals.

Precautions for Packing and Storage of Seeds

Following precautions have to be observed during the packing and storage of seeds:

1. Seeds should be clean, true to type and of a specified variety. It should be free from diseases, insects and unwanted materials. Diseases or insects can activate during storage so due care has to be taken.

2. If there is excess moisture in the seed, it may get swell during storage as the stores have ambient conditions. Swelling of the seed is first step towards its germination. Seeds can not grow further in store so the germination is arrested, the embryo gets killed and these seeds will never germinate when sown after the storage. Therefore, seeds with minimum quantity of moisture should be stored. In general, the relative humidity should be less than 40%.

3. Packing must be airtight and the packets be sealed properly. Excess of air is not beneficial for the seeds. Since the seeds are living being, they respire which means they can absorb oxygen from the atmosphere and then lose carbon dioxide. When there is excess of oxygen, there will be more of respiration, i.e. breakdown of complex substances and release of energy while the lack of oxygen and excess

of carbon dioxide limits the respiration. When there is less respiration, there is little loss of energy and so the seeds remain as such or dormant in a store. Thus, proper sealing helps in the reduction of respiration resulting in extension of life of seed.

4. Some of the containers cannot be packed airtight, e.g. gunny bags. They have to be stored as such. In such cases, the stores have to be kept locked, i.e. closed. No frequent opening should be there.

5. Labelling of the product on the cover of each package is a must. It provides information pertaining to the variety, kind, quantity, date of packing, germination percentage, etc. Some commercial nursery growers even mention the salient characters of the variety on the cover and make it quite attractive.

6. Seed packets and containers should neither be kept in humid places nor should be exposed to dry winds because both these conditions are unfavourable for embryo. Store should be free from the attack of rats, insects and other such calamities. It is better to mix some quantity (about 1-2%) of any insecticide like Aldrin, BHC, etc. with the sample before sealing or placing it in the store. It is advisable to fumigate the store before storage. The dose of the fumigant should be optimum and not lethal for the user.

7. Whatever container is used for storage of seeds, it should be well-sealed and airtight. It is always better to put a label giving details about the product, date of sealing, variety, quantity and other details, if possible.

8. Store should not be frequently opened, rain water should not be allowed to enter or it should not seep into the store. Floor should be cemented and without cracks. It is better to store the seeds in a cool chamber after packing them in a waterproof container.

9. Treated seeds should be kept away from the reach of children and animals.

Storage Life of Seeds

Depending upon the environmental conditions and the nature of seeds and species, the life span of seeds may vary from one week to three years. The seeds should be stored in such conditions, that they remain active, able to germinate after storage and produce healthy plants. It is possible only when the seeds have been collected from a healthy plant, are matured and are in good condition.

Generally, seeds are stored for one season, i.e. the period from the seed collection to sowing is only one season. In such cases, the life of the seed sample is only for few months. These seeds may be stored or kept in polythene bags or tin containers that are sealed and no extra humidity finds its way into the seed sample.

In some cases, seeds may need some period for rest to overcome dormancy and may need after-ripening. Seeds needing a rest period to complete the dormancy are usually of the temperate region. Apple, pear, plum, cherry, peach, etc. need a period of rest of about 60 to 90 days under chilling conditions to complete their dormancy. In some other cases, the seeds are retained in their fruits and taken out just a day or two before they are planted.

Most of the annual crop, vegetable and ornamental plant seeds can be stored for two years as after this they may lose their viability and vitality. Forest species are bit hardy and their seeds can be sown after their collection and storage.

Fruit seeds

The following table shows some of the fruit seeds with their storage longevity.

Common name	*Longevity (years)*
Almond	5
Apple	2-3
Crab apple	2-3
Apricot	5
Cherry (sweet)	1-3
Cherry (sour)	1-3
Citrus	1
Mango	30 days
Papaya	Immediate sowing is best
Peach	5
Pear	3
Pecan	1-3
Plum	4-6
Walnut	1-3

Flowering plants

Storage life of flowering plants is generally 2-3 years, but if kept under good storage conditions, it may be upto 10 years. Long storage should be avoided as it causes aging of the seed that may result in irregular stand of the crop on germination due to slow and prolonged period of germination under field conditions.

Vegetable seeds

The following table shows some of the vegetable seeds with their life span.

Common name	*Life span (years)*
Asparagus	3
Beans	3
Broccoli	5
Brussels's sprout	4
Cabbage	6-9 months
Cauliflower	4
Chinese cabbage	3
Celery	3
Cucumber	5
Cucurbits	3-4
Egg plant	4
Gourds	4
Lady's finger	2-4
Lettuce	6 months to 1 year
Melon	2
Onion	1
Parsnip	2
Pepper	2
Pumpkin	4
Spinach	3
Squash	4
Tomato	4
Water melon	2

Forest and avenue trees

Storage of seeds of forest and avenue species is not very common since they easily germinate in the coming season. Some of them if kept under cool and dry conditions, may retain their viability for two years or so. In practice, they are collected when mature and sown in their normal period of sowing.

Seed Treatment

Most of the types of seeds will germinate on getting suitable conditions for their germination like the air, moisture and temperature when placed in a safe or suitable medium—soil, pot or artificial medium. Seeds are having seed-coats under which is the embryo along with some food material stored in the cotyledon for the young seedling to become a full-fledged plant. This food material is available till the young plant gets the new leaves. Seeds that start germination out of their normal season do not grow into plants but soon wither away. But there are some species, which need some special treatments to overcome their shortcomings like after-ripening, dormancy, hard-coats, etc. Nature has provided some special mechanism for these seeds to prolong their life span since they are to pass through adverse climatic conditions and other vagaries of nature.

Under natural conditions, seeds may have to face some adverse conditions but to get suitable germination, they are given some special treatments to protect them against fungus, insects and pests that attack during storage and then during germination. The aims of treating the seeds is to provide them long life and protection against unfavourable conditions so that they give uniform germination to yield healthy crop and quality produce.

Seed treatments are usually given prior to sowing and hence are known as pre-treatments. Following are the common seed treatments.

1. Treatment with Pesticides

The seeds may have spores of the fungus on their surface at the time of collection. These spores can multiply on getting suitable conditions in the store and then in the field. The conditions conducive to seed germination are generally highly conducive for the multiplication of the spores of pathogens. Thus, seeds are treated with a suitable fungicide before being placed in the store so that they remain safe during the storage and then in the field as they are protected against the soil-borne diseases.

On the other hand, the eggs or other forms of insects may get activated during the period of seed germination. In order to make the seeds free of insect attack, they are treated with a suitable insecticide prior to their storage. Seeds stored when treated with suitable pesticides do not need these treatments at the time of sowing while other seeds must be treated with a pesticide so that no pathogen appears on the plants produced by these seeds.

Treated seeds are able to protect themselves from the soil-borne diseases and insects in the beginning. If there is danger of nematodes in the soil, suitable chemical killing the nematodes must be used prior to sowing of seeds. Seeds should be treated with suitable chemicals as per recommendations and need. Due consideration should be given to the dose of the chemicals; it should neither be too low nor too high. Low dose is practically ineffective while the high dose is lethal to the seed as it damages the embryo of seed.

Seeds may be treated in a container, which should not absorb the chemical. Use of such containers after treatment should be restricted and they should not be used for human or animal use even if they have been properly washed and cleaned. The container may be an earthen pot, plastic pot, glass pot or an iron drum or bin. Thc size of the container will depend upon the quantity of the seed to be treated. Avoid the use of metallic containers as they may get the chemical reaction that may erode the surface of the pot/ container.

For commercial use, seed dressers are available. Seed dressing drum in common has a lid and a handle. Seeds along with the desired pesticide in appropriate quantity are put in it and it is fully covered with a lid that fits over its mouth/opening. The handle rotates the dresser and so the seeds get dressed with the pesticide. The pesticide is spread in a thick film over the seed surface, which does not allow the attack of pathogens at the later stage. After spinning the drum, seeds are taken out for sowing or storage as the case may be. Great care should be taken during spinning the drum. The spinning or shaking should be gentle and it should not be violent, otherwise the seed is likely to be damaged. Seeds having pointed ends should be treated gently.

2. *Other Treatments*

Apart from treating the seeds with pesticides, they are treated with other chemicals, pure water and some other physical processes. These are:

Soaking in water

Sometimes the seeds are soaked in water overnight so that they swell up and germinate easily in the field. The pre-germination of tropical seeds such as those of oil palms, coconuts and rubber in well-watered germination beds is a natural method of hastening and this affords a ready means of selecting good viable seed. For such large seeds, the period of germination is thereby shortened and this hastens their direct planting in the field.

Cold water treatment

The seeds of some tree species like guava, *Terminalia arjuna, Syzygium cumini*, margosa, papaya, *Terminalia bellirica, Terminalia chebula*, *Madhuca indica*, custard apple, *Dalbergia sissoo,* Cassias, bamboo, etc., need to be put in clean water for 24 hours to induce rapid germination. Seeds floating on the water surface are usually immature or damaged by insects, diseases or by threshing. Such seeds are skimmed off and discarded. This treatment is given just prior to sowing of seeds. The water is drained off and the seeds are dried under shade to make them retain minimum moisture. Do not dry them in the sun.

Seeds with hard coats do not germinate easily as the water does not enter into the seed-coat rapidly and so the embryo is not activated. To make the water enter into the seed and to reach the embryo, the seeds are immersed in cold water for 24 hours, may be ice cold. The sudden change from normal to low temperature in water causes some crack in the seed-coat, which makes it permeable to water, and hence the embryo starts the activity. Seeds of some vegetables and forest species are treated like this.

Hot water treatment

Water at 40° to 50°C is used to expedite the germination and to arrest the growth of pathogens sticking to seed-coat. Seeds of acacias, *Delonix regia, Prosopis cineraria, Leucaena leucocephala,* etc. are immersed in boiling water for an hour or even upto 48 hours. Seeds coming to the top of the water are floated off, as they do not give good germination since they are of poor quality. Hard-coated seeds are given this type of treatment.

Celery seeds are often soaked in water at 45°-46°C for 30 minutes to destroy the fungus over their surface. At a slightly higher temperature, seeds of some Crucifers like cabbage, cauliflower, broccoli and Brussels's sprout are soaked in water for 30 minutes to treat them against seed-borne pathogens.

Alternate drying and wetting treatment

In some cases where the hard seed-coat is tough and can not be broken or cracked either with hot or cold water, seeds are soaked in water for 3-4 days and then dried and again soaked in water for 3-4 days and this cycle is repeated till the seeds show some signs of their swelling which is evident from their increased size. Seeds which swell have absorbed water and are able to germinate. In case of teak, these seeds are kept in such condition for about 45 days.

Acid treatment

Hard-coated seeds of green gram (*Vigna radiatus*) and senji (*Melilotus* spp.) and others are made to germinate after immersing them in 20% sulphuric acid for 20 minutes or in concentrated (95%) sulphuric acid for 10 to 30 minutes. Put acid in water and not water in acid. Acid should be added slowly and then the solution may be mixed with a glass rod. Good care has to be taken during their immersion.

For this treatment, earthen pot or glass pot may be used. For dilute sulphuric acid, plastic container can be used. Metallic or wooden containers should never be used as they are eaten away by the chemical reaction of the acid. Seeds should not be stirred in the acid with hand, but they should either be stirred gently or mixed with a glass rod. After the treatment, wash the seeds with clean water at least twice or thrice. No trace of acid should be sticking to the seed. Acid can be used again and again but it should be cleaned or passed through a sieved funnel to decant or ward-off the chaff or inert material out of the acid. Storage of acid should be at a safe place in a glass container. It should be away from the reach of living beings.

Seeds after washing may be dried under shade for a while by

spreading them over a mat to drain-off the excessive water. Drying for too long should be avoided as it arrests the growth of developing embryo, which may have started its activity during the treatment and washing. Treated seeds should be sown soon.

Instead of sulphuric acid, which is common, nitric acid, hydrochloric acid and other acids have been tried for breaking the dormancy with success to overcome the hard-coated condition of seeds. Even the mixture of two acids has also been tried with success. Since these methods are highly technical and need the exact duration of their immersion, they are of little commercial value.

Other chemical treatments

Like the acids, alkalies such as sodium hydroxide or potassium hydroxide have corrosive action on the seed-coat which makes it easier to imbibe moisture. It has not met with great success in overcoming hard-coated condition of seeds but it has proved highly successful for removal of superfluous seed structures like awns, glumes, hairs, fuzz, etc. These chemicals remove these structures and help in easy placement of the seed for sowing and leads to uniform germination.

Spinach, carrot, cotton and some ornamental seeds are treated with these chemicals. Concentrated solution to 20% dilute solution for 20 minutes to 24 hours, respectively, have been tried to remove the fuzz or other portions over the seed. This extra growth is provided to safeguard the seeds against some adverse conditions, but to have good and uniform germination, these have to be removed before they are seeded out. For large plantations or planting by dibblers or mechanical planting, seeds of uniform size are needed and this is possible only when the seeds have been separated from each other since they remain entangled with each other by their superficial growths which is good for seed dispersal but not for easy germination. Seeds treated with chemicals are sown soon after being treated and should not be stored at all.

Scarification

Seeds with hard seed-coats that are impermeable to water, i.e. seeds which can not absorb water when placed in water, are scarified either by physical, chemical or mechanical means. They may be scarified by pin pricking or by putting them in an earthen pot along with pointed pebbles or stones and then they are shaken thoroughly. With this shaking, the corners of the pebbles generally make a dent or pierce the seed-coat to such an extent that the newly-made holes have the ability to allow the passage of water or moisture into the inner parts of the seed, i.e. cotyledons. Now, these seeds are able to absorb water and can germinate easily. The time of shaking may vary with the speed of shaking. Generally, the seeds are shaken for 20 minutes. Scarification has to be done with little or no damage to the seeds.

Seeds that need this type of scarification are alfalfa, crotolaria, asparagus, clovers, okra, etc. Different types of scarifiers are available. Mechanical scarifiers allow the seed to pass over abrasive surface that may be stone or a sand paper or a disc rotated in such a way that the seeds are touched or rubbed fully.

Scarification can also be done with the help of chemicals but it is not used extensively. It is used in cotton where removal of cotton wool is necessary and further, this helps in rupturing the hard seed-coat to allow the passage of moisture.

Stratification

Seeds of temperate fruits like apple, pear, cherry, almond, peach, walnut, etc., and some forest species need some period of rest under chilling conditions, i.e. temperature below 7°C for about 60 days or so depending upon the species. Stratification may be done in two ways.

a) Indoor stratification: Seeds immersed in moist sand, kept loose and then sealed in a polythene bag are placed in a refrigerator. Small quantity of seed can be stratified in this way. Sufficient quantity of sand with ample moisture has to be kept in the bag. It should not be kept loose, i.e. open in a refrigerator; otherwise, the seed will be killed with freezing temperature. The temperature of the chamber should be below 7°C throughout the period of seed-keeping. In this way, the seeds get the anaerobic and chilly conditions for a specified period. After taking the polythene bag out of the refrigerator, it may be kept outside to bring the contents to room temperature. Later, the seeds are sown in the field or in the nursery.

b) Field stratification: Seeds of the desired species are placed in the field in a special way. A trench of the width of 30 cm and depth

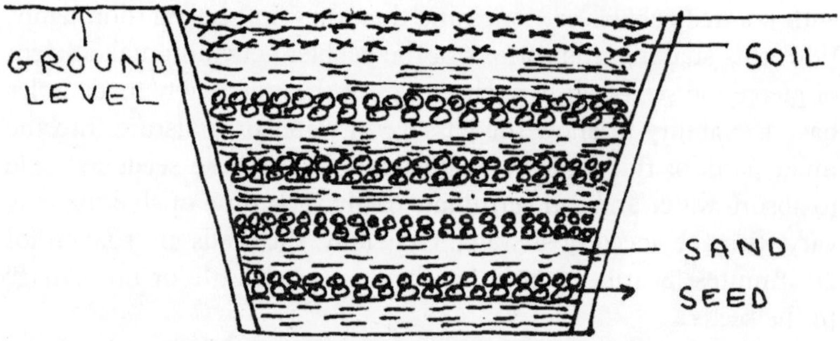

Fig. 12. Stratification of seeds in the open field.

of 30 cm is dug at a convenient place in the field. A layer of sand, 5-6 cm deep, is placed at the bottom of the trench and then seeds are spread uniformly in a layer. The layer of seeds is covered with a layer of sand, which may be 6 cm or more in thickness. Another seed layer can again be put on the second layer of sand. In this way, the seeds are in between the two layers of sand, which are 5-6 cm thick. Ample moisture is provided to the sand layers so that the seeds do not get desiccated during stratification. Top layer is covered with a soil layer. Thus, the seeds remain in the trench for a specified period. The period of stratification will depend upon the kind of species and the prevailing conditions.

A precaution has to be taken during stratification in the field. Soil should not have remains of diseases or insects. It may be sterilized, if possible. Excess moisture in the trench has to be avoided, as it will reduce the movement of air circulation. During winter, the moisture of the trench should not turn into ice, which may be harmful for the seeds. Normally under low temperature conditions, pathogens are inactive but be sure that no pathogen should be present on the seed during stratification. This method is common where the temperature goes/remains below 7°C during the winter for a period of about 60-90 days. This is possible only in high hills where the atmospheric temperature during winter is usually near the freezing point for a period of 3-4 months. Moreover, large quantities of seed can be stratified in one lot under field stratification. After stratification, the seeds are taken out and sown in the nursery.

Another method is the sowing of seeds during the early winters. Under field conditions, the seed gets the requisite hours of chill and will germinate after the expiry of the chilling period. Since there is no surety about the percentage of germination of the seed, more quantity of seeds have to be put per line. Moreover, congenial conditions have to be provided during whole of the period of natural stratification. Further, the need for look-after and care of the seedbeds have to be taken during this period that involves extra expenses. Therefore, field stratification in trench is of commercial use.

Seed Dressings

Analogous to seed treatment, there is another process by which the germination of the seed can be quickened and later the young plantlet is able to have its food from the adjoining area. In this case, chemicals like growth hormones, activators, bacteria culture and fertilizers are coated on the seeds of some species.

In order to ease the sowing by removal of awns, fuzz, glumes, hairs, etc., the seeds may be treated by cow-dung manure or with soil. They are rubbed with this substance and during this process, their awns, hairs, etc., are removed and they can be sown easily.

Small seeds are pelleted by coating their surface with useful, both active and inert, material. This increases its size and makes it uniform, which is helpful in easy seeding. The material to be coated on uneven and small seeds is made into slurry and the seeds are immersed in it and later they are shaken gently or rolled in a dry powder of calcium carbonate plus fertilizer to get their surfaces dried. Later, the seeds are dried under shade. Slow release nitrogenous fertilizer may be coated along with some quantity of calcium carbonate. This helps in the later stages, to the growth of young plantlet, which has emerged from the seed. Thus, the pelleted material provides the food material for the critical period.

Bacteria-culture is smeared on the surface of the seeds of some leguminous plants since these bacteria when added to the soil are able to utilize the nitrogen of the atmosphere through symbiotic relation for the benefit of the plant. This favours nodule formation in the roots. Thus, the young plantlet and later the plant is able to have good growth and development to become a robust plant.

Cultures of different kinds for various plant species are prepared in the laboratories. These are available from different sources. They are packed in envelopes, which are with instructions for their use.

The culture is mixed with sugar or gur and with the addition of little water to form a paste-like thick slurry. The cleaned seeds are soaked and mixed in the slurry for a few minutes so that the seed gets a coating of this mixture. This is enough for the seed. The seed is dried under the shade and not in the sun. If required, the seed may be rolled to get uniform size and round shape. These seeds are sown on the same day of their dressing. This helps in the early multiplication of the bacteria before the start of germination by the seed. When such seeds are placed for germination, the coating of the bacterial mixture gets moistened and the bacterial activity is enhanced. These bacteria take their food from the plant itself. Since they establish themselves in nodes and the roots become nodulated where these bacteria live and they fix the atmospheric nitrogen for the plant. They take their food in minute quantities from the plant but enrich it with nitrogen, which is vital for plant growth and green colour of the leaves.

Small and precious seeds are fixed on organic tapes at a suitable distance. The tape is put in the soil and covered by soil. Organic tapes, which disintegrate easily, provide nourishment to the plant at later stage.

Viability of Seed

A seed may look sound, bold, and attractive with all the requisite physical characteristics of the species and variety yet it may not be able to germinate when placed under suitable circumstances. In fact, it is the ability of the seed to remain alive. Under a highly congenial atmosphere, seed may live as long as five centuries as mentioned in some of the legendary books or may live only for a week or so if kept under unsuitable conditions of storage or is exposed to adverse weather conditions.

A viable seed is the one which is capable of germination when placed for germination under proper circumstances. Thus, the seed should be living but there is no consideration of the time taken by such a seed to germinate. It may germinate readily or in its normal period of germination and it may even take months to come into action. Therefore, the viability of seed is generally considered the ability of the seed to germinate in a reasonable period. Dormant viable seeds are the one which require a long period and even some treatment or processing to complete their dormancy and if this condition is not met, they can not germinate.

Germination of Seeds

All the viable seeds are able to become young plantlets. When such seeds are placed under proper circumstances and environment, they start absorption of water from the surroundings resulting in the swelling of seed, particularly the cotyledons and embryo. When the cotyledons increase in size due to absorption of moisture they need more space but, there is no space under the seed-coat and hence the seed-coat ruptures and splits up. Simultaneously, on getting congenial conditions, the embryo of the seed is also activated and there is emergence of radicle and plumule . Radicle is the first to emerge, which goes downward to form the primary root while the plumule comes upward to form the shoot. With the help of stored material in the cotyledons, the plumule is able to bring forth the tiny leaves which being green in colour, have the ability to manufacture their own food material from the atmospheric carbon dioxide. During this intervening period, the stored food material is almost finished and the fresh food manufacture starts. When more number of leaves emerge, the plant becomes independent and is able to survive and thus, the new plant starts functioning. In other words, the germination may be defined as the resumption of growth on activation by the embryo and development of a young plant from the seed. That is why, the proverb goes "reap as you sow", i.e., whatever you have sown will be ready for reaping. Good seed will give good crop.

Physiological Changes

During their dry stage, seeds are almost inactive but they do respire at the lowest level and on imbibing water, the seed membranes and other parts swell. Some of the enzymes present in dry seeds are activated while more are synthesized and they convert the insoluble reserve food material to soluble forms, which is the reverse of maturation of seeds. Amylases change starch to soluble sugars. Lipases act upon fatty acids to change them to carbohydrates. The stimuli are provided by the radicle to bring or initiate these changes and as a net result the seed starts its visible germination.

Conditions Necessary for Germination

It is only the viable seed that has a dormant embryo, can germinate on getting proper germinating conditions. A non-living seed may absorb water, swell in size, seed-coat may burst open the cotyledon but there will be no plant as the embryo is either inactive or damaged. But viable seeds with dormant embryos will emerge into plantlets; thus, the first condition necessary for the germination of a seed is its viability. Generally, the labels on the seed packets have a mention of the percentage of germination under normal conditions and in no case should it be less than 80%, otherwise due compensation for the remaining percentage will have to be made and so more seed has to be used and more area has to be prepared. There is also more expenditure involved in maintenance and management of field.

Major conditions necessary for germination are moisture, air and temperature. None of these factors should become a limiting factor. All these factors have separate as well as combined effect. For example, when temperature is high, moisture may be less and the lighter air, which lacks oxygen, may be more. In other case, low temperature at freezing point will cause the freezing of water and solutes in the cell, which may need more space resulting in rupturing of the tissues and loss of cell sap. Thus, it is very vital that these conditions should be available in a highly balanced state.

Moisture

Most of the seeds need sufficient quantity of water for their germination but it should neither be too much to form a visible film around the seed nor it should be too less to arrest the development of embryo. When there is excessive moisture, all the pore spaces in the soil are filled with water and there is no space left for the air and as such the respiration by the embryo of the seed is reduced or restricted which may stop the germination process.

Seeds do absorb moisture from the humid atmosphere and may start to germinate in that condition. Most of the seeds will start their germination even if the moisture level in the soil is much lower than the required level and as such more quantity of water has to be added to complete the process of germination of seeds or other parts.

Apart from being the agent for swelling of seed parts, water is necessary for chemical transformations which take place in the tissues of the cells. Carbohydrates are broken into simpler compounds with the help of moisture; further, water is a carrier of food material since it is a part of cell sap. In fact, no movement of solute is possible without water and no absorption of minerals and other matter from the surrounding is possible in the absence of moisture.

The exact quantity of water needed by a seed will depend upon the kind of the seed, soil and its surroundings. In general, it should just cover the seed but not as a thick film over the seed.

Air

Air is a mixture of gases in the surroundings and in the soil. Mostly it contains oxygen and carbon dioxide, which are part of the plant system. Other gases like nitrogen, sulphur dioxide, hydrogen sulphide, etc. also exist which may be of little importance in germination. These are produced by decay of organic matter and are by-products of many other processes. Generally, oxygen is needed to speed up the germination. Deep placement of seeds restricts the use of air by the seed while when placed on the surface exposes them to various vagaries of nature. During respiration of seeds, oxygen is the main gas needed which the seeds can have from the dissolved oxygen in water or from the pore space of the soil.

Temperature

Generally, most of the seeds germinate at a constant temperature of about 22°C but some may have slightly high or low range. Very low and very high temperatures prevent germination. Fluctuations in temperature during the germination of seeds are highly undesirable as the processes started are hindered and the growth is arrested.

Seeds germinate over a fairly wide range of temperature but they may sprout promptly at lower or higher temperature provided they get ample quantity of moisture, since moisture plays an important role in the maintenance of temperature in the surroundings and in the seed. It is also responsible for the breakdown of complex substances into simpler compounds needed for the developing embryo. Temperature can become a limiting factor for development of embryo and germination of seeds, since many physiological processes like respiration, movement of solutes, transpiration, etc. are influenced by the fluctuations in the temperature.

Light

This factor is not very important for most of the seeds. Generally, seeds germinate under dark, i.e. anaerobic conditions under field and laboratory conditions but there are some species, which need some light, even an exposure for a short while to light will start the germination. Evening primrose, lettuce, many grasses, mistletoe and herb seeds will germinate when they get some exposure to light.

Once the seed has germinated and plumule has emerged, light is the most essential factor for its growth and development. In fact, light acts as a stimulating agent of germination and well-being of the plant. For germination of most of the seeds, light can be a delaying agent, if given earlier.

Germination Period

Under normal conditions, the seeds start germination as soon as they absorb moisture from the environment through the hilum, thus activating the embryo, swelling the cotyledons and increasing the breakdown process of food material, into simpler elements that are needed by the radicle and the plumule. The time taken for completing the emergence of tiny leaves from the leaves may be 3 to 5 days and to have an independent plant from seed may take 7 to 10 days. Seeds having hard coats, requiring scarification or stratification mat take longer time. Generally, seeds germinating after a specified period of about 3 weeks are not considered fit for plating. Germination has to be uniform and the late germinating seeds do not provide uniform stand of the crop.

10

Raising Plants from Seeds

It is the easiest method of multiplying plants in a short time with great ease. The seeds are sown in the filed or a bed where they germinate and yield seedlings. They may be planted *in situ* or in seedbed or nursery bed before being transplanted elsewhere for their normal growth and production. In sowing of seed to raising of seedlings many processes are involved.

Sowing of Seeds

Mature, clean and healthy seeds are sown for raising nursery plants. Soil or other place where the seed is to be sown may be prepared in such a manner that the seed can grow easily for few weeks. It should be easy to dibble or place the seed in the soil from where it should be able to draw moisture and get proper air needed for the germination in the early stages and take up the growth at a later stage.

Seeds may be pre-soaked or pre-sprouted and then sown in the field. These seeds become fragile and need handling with care. They can also pose problem for sowing, as small seeds are difficult to sow after soaking them in water. In such cases these have to be covered gently by a cover of sufficient thickness to conserve the loss of water from the seeds till they complete their germination or are independent plants. It is better to place the pre-sprouted seeds over the pot mix in the pot or polybag and then cover it with the same mixture.

For sowing of seed, method of seeding or sowing, depth of seeding and time of seeding are important considerations.

Methods of Seeding

Seeds are sown in the field or other containers to get plants of good growth on them, therefore, they must be sown at a suitable space and appropriate depth to have good germination and later good plants. Here are common methods of seeding.

a) Line sowing

A straight line may be dug by a tiller, *khilna* or any other hand tool and then seeds are placed or dropped at appropriate depth in that line, known as furrow. The furrow is filled up so that the pulverised sand covers the seed + soil mixture or may be covered

Fig. 13. Line sowing of seed and mixing of manure.

by a suitable media, which should avoid exposure to light and should not be a hindrance in the emergence of plumule. This work can be accomplished by working a tiller, plough or disc harrow followed by planking or covering by spade after sowing. This method can be adopted for sowing of seeds in pots, trays or boxes.

This method is good for large scale planting of bold seeds but when small seeds are sown, they have to be mixed with sand or well-rotten farm yard manure to ease their dropping at a uniform depth and proper distance. Most of the cereals, grasses, vegetable seeds, ornamental flower seeds, forest species and other seeds are sown with this method. Distance between the two lines has to be maintained as per recommendation.

b) Dibbling

Seeds may be dibbled or put into the soil either by hand or by a dibbler, which may be bullock-driven or power-driven. The seeds are placed in a row at an appropriate depth. During dibbling, the seed is automatically covered with the soil when the fingers are being taken out or the dibbler has put the seed. Generally, medium-sized seeds like that of apple, many forest species and landscape avenue trees are dibbled into the soil.

This method is also used for planting the seeds in polybags where 2 or 3 seeds are sown. For *in situ* plantation as in case of mango and many other species, the seed stone or seed is dibbled by hand. Seed can also be dibbled in pots and trays.

c) Broadcasting

Seeds may be broadcasted over the surface of a well-prepared seedbed or field. Great care has to be taken for spreading the seeds at a uniform distance. For small seeds, mix some inert material like well-rotten farm yard manure, sand or small pebbles equal to the size of the seed for uniform distribution and easy spread of the seed. Roughly equal quantity of inert material is mixed well before the start of sowing. The distribution of seed by broadcasting is to be done with great care since every grower is not well experienced and may not be able to perform this. Small quantities of seed can be distributed with ease but for large scale sowing it is difficult. When sowing has been delayed due to unavoidable circumstances, this method may be employed. This method is not systematic due to some shortcomings like, having no lines, having improper distance between the rows, and birds taking seeds due to not being fully covered by soil. All this leads to irregular stand of the crop. It is not a reliable method but can be adopted for sowing seeds in pots.

Depth of Seeding

Seed has to be sown at an appropriate depth so that on germination, the plumule should be able to rise above the soil level easily. No hard and fast rule can be laid but as a general practice, the depth of seeding is almost three times the size of the seed. Further, it will depend upon the extent to which the seedbed or the soil has been prepared. In well-prepared soil of clay-loam or sandy-loam nature having crumb structure, deep seeding can be a success while in other types like clayey, waterlogged and hard soils, deep seeding is not a success. If watering is to be provided immediately after the seeding and the amount of water given is too much, this is not desirous as the soil crust may form a hard cover, which may restrict the emergence and development of plumule. It is advisable and customary to plant the seed slightly deeper in sandy soil than clayey or heavy soils.

Time of Seeding

Though the seeds can be sown at any time under controlled conditions yet many factors have to be considered for field conditions. Maturity of seed, kind of seed, season of growth, weather conditions, nature of the species and agronomic practices being followed are some of the factors, which control the time of seeding.

Mature seeds germinate when provided with ambient conditions necessary for their germination. These conditions can be created artificially in a greenhouse but it is not possible under open field conditions. Seeds will germinate only when they get the desired conditions for their germination under field conditions in their specific season. They are sown in spring, summer or winter season according to their nature but their time can be slightly hastened or delayed depending upon the variety and the prevailing weather conditions.

Other details about sowing are being given under individual crops.

Covering the Seed

After sowing the seeds, it should be covered with a thin layer of pulverised soil or some other material like wood ash plus well-rotten farm yard manure. This will enable the plumule to emerge out of the soil crust easily, birds will not be able to pick the seeds, seeds will get anaerobic conditions and moisture loss will be reduced. This layer on decay will add fertility to the soil that will improve the water-holding capacity of the soil, which in turn will help in providing better nutritive conditions for the young plants.

The thickness of the layer will depend upon the type of the seed and the availability of raw material for this purpose. In any case, the upper cover should not exceed 1 cm thickness.

Watering the Bed

If there is less moisture in the seedbed at the time of sowing, water may be given very gently so that the seeds are not displaced. Watering can be given through a sprinkler or a very fine nozzle fitted to the hose pipe to create moist conditions. When the nursery is being grown under greenhouse conditions, misting is best but for other types, water is to be given by watering can or sprinkler. In summer, watering may be given once or twice a day for the first three days or more and then once a day for a week and later on, the interval may be increased depending upon the weather and soil conditions.

During winter, the frequency of watering can be reduced to once a day for the first three days and then on alternate days followed by twice a week and then once a week. For rainy season, one has to watch the weather conditions. A great care should be taken to see that the water does not stagnate in the nursery seedbed or pots. Excessive water has to be drained off as soon as possible.

Avoid excessive watering and do not force the seedlings to drought conditions. Once the germination has started, sufficient water is needed, otherwise the growth will be arrested for want of water.

Failure of Seeds to Germinate

The grower may check the reason of low germination rate of seeds as the following are some of the reasons that are responsible for this:

1. Seed may be old and may not be viable.
2. Seeds produced under unfavourable and adverse conditions are either immature or over-mature and may not remain viable.
3. Seeds are damaged, their embryo may be inactive.
4. There may be either too little or too high moisture in the soil.
5. Temperature may be too high or too low.
6. Presence of growth inhibiting substances like the residues of herbicide, weedicides, etc. in the soil.
7. Seed planting has been too deep that may have arrested the activation of embryo.
8. Attack of damping off.
9. Seeds have no contact with the soil.
10. Lack of light or over-exposure of light to the seeds during their germination.
11. Seeds may not have completed their dormancy.
12. Seeds have been sown out of their normal season of planting.

11

Propagation of Plants

There are number of plant species which either do not flower or the seeds produced are not viable. In some cases, there is lot of variation in the plant characters that are raised from seeds. This is particularly important in horticultural crops like the fruit trees of citrus, mango, apple, pear, cherry, almond, walnut, plum, loquat, litchi, etc. Thus, nature has provided these plants with a gift of being propagated or multiplied by other means of multiplication than seeds. These parts may be stems, leaves, roots or buds. Plants multiplied by their vegetative parts are known as 'Vegetatively Propagated' or 'Asexually Propagated' plants.

These plants are in no way inferior to the plants raised by their seeds but they are better in many respects since they provide uniform stand of the crop and are smaller in size than seedling plants and are easily manageable. Different methods of vegetative propagation are: (1) Cutting, (2) Layering, (3) Grafting, (4) Budding, (5) Other means, (6) Micro-propagation.

Cuttings

This is a piece of wood of active or living branch, which is usually 10-15 cm long with 2-3 buds on the nodes and the thickness is equal to a lead pencil. When this is placed under good conditions of sprouting, gives rise to new plants. Generally, portion of the stem, root or leaf that can give rise to an independent plant are collected and planted in the well-prepared soil in a bed, in the field or glass-

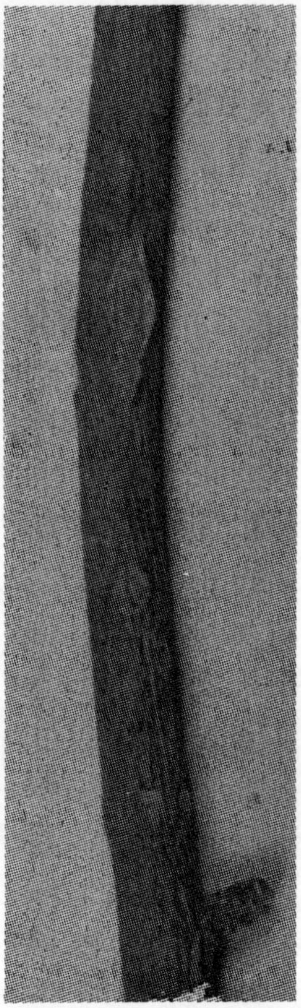

Fig. 14. Stem cutting.

house. The depth of planting is mostly 2/3rd in the soil. On getting suitable moisture, the cuttings start callus formation to form the roots and the buds swell to give rise to leaves. In due coarse, there is an independent plant. Apple, cherry, carnation, chrysanthemum, tung, ruscus, etc. are multiplied by their cuttings.

Cuttings can be collected from either the stem or root but generally the stem cuttings are used for multiplication of plants.

1. Stem cuttings

These cuttings are collected from the growing branches of trees, which may be of softwood, semi-hardwood or hardwood. These names are given according to their degree of maturity. Softwood cuttings are of the present season's growth and are towards the ends of the branches, while the semi-hardwood cuttings are from the last season's growth, which is usually 30 cm or more below the softwood. This wood has not matured fully. Hardwood cuttings are fully matured and they are from the last year's growth. They are further below the portion of semi-hardwood cuttings.

All these three types of cuttings are used for getting new plants since these have matured buds on them that are capable of giving rise to new plants. These are only the vegetative buds, which yield plants. A cutting with 2-3 active buds is selected.

Crops propagated by means of stem cuttings are: apple, peach, pecan, citrus, cherry, walnut, tung, junipers, crab apple, carnation, chrysanthemum, geranium, iris, grape, pomegranate, etc.

2. Root cuttings

These are pieces of wood taken from the roots of the plants. Their shape and size is like that of stem cuttings. Usually black berries are propagated by their root cuttings.

Collection of Cuttings

Cuttings are usually collected at the time of pruning. This is the best time because the wood is mature and there is no pressure of wood removal on the branch or tree since they will resume fresh growth in the next season. Shoots of temperate trees are leafless at this time. These can be stored for few days under proper storage conditions, i.e. cool, dry and free from pathogens. Waxing to avoid evaporation of water and attack of pathogens during storage may seal both the ends.

Preparation of Cuttings

Cuttings may be prepared for two purposes: (a) for rootstock, and (b) for vegetative propagation.

a) For rootstock

Cuttings of any type, i.e. hard, semi-hard or soft-wood from the healthy stems are planted in the soil or some other medium. Length

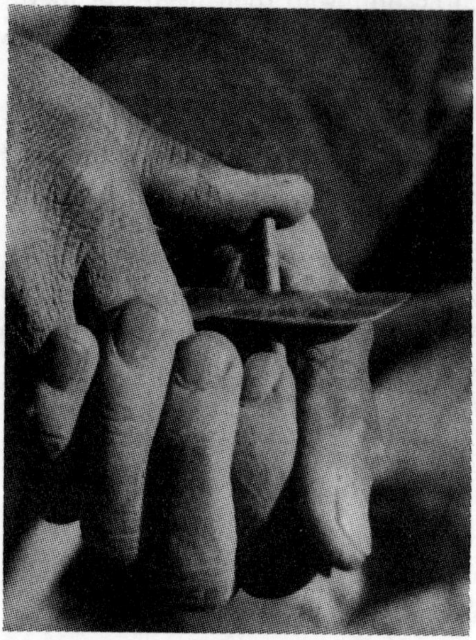

Fig. 15. Preparing a cutting.

of the cutting should not be less than 10 cm and thickness of 1 cm or equal to lead pencil. Such cuttings do have 3-4 buds. Lower end of the cutting is given a slanting cut while the upper end is given a horizontal cut. Slanting cut on the lower end of the cutting provides more contact with the soil to establish early, which facilitates the formation of roots after the formation of callus. In order to hasten callusing, growth hormones like NAA or IBA may be applied on the lower ends of the cuttings. These may be dip in 2000 ppm solution of NAA or IBA for 5 minutes or in 500 ppm for 12 hours. It will depend upon the kind of the cutting and the species. Now-a-days, readymade formulations of these chemicals in the form of powders like Rootone, Seradix, Rhizone, etc. are available. First of all the lower end about 2-3 cm in length of the cutting is dip in water to moisten it and then immersed in the powder. In this way the required quantity of the chemical sticks to the cutting. Treated cuttings are planted immediately after treatment.

b) For vegetative propagation

These cuttings can be prepared in the manner outlined above. For grafting of almost of all kinds, a budstick is prepared in the usual manner. Differences in the preparation for a particular type or special method will be described under that method.

Cuttings are usually prepared when they are to be used, i.e., on the start of cell sap in the spring or start of rainy season.

Planting of Cuttings

Cuttings taken from the stem portion or root portion of the plant or a tree of active growth are planted in the soil or some other growing media. These methods have been described in the earlier chapters.

Generally, 2/3rd portion of the cutting is immersed in the moist soil. The planting may be straight or slanting but straight planting is much favoured. Cuttings are planted in rows, which may be 15 cm apart while the distance between the two cuttings in the row may be 10-15 cm. This will depend upon the variety, species and type of the medium used.

Aftercare of Cuttings

Since the cuttings are planted in moist soil or other medium, they come in direct contact with moisture, start absorption of moisture, cuttings do start the absorption of water through their lower ends. This water reaches to other portions of the cutting. Buds are mature in every respect. On getting slightly higher temperature and humidity, the bud swells up and the inner portions burst open. The bursting of bud releases a lot of pressure. All this is due to acceleration of physiological and physical activities going on in the cuttings.

Softwood cuttings are the earliest to sprout but depending upon the stored food, buds may start their activity soon. These cuttings are useful for planting of pomegranate, geranium, carnation, coleus, impatients, berberry, spirea, azalea, junipers etc.

Hardwood cuttings, sometimes known as deciduous cuttings are late to sprout. They have enough food materiel, which is sufficient for a fairly longer period on the establishment of the cuttings. These cuttings are planted in the beginning of winter season and their buds usually sprout before the onset of spring season. Currants, figs, grapes, gooseberries, flowering peach, etc. sprout in the end of February or early March in low or mid hills but may sprout in the end of March or early April in high hills.

Cuttings do need fair amount of water for swelling of the buds and activation of the stored food material needed for the sprouting of their buds and for other physiological processes within the cuttings. In summer, these cuttings need plenty of irrigation, which can be regulated by providing mulch, and irrigation depending upon the source of water. In general, for the first week, daily watering is essential and then it is thrice a week, i.e., on alternate days followed by twice a week and then once a week. This can be adjusted according to the need of the cuttings and the plants, which are the result of successful sprouting of cuttings.

In temperate region, the weather is usually cool and the irrigation facilities are mostly not available and the cuttings are grown under rainfed conditions. These places do get snowfall, which supplies sufficient moisture for the cuttings. Thus, by the end of February or mid-March, no irrigation may be given. Later mulch of dry grass may be made to conserve the soil moisture.

Once the buds have started to sprout, i.e. they have swelled up, the cuttings should never be forced to drought. Suitable arrangements for the conservation of soil moisture should be made. Overwatering should also be avoided as it leads to damping off and other fungal diseases. Lodging can also be there.

Earthing-up, if necessary, may be done before irrigation. Similarly, weeding may be carried on as and when necessary. Hoeing is necessary for breaking clods and upper crust of the soil layer, which loosens the soil particles beneath, and around the root zone that helps in the easy movement of air and water in the pore spaces. This helps in the quick absorption of solutes from the soil/medium.

Sprouted cuttings become established in about a period of one month; they need all the care and attention, which the young plants need, so they should be cared properly.

In the coming season, these cuttings get themselves fully established. They can be used as seedlings or planted as such. For forest trees, such plants are useful while for fruit trees, they may be budded or grafted by a suitable scion.

Layering

This is an another method of propagating plants by stems. This is possible in plants that can have adventitious roots from the nodes and when placed under moist and slightly warm conditions. On coming in contact with the soil or some other growing medium, the stem portion can give rise to roots after callusing. From this place leaves may emerge in a few days' time. On successful establishment, the new plant can be separated from the parent plant.

Kinds of Layering

There are various kinds of layering, viz.

1. Tip layering
2. Simple layering
3. Trench layering
4. Mound layering
5. Pot layering

1. Tip layering

In tip layering, the tips of the growing plant that has bendable shoots are allowed or made to come in contact with the soil, i.e. their tips are covered with moist soil. A cut or a scratch can be made on the stem before bending and covering it with soil to hasten callus formation. Thus, roots and shoots develop from this place and as such in the coming season, a new plant is ready which is separated from the parent plant. The number of plants that can be had in one year will depend upon the bendable branches that can reach the soil level. Raspberries, blackberries, loganberries and similar plants are propagated by tip layering.

2. Simple layering

In this method, rather than putting a portion of the bendable stem, more than half, i.e. about 30 cm or more is covered with moist soil while the tip is kept outside. Notching may be done. Application of growth hormones is quite beneficial. Naphthalene Acetic Acid,

Indole Butyric Acid, 2, 4-5 T or some other root-inducing hormones may be applied for hastening the process of callus formation.

There is another method, which is an improvement with modification of this method. It consists of covering the stem alternately, i.e. some portion is kept outside while some is kept under the soil cover. In this way more number of plants can be made from a single stem. Moreover, the portion, which remains out of the soil, is photosynthetically active and thus, there can be no shortage of food. This method is known as 'Alternate Layering'.

3. Trench layering

A small trench usually 3 to 5 cm deep and 2 cm wide is prepared near the base of the tree. This may be prepared even in the basin. Generally, middle portion of the branch that can bend to reach the trench is covered in the trench while the basal and the tip portion remain outside. In due coarse of time, suitable moisture and other conditions facilitate the meristem to send roots and stem from the node. In this way, each node can give rise to individual but separate plant, which can be separated from the parent plant, when the new plant seems to be independent. Rose, spirea, rhododendron and some other deciduous plants can be multiplied by this technique.

4. Mound layering

A small mound which is a heap of soil, is placed over the stump of the plant in the non-growing season, i.e. when the plant is dormant. Before covering this, stump is cut off slightly above the ground level, i.e. 2-3 cm stub is left. These stubs, which are actually the growing stems, send new roots downwards and the new leaves may emerge out of the mound. These can be cut or separated in the following spring season. Apple rootstock is generally multiplied by this method. This process can be repeated year after year on the same plant. Gooseberries, quince, etc. are multiplied by this method.

5. Pot layering

In this method, the soil or some growing media is brought near the stem, rather than taking the stem to the growing medium. Last year's fully matured stems or a part of branch is given a notch and then covered by moss or some other inert material which provides sufficient amount of moisture to the covered portion. Notch can be a ring of less than half a cm width. Roots will emerge near the ringed portion. The stem remains fully active in growth. The new plant is ready after being removed below the ring. This method is usually employed for propagation of litchi, mango, *Ficus* spp., etc.

Precautions during Layering

1. Generally, only one-year-old mature branches that can bend easily should be used, otherwise they are likely to crack and break which invites unnecessary loss to the plant. Cracked portions are liable to be attacked by pathogens.
2. Cuts, notches and rings should be made with a sharp-edged knife under aseptic conditions. This helps in controlling the spread of diseases, viruses and other pathogens.
3. Immediately after making a cut on the stem, it should be covered with a rich soil, which should be able to conserve the soil moisture and supply fair amount of plant food material for the new plant.
4. Stems, bendable shoots should not be covered by a thick layer of hard soil but it should be sufficient loose to provide sufficient scope for exchange of oxygen and other gases which are needed by the plant to continue its living.
5. As soon as it is felt that the young layered plants are independent and can start their own life in a new place, they may be separated from the parent plant. If needed, it may be planted in a pot or polybag and then transplanted.
6. No damage should be done to the parent plant at the time of covering its stem and then at the time of separation of young plants.
7. Sanitary precautions and irrigation should be given due preference. Slight carelessness can cause heavy losses.

Grafting

This is an art of fixing a cutting over a seedling or a plant raised from rootstock. In fact this method is employed for improvement of the stock. In this case, the top of the plant to be grafted or joined to the seedling is known as scion. For successful grafting, following things are necessary:

1. Good scion
2. Good rootstock or seedling
3. Grafting tape or alkathene strip
4. Grafting knife with a sharp-edged blade and a sound handle
5 Grafting wax
6. Efficient and expert grafter
7. Suitable environment

1. Good scion

Scion is the portion which provides the desired characteristics to the plant. It should be of an improved variety, i.e. which yields better and uniformly than other varieties. It should be free from diseases and insect infestation. Scion should provide sufficient plant food material to the young emerging leaves till they are independent and can have link with the rootstock. Generally, it has 3-4 buds, which are active while the length may be 10-15 cm, or even upto 20 cm with thickness equal to normal lead pencil, i.e. diameter of 1 cm.

2. Good rootstock or seedling

Rootstock generally referred to as stock, is the portion of the plant, which has a small stem on which the top is fixed. It has a well-developed root system that is capable of absorption and adsorption of solutes from the soil very efficiently so that there is a healthy link with the scion. Since it is a living thing, every care should be taken to ensure that it is disease-free and free from the attack of insects and pests. Rootstocks are used in horticultural plants because they affect the quality of scion to a large extent. Some of the rootstocks are resistant to insects attack like the Malling or Malling Merton series of apple stocks that are resistant to Apple Woolly Aphid, which causes knots on the roots that restricts or inhibits the movement of solutes. Usually stock is of the same thickness as that of the scion, i.e. with diameter of 1 cm. The height of the stock does not carry much weight but the point of grafting should be at least 25-30 cm above the ground level and mostly a normal stock of 1 cm diameter has a height of about 60 cm.

Growth and vigour of the stock is dependent upon the soil conditions and the nature of the stock. Due consideration should be given at the time of selection of stock material for grafting.

3. Grafting tape

It is usually a strip of polythene or alkathene about 2-3 cm wide, which is tied around the graft union or bud union to protect it from the attack of pathogens, insects and unwanted pests. It also provides close contact of the stock with scion so that cambiums of the two tissues unite or fuse together. An added advantage of the tape is that it protects the entry of water into the tissue on one hand and also helps in the reduction of water loss on the other hand. It is wrapped around the union of stock with scion loosely but sufficiently tight to have the two tissues together. The tape may be removed as soon as the new plant becomes independent. Keeping it for a longer time, may lead to girdling below the place of union.

4. Grafting knife

Generally, grafting knife has a sharp-edged blade of steel which is about 6-8 cm long and 1 cm wide fitted with a 6-10 cm long handle on one end while the free end may be tapering or slanting. The edge of the knife is sharp and the back of it is thick and blunt. Handle should be smooth and strong. It should be preferred to have a plastic handle rather than a wooden handle.

5. Grafting wax

It is a semi-liquid paste-like substance which is applied on the surface of a cut portion of a plant to protect it from the attack of insects, pests and diseases and to safeguard it from unfavourable climatic conditions like dry weather, heavy rains etc. It may dry when exposed to natural conditions. To some extent it works as a wound-healing agent.

Grafting wax may be prepared locally by mixing the following ingredients:

1. Melt 5 parts of resin and one part of bees' wax and mix it with 1/4 part of linseed oil.
2. Melt 4 parts of resin and two parts of bees' wax, when cool add one part of lanolin and mix it thoroughly. It can be applied at the room temperature.
3. Ten parts of resin and 2 parts of bees' wax are melted together; when at room temperature add 1 part of talc and mix thoroughly to form a paste.

4. Equal parts of clay, sand and cow dung are mixed with a little water to make a paste.
5. Tree paint may be applied but it can crack under freezing conditions. So it has to be repainted.

6. Expert grafter

A man who can perform the operation of grafting with success is preferred. Though everybody can do this job of uniting the stock with the scion after giving the desired cuts but it needs expertise in slicing or giving cuts. Further, work has to be carried on swiftly, so the man responsible for doing this should be efficient and expert. It is better to practice the grafting on bud-sticks of plants, which are not required. Even branches of some bushes growing in the wild can be tried. A grafter can graft about 100-150 plants in a day.

7. Suitable environment

This includes the weather, social and local conditions. In a congenial atmosphere, more number of plants can be grafted in lesser time that is usually successful, less tiresome, easy and swift. Dry weather, hot or chilly winds and rains do hamper the process while cool and slightly humid climate invigorates the grafter to do more work and the grafts made are usually a good success. Other conditions like the behaviour of the person, animals, birds, noise, etc. do affect the grafter, which may indirectly reflect on the grafting.

Process of Grafting

Grafting consists in uniting, joining or placing very close the cambium of two different plants, i.e. stock and scion in such a way that the two tissues fuse and start the manufacture of more cells of cambium on both the sides. It is the ability of the cambium to divide and multiply to form phloem and xylem. Thus, the grafting is limited to only those plants, which have the compatibility of fusing together to have the growth of the scion.

Generally, when two pieces of living shoots with appropriate cuts are joined together in the right season, there is callus formation on both of them which fuses resulting in the formation of cambium by few cells and on successful intermingling the two cambia layers are connected with each other and the growth starts. On successful grafting new plant emerges out of a bud.

Fig. 16. Grafted mango tree.

Kinds of Grafting

It is the process of joining a twig or stem piece having 2-3 vegetative buds to a seedling or another stem, resulting in the emergence of a new plant having the characteristics of the twig. There are two possibilities, i.e. either the scion is taken to the rootstock or the rootstock is brought near to the scion as in case of bridge grafting. Generally, scion is brought near to the stock. There are two major types of grafting:

1. Having equal diameters of stock and scion.
2. Unequal diameters of stock and scion.

Under these two categories, there are different methods. Mostly, the first kind is most preferred for improvement of the material, i.e. seedlings that are used in commercial nursery production. Detailed description of various methods is as follows.

1. Whip grafting

This method consists in preparing a scion with an oblique or slanting cut about 2 cm on the lower portion of the scion. Similar cut is made on the rootstock and both are placed in such a way so that cut of one is over the other, and then tied with a grafting tape. Maximum possible slanting cuts provide maximum contact of the two tissues and hence there are fair chances of their success.

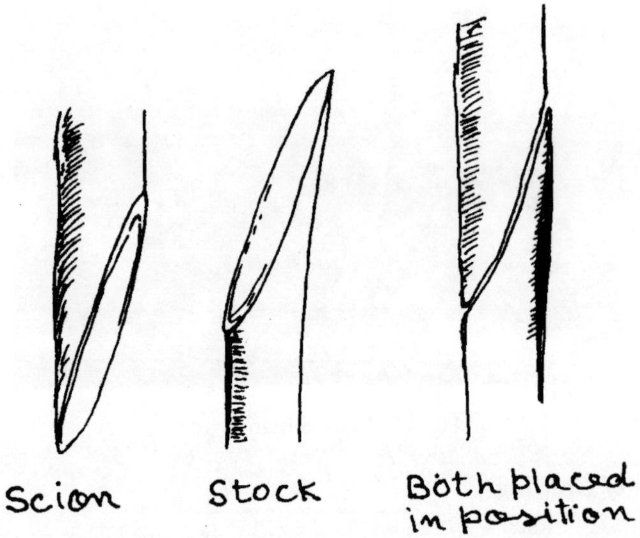

Fig. 17. Whip grafting.

2. Tongue grafting

In tongue grafting, stock and scion are prepared in the same manner as for the whip grafting but another vertical cut on the stock and scion is also given. The two (stock and scion) are fused together and tied with a grafting tape. This provides more contact of the two

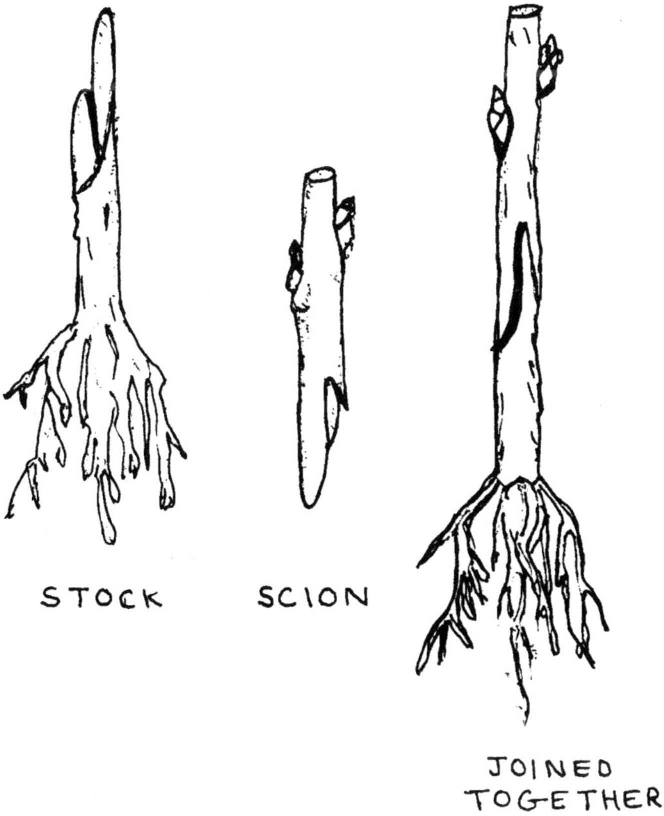

Fig. 18. Tongue grafting.

pieces. Further, this provides extra strength since stock and scion are forced into each other. Apply grafting wax and then tie the joint with a grafting tape. On successful graft, new plant emerges, i.e. the top gets itself established.

3. Side grafting

For grafting large branches, i.e. when the stock size is bigger than the scion, this method may be employed. An oblique cut on the stock is made which is usually 2-3 cm deep. The prepared scion, i.e. scion with a slanting cut on lower end is pushed gently into the cut of the stock. Later grafting wax is applied, followed by putting a grafting tape on that union.

Fig. 19. Side veneer graft on mango.

4. Side veneer grafting

Rootstock is prepared by making a shallow downward cut, about 3-5 cm, which is at least 10 cm above the ground level. Make another cut of the same size but with the upper end at the same place to form a chip. Gently remove this chip. Cut should not be very deep but slanting from top to bottom. Now a cut on the scion is made equal to the cut made on the stock. Both should be equal in size. The stock and scion are joined by placing their cuts parallel to each other. Apply grafting wax followed by grafting tape. On successful grafting, tape may be removed and the top of the stock is also removed. In this case, stock of bigger size than scion is used. Evergreen trees can be grafted. It is good for conifers.

5. Cleft grafting

When the stock is comparatively much bigger, i.e. the diameter may be more than 8 cm or so, vertical cut is made on the stock after cleaning the top of the stock. One or two prepared scions are inserted into the groove made on the stock. A chisel may be used to open the cut on the stock. Too deep cut should be avoided. After inserting the scions, the chisel may be taken out and the place filled with a grafting wax. This portion may be covered by a piece of polythene sheet, or may be covered with a plaster to avoid further cracking and attack of pathogens at this place. This will also help in keeping the stock moist and not exposing it to water evaporation.

6. Wedge grafting

In this method, small V-shaped wedge of the tissues near the bark is removed and the prepared scion is inserted into this place in the rootstock. More than two scions can be planted on one stock. The cut is usually sufficient to accommodate the scions.

7. Bark grafting

Bark of the rootstock is split open in the vertical direction and the scion after giving a slanting cut is introduced into the cut made near the bark. This method is applied only in the spring season when the sap of the cells in the plant has started its movement. Grower or grafter can use the scions, which have been collected during the winter.

8. Notch grafting

Rootstock is given a notch near the bark. This cut is vertical. Prepared scion is put there which may be nailed with the bark of the rootstock. It is waxed and then sealed. This method has the advantages of both the cleft and bark grafting.

9. Approach grafting

Stock and scion are grown in pots and they are independent on their own roots. Bark along with some wood is removed/sliced from the stock and scion keeping in view the size since both should have the cut of the same size. Both the stems of scion and stock are

Fig. 20. 'Gutti' graft in litchi.

brought close to each other and pressed and then tied after putting grafting wax. On successful grafting, lower portion of the scion and upper portion of the stock are removed. This may be done in stages. The plant may be staked and the tape removed when it is felt that the union is strong.

10. Bridge grafting

When the roots or lower part of the stem near the ground level of the scion/tree is damaged due to insects, rats or some other reason, this grafting method is employed in order to save the grown-up trees.

Depending upon the size of the trunk of the tree, 1-3 scions (planted with their own roots) are grown near the base of the tree for a season so that they are independent. By making suitable cuts on the stock and scions, the rootstocks are inserted into these cuts. These contacts are usually made above the injured part of the tree. Grafting wax may be applied. In one season, the old tree will be able to maintain contact with the soil. Roots of the plants (seedlings) planted in the basin provide anchorage and solutes from the soil to the top.

Apart from these kinds, grafting may be Stub, Inlay, etc. which are of academic value only.

Care During Grafting

Since it requires a success of joining the tissues of two living materials it is necessary that both should be compatible, i.e. their cells can fuse or intermingle with each other to give rise to another plant. Following precautions may be observed during grafting.

1. So far as possible, seedling-stock should be equal to the size and vigour of scion. Under-sized, over-sized, weak, diseased, insect-infested and virus-affected material should not be used.
2. Contact between the two tissues should be close to inter-mingle with each other.
3. Cuts on the stock and scion should be made with a sharp-edged knife under aseptic conditions. It is advisable to have a smooth cut with only one stroke.
4. Immediately after making suitable but matching cuts, both

the tissues should be placed side by side and slightly pressed together.

5. Apply the grafting wax to cover the exposed and adjoining areas.
6. Grafting may be done on a cloudy day but should neither be on a rainy day nor a sunny day.
7. Grafting tape or polythene tape may be fixed on the union and should be removed as soon as the plants seem to be independent.
8. Removal of the stock-top or scion-top, as required, may be done as soon as it is needed. Keeping them for a long time may cause trouble in the near future. This may be done in steps.
9. Support, if necessary, may be provided but it should neither be too weak nor too deep in the soil. It should be of dry wood/ branch, which should not get established in the soil along with the grafted plant.
10. Ties should be removed when they are no more required.
11. Soil should have ample moisture and nutrients to feed the growing plants.
12. If needed, suitable plant protection measures may be carried out.
13. Use only the recommended method of grafting since it has been tried under various conditions. One may try any other method of grafting at own level but for commercial nursery production, only the efficient, easiest and successful method should be used.
14. Season of grafting is most important. Though the grafting may be done at any time but it is preferred at the close of the winter or just start of spring when the cell sap is to start its movements. Bleeding should be avoided. Stubs or root-stocks should not be cracked and if cracked, may be repaired and smeared with wax.

Budding

It is the technique of taking a bud of one plant and inserting it on the stem of another plant. Since the physiological processes involved in uniting the two meristematic portions are the same as in that of grafting, this type of propagation is sometimes known as 'Bud grafting'. The objectives underlying budding are identical to that of grafting. Good contact between the bud and the rootstock is most essential so that further growth of newly formed tissues is possible. Following materials are required for budding: (a) Bud, (b) Rootstock, (c) Budding knife, and (d) Tape and Grafting wax.

(a) Bud

Bud may be a vegetative bud or a flower bud or combined, but for the purpose of propagation, vegetative buds are used which are small under-developed shoots in dormant condition waiting to grow into a leaf or a stem. Due care should be taken while selecting a bud for propagation use. Following points may be kept in mind while selecting a bud:

1. Bud should be healthy and of an improved variety.
2. It should be compatible with the stock.
3. Bud should neither be too young nor too old since old buds are difficult to take, insert and establish.
4. Bud should be of normal shape and size. Colour may also be considered. Since the buds are inherent, they look alike in colour and so may be taken from only one-year old wood.
5. It is better to collect the buds from the middle portion of the one-year old shoot because the buds near the tip of the shoot are weak and under-developed and lack stored food material, while buds near the base are usually woody and are not easily pulled. Moreover, they do not establish easily and early.
6. Avoid the selection of thorny buds, dormant buds and abnormal buds.
7. When there is more than one bud, select the middle one, as in the case of peach where there are three buds at one place.

Storage of buds/budsticks: Buds can be stored for one season. Pruned wood is collected and out of that, budsticks of one-year growth are selected. They may be wrapped in a moist peat moss and then wrapped in polythene sheet and placed in a refrigerator. Buds should not be stored for a long period since they lose their viability after one season. The free ends of the budsticks can be

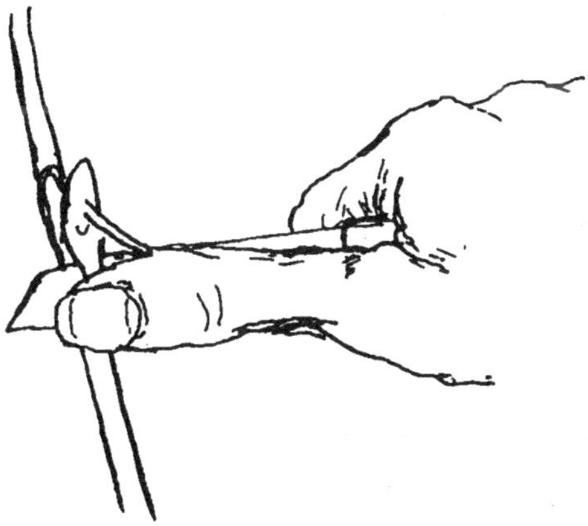

Fig. 21. Taking a bud.

immersed in wax before storage so that they do not rot during storage. They need full protection from pathogens and insects during storage.

(b) Rootstocks

Qualities of the rootstocks for selection are the same as for grafting, but the bark of rootstock must come up or split up easily. This method cannot be used where the bark of the tree does not peel off, i.e. it remains sticking to the inner tissues.

(c) Budding knife

It is a knife, which has a handle that has a blade on one end and a plastic or blunt iron piece, lifter on the other end. With the tip of the blade, various cuts are made while with the help of the lifter, the bark is lifted and even the bud is taken out of the wood. Top of knife is also used for removal of excessive wood beneath the bud.

(d) Tape and grafting wax

This material used for grafting can be used for budding also since the aims of both the processes are the same and they do occur in the similar fashion.

Kinds of Budding

For the insertion of bud to the rootstock, many methods are

employed which are described here. In all the methods, bud is taken out cautiously without injuring the budstick and the bud with the help of blade of knife, the cut starts half a cm above the bud and goes below the bud about half cm on both the sides and the bud with wood is sliced off. With the help of the tip of the blade and the blunt end of the handle of knife, the bud-wood may be removed carefully. Some wood may be retained with the bud. Lower end of the bark may be made into an oval shape, which should have sufficient bark. This can be learnt through experience. One can practice the budding on the pruning sticks. It is most necessary that buds should remain alive, without any damage and dormant while taking out and insertion during budding. Following are some of the methods of budding.

'T' budding

A horizontal cut of 3 cm length is made on the bark of the rootstock, about 30 cm above the ground level. Another cut starting from the middle of the first horizontal cut in the vertical direction but downwards is made which is also 3 cm in length. Thus, we get the cut of 'T' shape. With the help of the tip of the blade, the bark may be separated and lifted to insert the prepared bud into this cut. Thus, the bark that has been lifted works as a shield, i.e. protecting the inner wood. The method is also known as 'Shield budding.'

After the insertion of the bud, grafting wax may be pasted and then grafting tape may be tied.

Inverted T (⊥) budding

In localities where rainfall is plenty and there is danger of entry of rain water into the union, vertical cut in the upward direction is given. Other details are same.

Similarly, I or H budding are made. It is the only difference in the shape and manner of cuts being applied.

Flute budding

Identical to this method are Patch budding and Flap budding types. In this method the bark around the bud is given the desired shape and the same shape of bark is removed from the rootstock. Great care should be taken that no place is left uncovered. Moreover, bark of bud should not overlap the bark of the rootstock. Imme-

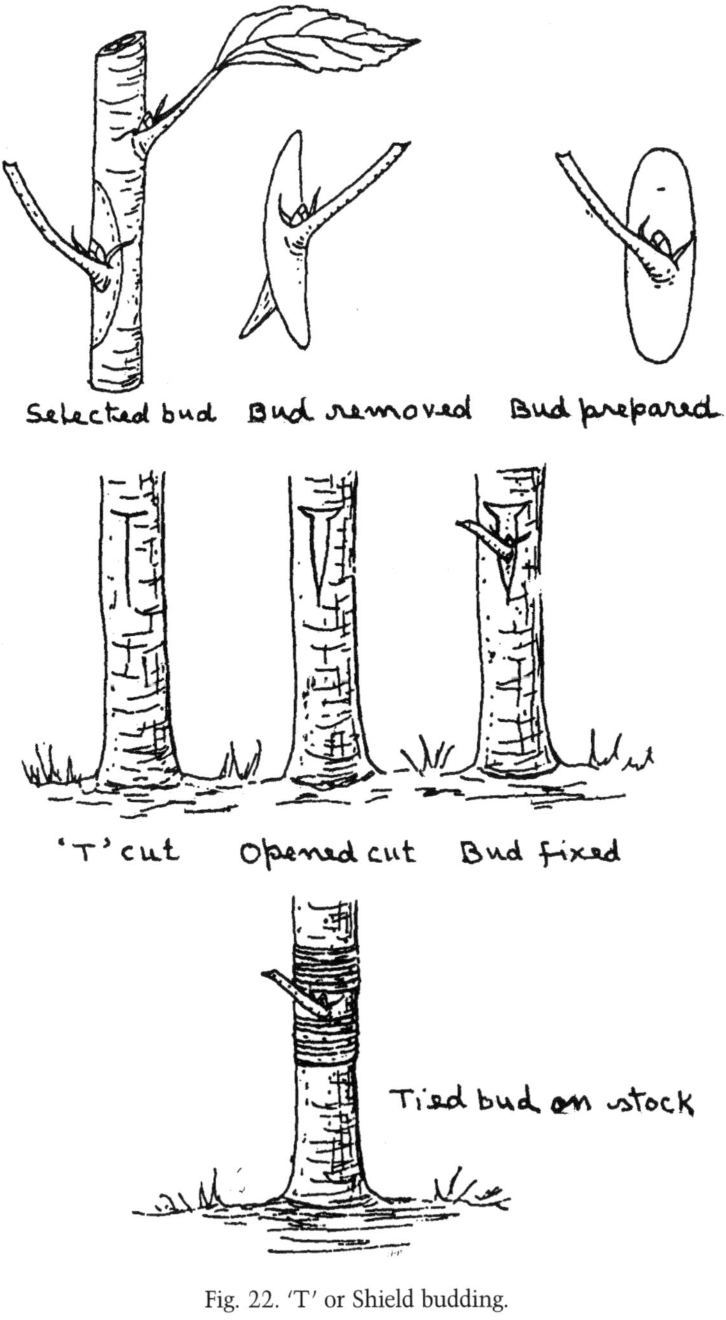

Fig. 22. 'T' or Shield budding.

diately after placing the bud piece on the rootstock, it is covered by a grafting wax, which should be then tied by a grafting tape.

Ring budding

Bud along with the ring of the bark is removed from the budstick and is then placed on the rootstock that has already been given same type of cut, i.e. the bark in the form of ring has been removed. This is also known as 'Annular budding'. Waxing and fixing the tape is a must.

Chip budding

In some cases, where bark of the tree cannot be separated, some pieces of wood along with the bark known as a chip is removed both from the rootstock and the budstick. Generally a triangular piece in the form of chip is sliced-off from the rootstock. An identical-sized chip along with the bud is placed on this piece. They are fused, pressed together and then tied.

In addition to these methods, many scientists have tried some modifications. But is general practice, T budding, Patch budding and Chip budding are carried on since they are easy and have great success.

Precautions During Budding

Most of the precautions to be followed are identical to grafting. Readers are advised to follow them. In addition to those, following points must be kept in mind.

1. Bud should be compatible, healthy, disease and insect free.
2. After taking out the bud, it should be inserted immediately.
3. Stock and bud should not be damaged during the whole process.
4. Inspect the budded portion after two weeks. If there is girdling, grafting tape may be replaced. If there is a success of union, tape may be removed. If unsuccessful, budding can be done again on another place.
5. Thinning of leaves of the rootstock may be done prior to budding but it should be only a day or two before the actual budding.
6. If needed, support may be given to see that the stem emerging out of the bud is straight.

7. Top of the rootstock above the bud union place may be removed on the successful budding, but removal should be in steps rather than in one go.

Other Means of Multiplication

Plants have some modified parts, which have stored food material with them and are capable of giving rise to new plants when planted indoor or outdoor. In general, these structures are the modifications of stem, root or leaves but mostly stem modifications are used for propagation, as they are easily available in plenty. In some cases, the plants either do not produce seeds or the seeds may be a few in number or are non-viable. Thus, these structures are needed for propagation.

Bulbs

These are specialised underground stems, which are usually disc-shaped and have scaly leaves called scales and the roots develop from the stem. There can be different kinds and sizes of the bulbs, but generally, the bulbs are tunicated which have fleshy scales like that of onion, tulip and daffodils while the other kind is that of non-tunicated bulbs, the fleshy scales form separate organs capable of producing new plants, e.g. garlic, lily, etc.

At the end of current seasons growth, small bulbs appear around the mother bulb. These small bulbs are capable of producing young plants, when planted in the field.

Corms

These are round, swollen stems covered with a papery tunic. These are solid with a bud on the top that produce leaves and flowers, e.g. crocus, gladiolus, etc. Small corms called cormels are separated from the mother corm for planting or raising new plants.

Tubers

An individual tuber is an underground short, thick, fleshy stem that has eyes or buds from which leaves and flowers emerge when planted. Large tubers like that of potato and artichoke can be cut into small pieces so that each piece has 2-3 eyes. These eyes develop into shoots while the roots emerge from the sides and thus give rise to new plants, which are identical to the mother plant. Number of plants that can be had from a single tuber will depend upon the number of eyes present on the tuber.

Rhizomes

These are the horizontal stems, which may be fleshy or non-fleshy. Roots grow from the bottom of the rhizome while leaves and flowers sprout from the top. Nodes and internodes are sometimes visible. These are found in plants, which mostly grow horizontally, i.e. the stem is parallel to the ground level. Bamboo, sugarcane, banana, many ferns, ornamental plants like aster, hollyhock, violet, phlox, delphinium and many grasses are multiplied by rhizomes.

Fleshy roots

These may also be known as 'Tuberous roots' since the roots are fleshy and swollen which have a pointed bud on the top that develop into a shoot while the roots emerge/sprout from the bottom. These roots differ from stems in respect of absence of nodes and internodes on them. Sweet potato, dahlia, etc. are propagated by their fleshy roots. Great care has to be taken while selecting these tuberous roots for propagation; they must have a crown, i.e. bud at the end without which they cannot emerge as new plants. Fleshy roots have enough stored food material for the use of future plant.

Planting

All the above-mentioned parts suitable for multiplication are placed in well-prepared soil or a pot. Details of the soil preparation methods have been described earlier. Single piece is placed at one place. The depth of placing these parts depend upon the size of the tuber, bulb, corm, root or the other portion but it must be in the soil by keeping the bud upside so that the emerging leaves from the part may easily come out. The distance between two tubers, bulbs, corms, etc., depend upon the species and the time for which a plant is being grown in the container or the soil. In soil, the distance is usually 20 to 45 cm according to the species.

At the time of planting there should be sufficient moisture in the soil so that the tuber, bulb, etc. get swollen and the food stored in them is converted into simpler compounds for the utilization of the new plant to be taken. In few days, there will be a new plant. This plant is looked after as the seedling. They may be allowed to grow at the same place or transplanted elsewhere as the case may be.

Micro-Propagation

It is the technique of growing plants from small bits of most active tissues. It is the fastest, sure and best method of producing large number of plants in a short span of time but needs completely asceptic conditions during their early stages of growth. The technique is also known as 'Tissue Culture Technique'. Virus, disease and insect-free plants can be produced.

This technique involves the growing of small pieces of plants such as their stems, seeds, shoot tips, root tips, callus, etc. in an artificial medium where they get all the desired conditions for their growth and multiplication under completely sterile conditions.

At its simplest, micro-propagation consists of excising small pieces of actively growing tissue, and, under sterile conditions, transferring them to a growing media. In this they develop into plantlets, which then are taken from the laboratory and hardened, to make them fit for growing in the outdoors or field conditions.

After an initial adaptation phase of nine to twelve months in the

Fig. 23. Micro-propagated plugs.

test tube environment, the tissues are encouraged to develop multi-shoot structures. When sufficient number of shoots has been obtained, they are subject to root initiation. These plantlets are then moved to greenhouse on a sterilized rooting medium having high organic matter, under high humidity, low light and optimum temperature. After about 3 to 4 months, these plantlets are ready for transfer to the pots or for planting in the ground.

For production of virus-free plants, meristem culture is primarily used that must have the back up of indexing facilities to confirm virus freedom.

Basic Needs

The equipments needed will vary with the amount of material being handled and the production system employed and the plant species grown but as a general guideline these are:

Equipment

- Autoclave
- Balance
- Refrigerator
- Laminar air flow cabinet
- Sterilizing oven
- Drying cabinet
- pH meter
- Deioniser
- Stereomicroscope
- Magnetic stirrer

Glassware

- Beakers
- Bottles
- Glass rods
- Measuring cylinders
- Funnels
- Aspirator
- Reagent bottles
- Pipettes
- Test tubes with caps

Chemicals

- Agar
- Sucrose
- Ethanol
- Methylated spirit
- Sodium hypochlorite
- pH buffers
- Wetting agent
- Prepared media
- Hormones
- Hydrochloric acid

Tools

- Scalpel handles
- Forceps
- Needle holders
- Gas burners
- Gas lighter
- Filter holder
- Vial racks
- Test tube racks
- Magnetic followers
- Syringes

Miscellaneous articles

Jars	Petri dishes
Plastic containers	Tissue paper
Gas cylinders	pH papers
Autoclave tape	Filter papers
Disposable gloves	Scalpel blades
Markers	Tin foil
Plastic trays	Pots

By tissue culturing, nurserymen can raise micro-cuttings, plant plugs or hardened plants. In a year about 70,000 plants can be multiplied. This method is difficult, needs thorough knowledge of the technique, expertise and money. Interested grower may take up this as an avocation but one has to find a ready market. The cost of production of plants by this method is almost 3-4 times more than the ordinary method but the work is fast. This work needs great care and timely attention. There is no doubt that the plants multiplied through this technique are true to type, virus-free, disease-free, uniform in size and production.

12

Management of Nursery

Nursery plants are living beings and tender in nature, and are suppose to get due care and attention after they have either emerged from the seeds or have been raised from other sources like rootstock or through tissue culture technique. Since they are in the second phase of their life which is active, they face various agro-climatic conditions. Generally they are grown in the open field under the protection of Mother Nature where they should be able to face the local environment and other conditions.

It is the duty and main objective of a commercial nursery grower to supply the nursery plants with suitable conditions necessary for their normal development and growth. This is the major work of management in the nursery, which includes all such operations right from the emergence of young plantlet till they are fully grown-up or are ready for uprooting and transplanting out of the main nursery.

Breaking the Crust

Usually after light irrigation, particularly, in the summer months, the upper crust of the soil of the seedbed or transplanted site, may be a pot or a tray, gets dried up in such a way that it forms a protective layer which does not allow the movement of air in and outside the soil which arrests the emergence of plumule. So, it is necessary to break this crust as soon as it is seen. This work can be accomplished with the help of a hoe, rake, *khurpa* or *khilna* but should be done gently so as not to disturb the swollen seeds or the emerging radicle and plumule.

Irrigation

Plants can take up the mineral matter and other nutrients needed for their development and growth only when these are in the solution form and as such the roots of plants should be in the vicinity of water i.e., in direct contact with the water but it should be sufficient/enough to dissolve the material. Irrigation is the process of supplying water/humidity to plants.

Irrigation can be given in two ways, i.e., over the surface of the soil and under or sub-surface of the soil. In the former method, watering can be done by a can or flooding the bed through a water channel or by sprayer or sprinkler which are mechanically operated. These supply water over the surface which percolates into the soil and thus, wetting the soil.

In the sub-surface irrigation, watering is given through special method, i.e. drip irrigation system in which the pipes are usually laid underground about 2-3 cm deep in the soil and are covered by the earth. The laying of pipes, etc. is laborious and if the water used is not clean, it can clog the pipes and joints. So regular checking of the pipes, distributors and joints is a must. Amount of water required is very less as there is no loss by evaporation.

For newly emerged and young plants, which are 3-4 weeks old or have established themselves fully, surface irrigation method consisting in supplying water through sprinkler is best suited. Through a sprinkler, the amount of water released is less and is with minimum force. Seedbeds being smaller in size cannot be irrigated by sub-surface irrigation method.

For older plants, which are in the nursery beds and are in pots or polybags, irrigation may be given by mechanical sprayers.

For more grown-up plants like those which have been budded or grafted, irrigation can be given through the sub-surface method. Since some of the plants are to be removed with earth-balls, this method is not recommended. Only flooding method or surface method of irrigation should be used.

Amount of water to be given to the plant will depend upon many factors like the nature of the plant, age of the plant, and kind of soil and weather conditions. A nursery grower has to use his own experience to calibrate the amount of water needed by a plant. As a general rule, plants should never be forced to drought and on the other hand over-watering should also be avoided.

General Recommendations of Irrigation

1. There is no need of irrigation if there is suitable moisture regime in the soil at the time of seeding.

2. Apply water everyday for the first week after sowing of seeds or transplanting of rootstocks or cuttings.

3. The interval between two irrigations may be enhanced to 48 hours, i.e. alternate days. This may continue for 10 days.

4. Later the duration/interval of watering may be increased to 72 hours or twice a week for the next 10 days.

5. The irrigation after this may be once a week.

6. All irrigations may be regulated according to the prevailing climate. The duration may be increased or decreased depending upon the rain or precipitation.

7. In greenhouse, mist chambers and other growing structures, the amount of water and the frequency of irrigation may be regulated.

8. A day or two before uprooting the plants, light irrigation may be applied to ease the uprooting. It will also help in the preservation of the roots during the uprooting of plants.

Nutrition

It is an important aspect since without having proper feeding, the plantlets cannot develop and grow in the normal way. In fact, it is the essence of vigour of plant life. Plant can have the food material only in the liquid form, that too mostly from the soil and only under emergent conditions through their leaves. Generally, a seed may be tiny or bold as per species, has enough stored food material to feed itself till the emergence of new leaves from the seed. It depends upon the maturity of the seed and the prevailing conditions. Mature seeds have sufficient food material, which is digested during the seed germination by the interaction of water and then the breakdown of complex substances, to feed the primary emerging leaves. The stored food is depleted with the emergence of these leaves. New leaves start the manufacture of food material themselves. In dry soil and poor soil, the availability of these substances to the seeds may be reduced. It is only due to this fact that viable, mature and healthy seeds are recommended for sowing.

Generally, the plants need nitrogen, phosphorus and potassium for their general growth and proper development. Nitrogen is an integral part of various food materials found in the plant. It is essential for protein that is necessary for vegetative growth. In fact, the green colour in the leaves is due to chlorophyll, the green pigment needed for photosynthesis, which is resultant of nitrogen. Over-dose of nitrogen should be avoided since it causes lanky growth, weak stems, soft tissues, susceptibility to diseases and finally lodging of plants. It is, therefore, generally advised to use nitrogen in two split doses to make it available at regular intervals. Phosphorus and potassium are also part of many compounds found in the seed and plant body, which are part of proteins, many enzymes and other substances necessary for growth and development.

Apart from this, the plants may need other elements like calcium, sulphur, magnesium, iron, boron, zinc, copper, manganese and molybdenum in small quantities, may be in traces, but they are essential. Therefore, soil sample may be got analysed before the start of the business and then it should be repeated at least on every alternate year. This will provide information about the quantity of each element present in the soil and one can add the desired quantity to bring the fertility level of the soil to the optimum level.

Time of Application of Fertilizers

The plantlet will need the manures and fertilizers, which supply the requisite elements, when they are with primary leaves. Primary leaves on becoming green are able to manufacture the food material for themselves from the external sources. Moreover, the stored food material is depleted by this time. So, to make the food material available to the plants, these manures and fertilizers should be supplied to the plants. Most of the manures like farm yard manure, compost, green manure, and fertilizers like Super Phosphate, Muriate of Potash, etc., need a time of about 1 to 1½ months to come in the form suitable to the plant, so these are added at the time of preparing the land or making a soil mixture or pot mix.

Well-rotten farm yard manure or compost is added along with the Super Phosphate and Muriate of Potash. Other materials may be added as and when needed. If there is deficiency of a particular element, it can be sprayed on the leaves. Nitrogenous fertilizer like CAN (calcium ammonium nitrate) is added to the soil a day or two prior to sowing of seeds while urea can be given on the day of sowing or it can be given as an aerial spray.

Dose of Fertilizers

Soil mixture or pot mixtures are generally prepared in such a way that necessary ingredients of plant food in a balanced way are included in it. Different mixtures have been described earlier for pots, trays and other containers; the quantity of organic matter added is sufficient.

When seeds are sown in well-prepared seedbeds, 5 kg well-rotten farm yard manure, cow dung manure or compost, 120-150 g of CAN, 125 g of Super Phosphate and 20-25 g of Muriate of Potash are mixed in a square metre area. This amount can be increased or decreased according to the need of the soil and the plant species. In the same way beds for planting of other plant parts for propagation are prepared.

For spraying, urea @ 0.5 to 1.0% may be used. Urea is dissolved in required quantity of water and then sprayed on the foliage taking care that the solution is stirred during the spraying operations so that the spray is uniform. If needed, the spray may be repeated after few days.

Methods of Application of Fertilizers

Ingredients to be added in the soil mix are ground with a wooden mallet or some other thing so that they are small and uniform in size.

Farm yard manure is spread in the field and then mixed with a furrow turning plough or disc harrow. For small areas or plots, this may be mixed with the soil with the help of a spade, rake, *khilna* or *khurpa*. Similarly, the Super Phosphate and Muriate of Potash are mixed prior to sowing of seeds or planting of vegetative parts.

In case the deficiency symptoms of an element appear on the leaves of young plantlet, the solution of same element may be made in clean water @ 0.4 to 0.6% and sprayed on a clear sunny day. Urea @ 0.5 to 1.0 per cent is dissolved in water for spraying on the foliage of the weak plants. This may be repeated if the plants are still weak as will be evident from their light green colour and small-sized leaves. Solution of other nutrients may be sprayed on the foliage on a clear sunny day to correct the deficiency symptoms. The spray may be repeated, if there is a need.

Care During Manuring

Manures and fertilizers need to be added with great care. Since most of the fertilizers are chemicals in nature, they can be harmful if their dose is in excess. There may be spots on leaves, leaves may shrivel and dry, droop down or curl upward, marginal necrosis and many other symptoms may appear. Following precautions must be observed.

1. Use the right dose and correct method at the best time of the use of fertilizer.
2. Farm yard manure and other organic manures should be well-rotten since half decomposed manure invites white ants and other insects. Fungal diseases may also appear.
3. Do not use chemical fertilizers when the soil is dry or rain is not expected after their application. They need to be added when the soil is moist or irrigation is to be applied immediately after their application.
4. Chemical fertilizers should not stick for a long time on the leaves and other aerial parts of the plants. When the dose is in excess, it badly affects the leaves and other parts of the plant.
5. Dry fertilizers should not come in direct contact with the parts of the plants.
6. Only aqueous solution of the fertilizer, i.e. when the fertilizers are in solute can be absorbed or adsorbed by the plant cells.
7. Spray should be made on a sunny day. Wetting agent may be mixed with it. This increases the sticking capacity of the fertilizer and also increases the efficacy of the chemical.
8. Thorough drenching of the plant with a nutrient solution

should be done but it should be done smoothly and gently by means of a fine nozzle sprayer.

9. Solution should be made when needed and the leftover may be put in the soil of other area.

Rouging

It is the process of removal of plants of other varieties or unwanted plants from the nursery. Though it is a difficult task to do in the early stages since all the plants may look alike. Most of the varieties show some characteristics in the young plantlets. Difference in margins of the leaves may be recognized in the early stages. In case of seedlings of fruit plants, there can be some distinction as difference in wild and other varieties in certain characters do exist. Off-type plants are usually different, may be weak, sick or bolted. It is better to rouge the vegetable and flower plants before being uprooted from the pots or soil for transplanting in the field. It will save time, labour, space and fertilizers when they are grown outdoors. Moreover, it is economical to plant less seedlings rather than having so many plants that include off-type plants. Single rouging will be sufficient.

Weeding

Weeds are unwanted plants, which come up in the nursery beds or pots. Their seeds may come either with the soil mixture that has been put in the pot or the manure, which has been used for enriching the soil. These may also come along the seeds of the main variety or species. In many cases, weed seeds look similar to the main variety so they are difficult to distinguish and eliminate from the seed sample.

Weeds compete for soil, irrigation, fertilizers and other management practices with the main plants, hence their removal from the nursery is essential. It is easy to remove them at the early stage as they are young and have not robbed much the requirement of the variety.

To avoid the weeds, seed sample may be examined thoroughly before sowing. Soil or soil mixture may be prepared under strict supervision. So far as possible, the seeds of weeds should not reach the seedbeds through irrigation or other means.

Weeding in the early stage should be done with manual labour, which is commonly known as hand weeding. Though, it is costly but is a sure method of removal of weeds. Light irrigation may be given before weeding so that the weeds may be uprooted easily and the process should not damage the main plants.

Chemicals known as weedicides may be used with care. These are either used prior to emergence of weeds or when they have already appeared in the field, the former is known as pre-emergence treatment while the later is post-treatment. Weedicides are selective in their action; they either kill the broad-leaved or narrow-leaved plants. So selection of the weedicides to be used will depend upon the kind of weeds present in the seedbed or nursery beds. Simazine, Atrazine, Goal, Gramaxone (Paraquat) 2, 4, 5-T, 2, 4-D are common weedicides, which can be used with advantage.

Mechanical weeding is possible for the grown-up nursery plants of fruits. They are usually planted about 30 cm away in lines from each other and as such space is available for the movement of plough or harrow in the field. Moreover, these plants have established fully in the field and can tolerate some pressure of being disturbed during weeding. Great care should be taken since some plants are likely to be trampled by animals and men who are part of this type of weeding.

Number of weedings to be carried out will depend upon the type of weeds present in the nursery or pots. After every weeding, the uprooted weeds should be collected and buried in a pit or burnt so that they are not able to multiply further. They should be removed along with their roots before flowering.

Hoeing

This operation is carried out with the help of hoe, rake, *khurpa* or *khilna* with the aim of loosening the soil particles around the roots of the young and old plants. This operation increases air spaces, which on watering can have more moisture, retained near the root zone and this is essential for the proper growth and development of plants. Exchange of gases near the roots is very important, as roots cannot grow under limitation. Great care should be taken during hoeing that the plant roots and tops are not damaged. Light hoeing will be sufficient. Frequency of hoeing will depend upon the soil and moisture conditions; heavy soil may need more number of hoeing while dry soils may need less hoeing. Usually after every hoeing, light irrigation may be given.

During weeding, hoeing is also done automatically because when weeds and unwanted plants are being uprooted, the neigh-bouring plants do get the hoeing. It is better to combine both these operations together to save time and labour.

Earthing-up

When the soil is moistened, it may settle down to some extent, particularly near the main stem, so to provide some support to the stem, soil is raised a bit which forms a mound around the stem. This is essential for grown-up plants and the plants which are being raised through their vegetative parts like tubers, rhizomes, bulbs, etc. Developing bulbs, corms, offsets, runners, etc. are also earthed-up to increase their size and development. This operation indirectly helps in increasing the air circulation near the root zone of the plants.

In small beds, nursery beds or seedbeds, this work is done manually but in large beds where plants are spaced at a wider

Fig. 24. Earthing-up or mound layering in apple.

distance, ordinary plough, harrow or hoe may be used which can hoe and earth-up the plants. Earthing-up in the form of mound is usually done for raising/multiplication of rootstocks from the cuttings. It may be done when there is a need for it, which a grower will feel himself on seeing the bed, which is sinking. It is better to earth-up before applying irrigation. After heavy rains, earthing-up with dried soil is a must.

Earthing-up should not be much. In case of mound layering, when soil is being earthed-up, the top of the plant must be visible out of the soil (Fig. 24). Crowns of plants must be cared for fully. For grown-up plants, weeding, hoeing and earthing-up can be done simultaneously to save time, labour and energy.

Mulching

Moisture in suitable quantity is a must for every plant. It is needed to carry out various physiological and other activities in the plant without which there is no life. During dry weather in summer, there is too much evaporation of water from the soil, which forces the plant to grow under drought conditions. It is, therefore, essential that the plant must have sufficient quantity of water at its disposal for proper development and growth.

Mulch is provided to conserve the moisture available in the soil by covering the soil with a layer, which checks the evaporation of water from it. This layer may be of dry grass, polythene or of a chemical. Under our farming situations, mulch of dry grass and use of black polythene sheet is possible.

Dry grass without seeds or other propagation material is spread in a layer of 7 to 10 cm thickness over the soil. A layer of sawdust or soil may be spread over the dry grass to avoid sweeping away of the grass by wind. This helps in the reduction of water loss from the soil. This layer can be later used for making compost or any other organic manure.

Black polythene sheet as mulch can be provided to grown-up plants, which are spaced at a uniform distance. The sheet is spread and sides covered with soil so that with the pressure of wind, this may not be swept away. In chemical mulching, tar-like pastes are smeared on the soil and this has to be done after the planting of young seedlings. This method is not adoptable for commercial nursery raising since there is seed sowing and hoeing, etc.

Mulching, apart from protecting the moisture from loss, does not allow the emergence of weeds and other unwanted material. It has been found by experiments and experience that mulched plants do better than other plants.

During the early stages, i.e. after seeding, the seed is covered by a layer of sawdust + ash + cow dung manure. This layer helps in the easy emergence of plumule, and also serves the purpose of mulch.

Deshooting

Young seedlings of annuals like those of vegetables, ornamental plants and other medicinal plants which are to be transplanted when they are 3-4 weeks old, remain of a single stem but other plants when kept in the nursery after this period, need their single stemming, i.e. their shoots arising from the main stem upto 30 cm above the ground level are to be removed.

Deshooting or single stemming is most essential. The stocks to be budded or grafted should not have any other shoot from the main stem at least 25-30 cm above the ground level. In practice, budding or grafting should be done at least 25 cm above the ground level. In case of forest trees, this distance is also maintained by deshooting. This helps in keeping the main stem straight and sound.

Generally, any leaf or bud erupting out of the main stem upto 25-30 cm distance above the ground level is removed by rubbing it off with the fingers of hand. This rubbing should be smooth and gentle. For grown-up plants, this work has to be done by a secateur that should not damage the stem and there should be no wound. Young and small cuts do heal themselves but bigger cuts need to be painted with a wound healing paste.

Staking

Weak stemmed plants do need support to keep their main stems straight. It is most important in windy areas where the plants sway and tilt in the direction of wind, which causes a bend that may lead to a bent stem or crooked stem. Further, grafted plants may need support to keep the union intact and safe from the swinging effect of the wind. Great care should be taken in providing support; the support should be strong and should not start rooting/establishing

Fig. 25. Providing support.

there. If some bands are needed, they may be provided but these should be strong and soft. Cotton or cloth piece may be kept under a tie to avoid girdling. Bands should be removed when they are no longer needed (Fig. 25).

Transplanting

Many-a-times, young seedlings are in need of transplantation since they need better spacing for their development. Further, for improvement of the stock, they are to be propagated by grafting or budding. They may need top working. Under such conditions, the seedlings of the young plants are transplanted elsewhere.

Healthy, robust, disease-free plants are uprooted and transplanted in well-prepared nursery beds at a suitable distance so that they can be worked upon easily without damaging them at all. Soil should be well prepared like that of a seedbed but the requirement for manures may be halved. Artificial manures should only be given near the plants.

When the plants are uprooted with their earth-balls, site of the nursery beds should be changed after a year. Old site can be used again after enriching the soil with well-rotten farm yard manure. This soil may be got chemically analyzed for fixing the dose of manure. Soil is prepared in the normal manner.

A pit or a place for the transplanting of the young plant should be prepared in advance. This may be equal to the size of the spread of the roots. Transplanting of annuals is done by placing the plant in the furrow made by a marker or a harrow. Plants are kept straight. For larger seedlings, the depth of the furrow has to be 15 to 20 cm depending upon the size of the roots of the plants to be transplanted. Cover the root zone of the plant with a moist soil and the light irrigation may be done to make easy contact of the soil particles with the roots. Covering should be sufficient and it should neither be deep or shallow but it should be as it was in the nursery.

While transplanting in a pit, the soil around the stem of the plant may be pressed with the back of a spade or by feet so that the air space in the root zone is reduced. Light watering may be given soon. Keep the plant straight as far as possible.

Transplanting may be done in a moist soil either in the early hours of the morning or late in the evening. If moisture in the soil is less, light watering may be given. Avoid too much watering. Operations after transplanting are same as for other beds.

Hardening of plants

Young plantlets received through tissue-cultured technique from the laboratory are hardened, i.e., acclimatized to the natural conditions in the greenhouse and then in the open field or pots. These tender plants are planted along with their soil in the form of earth-balls; they are looked after like other plants except that they are grown under better conditions of their growth. They are supplied with most congenial conditions for their development. It may take about 3 to 6 months to harden them and to make them fit for growing in the field.

Pruning of seedlings

Young actively growing seedlings may be notched, i.e., dried leaves may be removed. Diseased and insect-infested parts may also be destroyed after removing them from the plant.

Sometimes their roots, which have dried after uprooting, may be pruned gently. Unwanted and intermingling roots may also be thinned or chopped. But this is possible only in case of plants that can have adventitious roots.

Like root pruning, the tops of the plants may be removed. By removing the top, the stem may produce side-shoot and thus the growth of the plant is directed towards side rather than upright. This is known as *Head Back*. This operation is important in temperate fruit trees to regulate their height and to get growth on all sides.

Since the process involves removal of living parts, plant protection recommendations should be followed. Generally, this work is done during winter and at the time of transplanting; there are less chances of attack of fungus due to very low temperature. Small cuts heal themselves while bigger cuts of more than a cm diameter may be smeared with a suitable wound healing paste. Other precautions have been given under the chapter Propagation of Plants.

Plant Protection

From the sowing of seeds or planting of other parts of plants for propagation, till they are removed from the nurseries for disposal, they are attacked by a number of pathogens and insects, which mar the quality of the plants. The nursery grower has to use many methods to protect their plant material from the attack of insects, pests and diseases.

Plant protection measures include the protection of plants from pathogens like fungus, bacteria, virus and insects.

Plant Diseases

The following are some of the major plant diseases that need protection measures.

Fungal Diseases

Different kinds of fungi have been reported to damage the plants at different stages. During the early stage of plant development, they may be present on the seed or in the soil. They are activated during the development of seed to seedling, i.e. during the germination of seeds. Later, the seedlings are liable to be attacked by fungi to affect the plant growth. These fungi can be carried by the affected plants to the field where they are transplanted.

Fungi spores are the main cause of their spread. On finding a suitable place for their attack, they enter into the body of the plant and on getting congenial conditions like humidity and temperature, they multiply after sucking/drawing sap from the plant and as a result, the growth of the plant is restricted. Depending upon the severity of attack, it can kill the plant.

Generally, fungi cause following five types of diseases: (i) Powdery mildews, (ii) Anthracnoses, (iii) Downy mildews, (iv) Leaf spots, and (v) Fusarium wilts.

Powdery mildew: Spores of the causal organism appear on the surface of the leaves and even on the tips of the affected plants. They usually appear as if wood-ash has been broadcasted over the surface since the colour of the spores is usually grey to greenish white. The leaves being covered over by these spores are not able to manufacture their own food due to lack of photosynthetic place and suitable environment, the leaves dry up and fall down. These spores can further spread by wind, water or by animals.

The disease is quite common with seedlings of apple, mango, grape, papaya, citrus, cucurbits, rose, zinnia, chrysanthemum, pea and number of other species.

There are two common control measures:

a) Collection of the affected parts early in the morning and then destroying them so that no further infection is passed on. In the early hours, the spores are inactive, i.e. they cannot move by wind due to lack of wind velocity and presence of dew or moisture in the surroundings. The affected portions are collected in a bag, burnt or buried deep in the soil.

b) Use of fungicides like Karathane (1 ml/L), Wettable Sulphur

(3g/L), Carbendazim (0.5g/L) or any other may be sprayed on plants before the formation of fungal spores. If needed, repeated sprays may be made but care should be taken to use different fungicide in the repeat spray. Two sprays are regarded sufficient to contain the disease.

Anthracnoses: The fungus causes small dead spots that often have a raised border and a sunken centre and that may have concentric rings of pink and brown colour.

In grape, small dark brown spots appear on leaves, which generally increase in size while in guava, pinheaded spots or dieback symptoms appear. In case of mango, dark brown sunken spots appear on leaves and may appear as dieback in citrus and cashew nut. In pepper and chilies, there is dieback.

Control is possible by selection of disease-free seed, rotation of crops, collection of affected plants and then their destruction but, avoid touching the affected plants when they are wet. Spray of Bordeaux Mixture (4:4:50), Captan (0.3%) or Zineb (0.2%) has been found to be very effective in control of further spread of the disease. Other fungicides like Dithane (Indothane), Maneb and cuprous oxide have shown good results.

Downy mildew: Generally white to purple, downy growth, usually on the underside of the leaves which turns black with age. Upper leaf surface has pale surface. The disease can remain in the soil for many years, if soil remains affected. Wind, rain and seeds spread it.

In case of grapes, it appears as irregular yellow spots on the upper surface of the leaves and white growth on the under surface. Later leaves whither and die. In cauliflower and cabbage, the young leaves may be affected while patches may appear on onion leaves. Greyish mouldy growth appears on sweet pea leaves. Lettuce and pansy leaves have also shown such symptoms due to downy mildew.

To control the spread of this disease, disease-free seed should be selected. Rotation of crops may be followed. Removal of infected plants is a must. Plants may be sprayed with Captan (0.2-0.5%), Copper oxychloride, Blitox (0.3%) or Bordeaux mixture (4:4:50). If needed, repeated sprays may be used.

Leaf spots: Various kinds of leaf spots may appear on the leaves of the plants. They appear in a small patch in the beginning and

Fig. 26. Apple scab symptoms on leaf.

go on increasing in size, thus restricting the growth and development of leaves, which finally leads to death of leaves. It is observed as apple scab (Fig. 26), cherry leaf spot, rose black spot, candytuft leaf spot, etc. It is common in most of the vegetables.

Resistant varieties may be planted. All dropped leaves should be collected and destroyed. Recommendations to control these spots by various fungicides are there. Different fungicides like Bavistin, Captan, Indothane, Zineb, Mancozeb, Dodine, etc. may be used. Repeated sprays may be adopted but for the repeated spray, earlier fungicide used should not be employed to avoid its resistance.

Fusarium wilts: These fungi cause seed borne-diseases and infest the seeds while they are developing on the plants in the field. During storage, they remain dormant since the moisture in the seed is too low for its multiplication, and when the seed is sown, it activates and as a result the fungus is also activated which leads to infection on the young seedlings. The seedlings wilt and die.

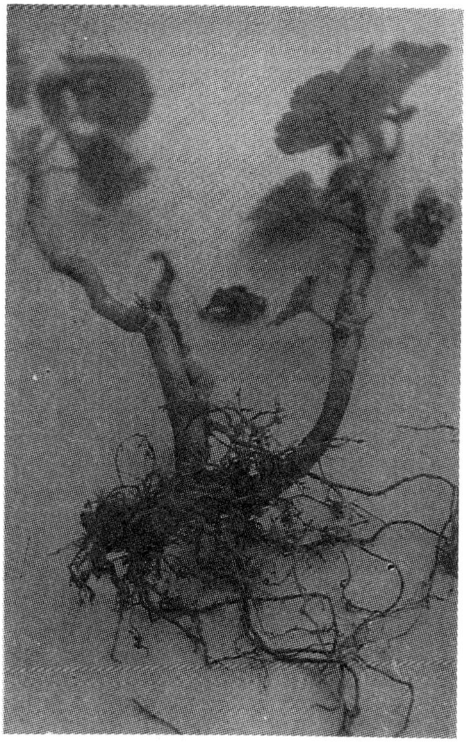

Fig. 27. Wilt in geranium.

Seeds of forest trees are usually infected but in other cases, some precautions are observed to keep the seed free from such fungi. These fungi have been found to attack a wide range of flowers, fruits, vegetables and ornamental nursery plants.

For the control of these diseases, it is better to use the disease-free seed and it should be treated before sowing with fungicides like Thiram or Captan. Rotation of crops is another way of controlling the spread of disease. Affected plants may be destroyed.

Other diseases: Blights, cankers, rots, rusts, moulds, etc., are also common in young seedlings. They can be controlled by mechanical means followed by spray of fungicides.

Bacterial Diseases

Bacteria are single-celled microorganisms, which reproduce by

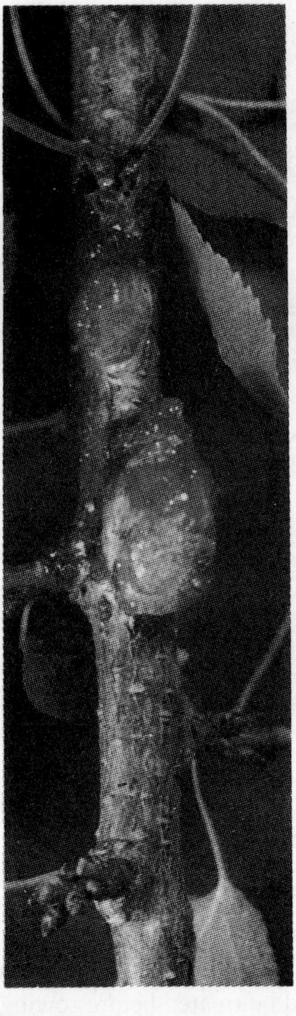

Fig. 28. Bacterial canker of stone fruits.

simple cell division. They are visible only under a microscope but their presence in the plant is easy to detect with the naked eye. They may spread by wind, water, insects, garden tools and other media. Bacteria are capable of living over the dead organic matter. They enter the plant through stomata, nectaries and wounds. Seeds affected by bacteria look normal.

Angular leaf spot of cucumber, bacterial wilt and bacterial canker of tomato, blight of pear, carnation wilt, crown gall in apple, bacterial canker of stone fruits (Fig. 28), bacterial gummosis, etc. are common bacterial diseases.

Many small dark spots appear on leaves and the spotted portion drops after drying and the leaf shows a hole. These symptoms are common in apricot, plum, peach, etc.

Bacterial diseases are more difficult to control than fungal diseases. To control these diseases, plant good varieties, use good stock, destroy the infected parts, follow plant rotation, adopt clean cultivation and spray of copper fungicide or Bordeaux mixture.

Viral Diseases

Viruses are small plant organisms, which are so small that they are difficult to see under a microscope. They are transmitted through insects. Virus multiplies within the cells of the suitable host. Once the plant is infected, plants propagated from it are usually infected. Infected plants usually grow slow; their leaves may curl or twist and develop mosaic pattern or mottling. Symptoms may vary from species to species but in general, the growth is slow and leaves show symptoms of mosaic pattern.

Common diseases are yellows in peach and aster, Panama wilt, greening in citrus, mosaic of tomato, apple mosaic, etc.

Control of the disease is possible with the use of disease-free material, use of tools under sanitary conditions, control of insects that spread virus, and removal and burning the infected plants. Growing of plants raised through tissue culture technique is the sure way of eliminating the disease since virus-free plant material is produced through this technique. Common fungicides can overcome these diseases to a larger extent.

Insect-pests

Number of insects of various kinds and habits have been reported to damage the nursery plants. They may cut, chew or eat away the portions of the leaves and tender shoots. They pass through four stages of their life, i.e., egg, larva, adult and pupa. Egg and pupa do not cause any direct damage but larva and adult damage the tissues since they suck the sap from the plant or cut the top of the plant. Their attack may not be visible at the first instance but when some part has been affected, plant shows slow growth and finally dries up.

Aphids, caterpillars, beetles, borers, cut-worms, bugs and scales have been found to attack the young plants. They show varied symptoms. The insects do have specific colour and shape. They can be identified easily by observing them closely.

Aphids affect pear, apple, vegetables, ornamentals and shade trees where they suck the sap from the tissues causing foliage to distort and drop.

Caterpillars chew the leaves, they eat away the margins of leaves of many nursery plants while different kinds of beetles defoliate the young plants and thus, kill them. Cutworms chew or cut the stem near the ground level. Borers make holes either in the main stem or in the roots. Bugs suck plant juices causing distortion of leaves. Scale insects also suck the sap that render them to become yellow, leaves are dropped and some sticky exudate may deposit on the foliage of the infested plant.

Common insect-pests found with the nursery plants are Woolly Apple Aphid, Sanjose Scale in apple; borers, defoliating beetles and thrips in apple and some stone fruits; Peach Leaf Curl affects peach and apricot; Weevil in nut crops; Scale and psylla in olive; Leaf Minor in Citrus; White Grubs and hairy caterpillars in strawberry; beetles in grape and cucurbits; cutworms in tomato and other Solanaceous plants; beetles, jassids, cutworms in ornamental plants.

Control of insects-pests is a problem. Various methods have been suggested. Agronomic or cultural practices include the destruction of eggs and pupa of the insects by ploughing or digging the soil so that the eggs and pupa underneath the soil may come to the top of the soil where they may be picked up or destroyed by birds. Exposing them to light and sun may also kill them. It is advisable to expose the soil for 2-3 days at the time of preparation of the beds or making soil mixture. The sun disinfects the soil and it may inactivate insects along with other pathogens. Infested portions should be removed, taking care that eggs or larvae are also taken out, and then destroyed.

Different chemicals have been recommended to avoid the attack of insects and to kill the insects found on the plants. The right type of insecticide to be used will depend upon the feeding habit of the insect and the time of spray of the chemical. Liquids, powders and granules of the chemicals known as insecticides are used. Metasystox, Metacid, Rogor, Monocrotophos, BHC, Aldrin, Gamaxene, Neuvon, Malathion, Parathion, Accothion, Endosulfan, Endocel, Thimet-IO G, Carbofuran, Ruban, Durmet, Chlorphyriphos, etc., may be used as per recommendation of the authorities. Spray should be done in the early hours or late hours of the day so that the effect is more. It should not be done on a rainy or a foggy day and should cover the whole plant. Repeated sprays may be made, if necessary. Chemical should not come in direct contact with the gardener and they may be stored in a dry but cool place. Chemicals that have become inactive or are of the expired date should not be used. Instructions given on the package should be strictly followed.

Nematodes

These are thread-like worms, which are microscopic and unsegmented. They suck the sap of the plant by means of a hollow tube called stylet. These are usually present in the root zone of the plants where they form knots on the roots that inhibit the movement of solutes, causing reduced growth, wilting and lack of vigour. Nematodes attack variety of crops including most of the vegetables and ornamental crops.

Control of their spread is possible in the soil by keeping the soil free from nematodes by sterilizing it with Formalene or the use of Thimet-IO G or Carbofuran granules in the soil. These chemicals on coming in contact with the moisture in the soil, release their active ingredients, which kill the nematodes. It is advisable to mix them 2 cm deep in the soil to have best effect.

Termite or White Ant

These are ants, which attack the lower portion of the plants. They thrive on the roots of the plants, thus, checking their growth and finally forcing them to dry and die. It is common in dry and valley areas. It is recommended that 20-25 kg of Aldrin 5% or BHC 10% per hectare may be mixed with the soil before planting of seed or making final preparation of the soil.

13

Uprooting of Plants

Nursery is the place for raising plants of different kinds, which are to be transplanted elsewhere in the field where they can grow to their maximum capacity so they have to be uprooted or taken out of their natural growing places for providing them congenial conditions for their development and growth since after transplanting they need less care and attention.

Plants which are raised by their seeds or other means of propagation in the soil are uprooted, i.e. they are dug from the soil while the plants raised in polybags are not uprooted but are transplanted after rupturing the sides of the polybag. Therefore, uprooting of the young or old seedlings is common in nurseries where the seeds or other parts are sown in the soil.

Young plants capable of transplanting are dug from the soil. They need care right from uprooting to their transplanting through transportation. Active roots are very essential for the plants since these absorb and adsorb water and other mineral matter from the soil, which is used by their tops, leaves and other parts of the plant. Roots provide physical anchorage and physiological support to the plants. Once they get damaged, they may not be able to get themselves repaired. It is only in some cases, where the adventitious root system may develop to take the place of primary root system but for initial establishment, original root system is a must and it should be the aim and primary objective to protect them while uprooting the plants.

Preparing the Seedbed before Uprooting

Generally, roots are tender so they need to be cared properly. A day prior to uprooting of plants, light irrigation may be given by any means, taking care that the soil of seedbed or nursery bed is soft and moist to ease the uprooting of seedlings without damaging their roots. The soil around the roots should neither be too wet nor too dry; wet soil does not allow the soil to stick well with the roots and it is difficult to work in such soils, while uprooting or pulling the plants their roots are damaged and broken which makes the plants unable to establish on transplanting. On the other hand, in dry soils, roots are damaged when being uprooted from dry soil.

There should be sufficient moisture in the soil to ease uprooting, i.e. roots may come out with a slight pull. But when earth-balls have to be kept along with roots, slightly thicker soil mix should be there. So farmer has to decide himself about the requirement of moisture in the soil at the time of their uprooting.

If there are weeds and other unwanted plants in the seedbeds or nursery beds, they may be uprooted and destroyed before the uprooting of the young seedlings. Generally, weeding is done at least a week prior to the uprooting of plants.

When to Uproot

Vegetable, ornamental and other annual plants are uprooted when they have attained the height of about 8-10 cm and have 3-4 leaves, which are quite active. At this time, their roots are almost 5-8 cm deep in the soil and their age is about 3-4 weeks. Such plants are able to establish themselves when transplanted elsewhere.

In case of fruit trees, particularly the temperate fruit trees like apple, pear, cherry, almond, plum, walnut, etc. the seedlings or the rootstocks are first uprooted when they are 6 to 8 cm tall. They are transplanted in the field where they are allowed to grow for a season so that their main stems are of pencil thickness and are of 45 to 60 cm height. They are fit for top-working for their improvement or fixation of a suitable scion. When scions have established, these plants are again uprooted. Thus, their uprooting is generally twice.

Sometimes, the uprooting has to be done for the sake of thinning the plants in the nursery beds. They are uprooted from one place and then planted at another place, which does not require a gap of time, and this process is known as gap filling.

Vegetatively propagated plants like the grown-up budded or grafted plants are uprooted when they are fully independent. They may be 1 to 1½ year old; their height may be 60 cm to 1 m or more depending upon the type of soil and the seedling. Root system of such plants is also fully developed and can be 60 cm deep or so. In case of evergreen plants, their height is about 60 cm while the root spread is about 20-30 cm deep. Same is the case for forest trees and other avenue trees. Such plants have the ability to establish themselves even if their roots are slightly damaged since they can have adventitious roots.

Season of Uprooting

The season of uprooting depends upon the season of planting. In general, the plants are uprooted in two seasons: (a) monsoon-rainy season, and (b) winter season.

Normally in plains, the major planting is done during the monsoon season, i.e. on the onset of rains. Evergreen fruit and forest trees are uprooted just at the onset of rains while the temperate fruit and forest trees are uprooted on the start of winter season. In both the cases, plants can get themselves established in the coming period under natural conditions.

If irrigational facilities are available, these plants can be uprooted and transplanted any time during the year but they need great care and attention during whole of the process from uprooting to re-establishment.

Annuals and other plants completing their life cycle in a season are uprooted according to their season of planting. This includes the vegetable, herbs and ornamental plants.

In-situ plantations do not need uprooting. Plants from polybag are also not uprooted.

How to Uproot

Uprooting is the process of pulling out the plant along with the roots out of the soil or growing medium without damaging the plant.

One can adopt any method suited to his convenience but should assure himself about the well-being of the plant.

Annuals like vegetable, herbs, paddy, ornamental and medicinal plants that are of 6 to 10 cm height are uprooted from the wet soil by a spade and then collected and washed in water before packing or transporting.

Young plants are uprooted with the help of a spade (Fig. 29). The

Fig. 29. Uprooting citrus plant with earth-ball.

plants along with the soil are dug to a depth of 20 to 30 cm or more and then the plants are picked up. If earth-ball is needed, then the roots are taken out along with the earth-ball of the soil, which was with that plant earlier. Earth-ball should not break or crack at all.

Small number of plants can be uprooted by manual labour, i.e. by pulling out the plants from the soil with fingers. Though plants can be uprooted and planted mechanically but under our conditions, it seems impossible or difficult at this stage.

Care during Uprooting

Uprooting of young or old plants seems to be a mechanical process. All the physiological processes being carried out in a plant condition the uprooting, so great care has to be taken during their uprooting. Slight carelessness can cause the death of the plant and economic loss to the grower. Following precautions must be observed while uprooting the plants.

1. Be sure that the plants have attained the right type of growth and are able to establish themselves after transplanting.
2. Plants should be able to tolerate the shock of their uprooting and then some damage during their transportation by any means.
3. Only the desired plants should be uprooted, others, which are small or under-developed, may be left in the bed to let them develop fully so that they are independent in the future.
4. Diseased and insect-infested plants should be removed and destroyed and should not be used for transplanting.
5. Sufficient amount of moisture should be there in the soil to ease the pull out of plants. Less watering is needed for the plants, which are to be removed with their earth-balls.
6. It is better to uproot the plants in the evening during summers as they get lower temperature during the night, which is good for their rest.
7. Tools to be used for uprooting should be sharp-edged which saves the labour. More work can be done in less time.

Care after Uprooting

Uprooted plants may be inspected for the attack of diseases, insects and pests. The affected and other unwanted plants may be removed. Plants of the same height and vigour should be grouped together in a single bundle of each variety.

Immediately after uprooting, their roots may be washed in water, if they are to be planted soon, or the soil may be kept intact which can be moistened as and when necessary. In all the cases, roots should be sound and well developed.

Plants may be kept under shade to provide them some respite to bear the shock of their removal from the soil. Their roots may be kept moist so that they do not dry up and break in the coming period, i.e. they remain healthy till transplanting.

Avoid keeping the plants in a store or a room, which is not properly ventilated. Storage period under normal conditions should be minimum. Plants may be packed as the need may be. Stacking of plants should be avoided.

Storage of Nursery Plants

Large nurseries may store the plants for some time to tide over adverse climatic and other conditions. Generally, plants at their proper stage of growth and development are uprooted from the nursery beds at the right time and are packed. They may be stored to arrest their further growth. Main aim of storage is to control rather to reduce the rate of respiration and transpiration of water from the plants so that they have minimum growth, and stay good in store and have longer life.

During storage, the temperature should be around 0°C to 3°C with relative humidity ranging in between 85 to 90 per cent with good ventilation for the exchange of gases given out by the plants and a good environment, i.e. hygienic, without any fungus or insect. At this temperature and other conditions, fungal and insect activities are at the lowest, i.e. there is no danger of fungal infection and insects.

A storage house may have three chambers or rooms:

1. *Working place* where plants can be prepared for placement in a store. The plants are pre-cooled before keeping them in the store while this place also serves for the warming up or bringing the cooled plants to room temperature before being sent out.

2. *Packing room* is the place where plants are packed for keeping in the store. Grading is also done here.
3. *Storage room* is used for the actual storage of plant material. It may have shelves, benches or some other infrastructure to accommodate maximum number of plants.

In fact, it is the storage room where plants and other materials are stored, thus, it must be fully fit for keeping the materials safe and sound.

Packing of the Nursery Plants

After uprooting the nursery plants whether seedlings or vegetatively propagated plants, they are immediately taken for transplanting. This is possible when the site of planting is very near and the number of plants to be transplanted is limited but under ordinary conditions, the site for transplanting of plants is far away from the nursery site and the number of plants to be planted is high. Thus, the plants have to be prepared for packing for being transported or moved to the site of their planting.

Preparing the Plants

Immediately after uprooting the plants from the nursery beds, young plants with bare roots or earth-balls are placed in a cool and shady place so that they lose the field heat. They can be kept here for few hours but they should not lose the moisture. If needed, simple watering through sprinkler may be provided to keep the earth moist and the plants under humid condition. This is most important during summer months since the rate of transpiration and evaporation of water from the plant and soil, respectively, is higher as compared to winter months.

Diseased, insect-infested, dried leaves and other parts of the plants may be removed either with hand or by a secateur without injuring the other healthy portions of the plant. Roots of the plants may be dip in fungicide solution to protect them from attack of diseases in the near future. Tops of the plants may also be sprayed with insecticides to ward-off attack of insects.

Plants of different heights may be placed under different heaps or stacks. No two varieties or species should be mixed together. It is very important to separate them now, as at a later stage it is impossible to differentiate the plants under normal conditions.

Packing the Plants

Packing is the method or way in which the young plants are tied or kept together till they are transplanted. They have to be packed in such a way that they do not lose their physiological activities like, turgidity and are able to establish themselves on the new site. Major aim of packing is to keep the plants safe and intact during transportation. In other words, good packing ensures their success on transplanting. Thus, packing has to be done in a simple but sound manner. In general, the nursery plants/seedlings are packed in the following containers:

1. Wooden baskets of stretchable stems
2. Wooden boxes
3. Plastic trays
4. Polybags
5. Pots
6. Other materials

1. Baskets

Baskets used for carriage of manure, seed and other materials may be used. These are with a flat base but with a circular rim and about 25-30 cm height. Diameter of the basket at the top varies between 30 to 50 cm. Plants are kept straight in them. These baskets can be carried to long distance when packaged and can be moved by manual labour to small distances. Plants are not damaged.

Wooden baskets can be re-used and are usually available at the farms. These are light in weight and are easily available, cheap and are made from the locally available material.

2. Wooden boxes

Young plants to be transported with earth-balls can be placed in wooden boxes of convenient size, which can be carried easily by a labourer as they are to be moved from one place to another. These boxes can tolerate long transport and jerks during transport. If suitable moisture content can be maintained, these plants can be kept in these containers for a period of 7-10 days.

3. Plastic trays

Instead of wooden boxes, plastic trays can be employed for this purpose. Trays of different sizes are available. Bare-rooted plants need a small-sized tray while the plants with earth-balls have to be packed in bigger trays whose base should be strong enough to hold the weight. Micro cuttings, plant plugs and seedlings are transported through these trays. The plantlets are allowed to grow there and then taken to the field. Similarly, in the tissue culture process, micro cuttings are planted in these trays but when they grow in size, can be shifted elsewhere.

It is a safe way of transport for long as well as short distances. Due care has to be taken for maintenance of moisture and provision of desired quantity of sunlight. These trays are strong enough to tolerate the vagaries of nature and can be reused if handled properly.

4. Polybags

Seedlings of most of the forest plants are raised in polybags of different sizes, which can be transported by placing them in wooden

Fig. 30. Watering polybags with a watering can.

on plastic trays. Great care should be taken to see that the soil or the soil-mix of the polybags is not disturbed during packing and transport. Sufficient amount of moisture may be maintained during their transport (Fig. 30).

Lower portion of the plants are wrapped in polythene bags. Few plants can be tied in a single bundle, say about 10 and then placed in the bag. The upper portions of the plants are usually kept open so that they continue their physiological activities as usual. Plants can be transported to long distances.

5. Pots

Earthen or plastic pots are also used for the transport of seedling and plants. Some of the potted plants are transported from nursery to other sites where they may or may not be transplanted. These pots should be strong enough to hold the plants in good condition during their transport and afterwards. Moisture maintenance is easy but being bulky 2-4 plants can be placed in a single tray for transporting.

In other cases where the seedlings are grown in such pots, they are moved as such to the new site where they are uprooted and planted almost simultaneously. Moisture can be maintained easily. Pots are reusable. Plastic pots can tolerate better transport hazards than earthen pots.

6. Other materials

In some parts of the country, particularly the central and southern parts, banana leaves are used for packing the plants with their earth-balls. This is useful for local transportation. Since banana leaves may not be available at all the times and places and they are liable to crack if mishandled, this package cannot be transported by rail, road or air, thus, it is limited or rather restricted to local use.

Plants with bare roots or with earth-balls may be tied in gunny bags or polythene sheets. This method is used for transportation of temperate seedlings since these are transported with bare roots and climate is cool which does not allow much evaporation of water. Plants being without leaves do not transpire much. They can be kept for few days without any loss. Watering to the extent of wetting the gunny bag is sufficient to provide enough moisture to the roots. Generally plants are tied in a bundle and then their lower ends, i.e. the root portion is wrapped or covered with the gunny bag, which is tied around the pack. Moss can be used with advantage for transportation of budsticks, young plants and other tender material for short distances. Moss can retain the moisture for a fairly long period but it has to be moistened during transport.

Whatever may be the material used for packing, plants have to be protected from adverse climatic conditions, vagaries of transport, excess of sunshine, darkness, etc. Packing should be strong enough to hold the plant material intact. Choice of the material to be used should be in accordance to the distance of travel, means of transport, weather conditions and nature of the plant material.

Labelling

After packing or during packing plants must be labelled in a comprehensive way, i.e. name of the species or variety must be indicated by attaching a semi-permanent label so that it remains intact during transport. In case the material for labeling used is ink, it should be indelible and handwriting should be easily legible. The package must be labelled, in case it is being sent by air, surface or rail. Name with address of the sender and the receiver must be indicated. Mark of indication of the nursery may also be made.

Precautions during packing

Since the plants are to be transported or dispatched to various places involving different types of climates and environmental conditions, it is important that plants should remain in normal conditions as far as possible during their transport or movement. Some of the precautions given below may be observed:

1. Healthy plant material, which is free from diseases, insect infestation and other pathogens, should be packed. If necessary, a dip of the root zone of these plants in a fungicide solution may be made before packing. Similarly, insecticide may be sprayed on the tops of the plants to safeguard them against insects. With these treatments, they are able to withstand the attack of some pathogens during transport and then after transplanting.
2. Under-sized plants should not be uprooted and packed for sale.

They may not establish when planted. Such plants can bring discredit to the nursery grower.

3. Plants of a single variety and single size should be packed in a single bundle. No two varieties are to be mixed.

4. Plants when packed along with their earth-balls should be packed individually. Care should be taken that the roots are enclosed in the earth-balls and the earth-ball is fully wrapped in the banana leaves, gunny bags or moss but should not be exposed to open conditions. If needed, a rope may be tied around the root zone.

5. Base of the earth-ball should be flat or round while the upper portion near the stem may be slanting towards the root zone. This helps in better conservation of soil moisture and packing.

6. In case of temperate plants where roots are usually naked, small bundles may be tied together and then gunny bags, polythene sheet or some other material may wrap their roots and half of the main stems. A rope or raffia may be tied around the root zone to keep the plants and bundle in shape. Another band may be applied near the top, about 3-4 cm downwards so that the tops are also together.

7. Plants in pots or other containers like plastic trays or polybags may be placed direct in the needed container. Grass or other material may fill up empty places like the corners. This helps in avoiding the jerks during transport.

8. Unnecessary exposure to sunlight or darkness and to winds should be avoided. All plants need sufficient amount of sunlight to continue their living activities. In the absence of light, they become etiolated, lanky and weak. Exposure to wind, cold or heat causes abnormal conditions of physiological activities, which may arrest the growth of plants.

9. To avoid the cracking of earth-balls and to maintain the moisture regime near the root zone, moss, gunny bag or some other moisture-retaining material is wrapped around which may be checked regularly during the movement of plants.

10. Avoid the use of big and bulky containers since they become heavy and difficult to handle. They may crack or break open during rough handling.

11. Tying of the rope should neither be too loose nor too tight as the loose one slips down while the tight one causes girdling on

the stem and cracking of earth-balls and in some cases prolonged tying causes the arrest of the development of roots.

12. Every care should be exercised to see that the roots of the young plants are not damaged during packing. Roots once damaged cannot resume their activities.

13. Labels should be of quasi-permanent nature as they are liable to face many adverse conditions during transport. The ink should be fast and deep. Writings should also be legible. Complete particulars must be provided.

14. Due provision for all sorts of expected damage by rough handling of the labour should be made which is possible when the packing is secure, proper and by an efficient packer.

15. When plants are packed with bare roots, it is advisable to pack them with moss having some moisture and again wrap these plants in polythene or waterproof cover. They may be put in a cardboard or plywood box, if shipped or air-freighted.

16. Keep the plants straight in the box or the container during all the processes.

14

Equipments and Accessories Required

Following materials including implements, hand tools and other accessories are necessary for an average nursery. Number or quantity needed of each material depends upon the size of the nursery and the number of plants being raised. For successful and economic nursery production, these things should be arranged well in advance.

1. Suitable place, sand, clay, pebbles, leaf mould.
2. Manures and fertilizers—Farm Yard Manure, CAN, Urea, Super Phosphate, Muriate of Potash, Lime, Copper Sulphate.
3. Fungicides and insecticides as per recommendation.
4. Different types of herbicides.
5. Growth promoters like Agromin, Multiplex, Agrigro, Hortigro, Rhizone, Rootone, Seradix, etc.
6. Seeds and propagation material.
7. Mother trees, if possible.
8. Polybags of different sizes and gauges.
9. Pots—earthen, plastic, wooden, clay or ceramic.
10. Seed trays, plant trays.
11. Wooden crates, moulded plastic trays.
12. Hand tools like spade, pick-axe, shovel, *khilna, khurpa,* sickle, grafting knife, budding knife, crowbar, hammer, secateur, mallet, *tasla*, hand hoe, hand rake, axe, saw, sieves.
13. Implements—plough, hoe, plank, harrow, stapler, spraying machine, sprayer, duster, hand sprayer.

Fig. 31. Equipments needed for plant propagation in a nursery and field.

14. Irrigational facilities—hose pipes, hand sprayer, lift pump, sprinkler.
15. Place for storage of seeds, chemicals, hand tools, implements, etc.
16. Arrangement for protection against wind, frost and hails.
17. Packing material—basket, gunny bags, straps, rope, labels, plastic sheet, polythene sheet, wooden box, paper-board cartons.
18. Technical know-how.
19. Money.
20. Labour.
21. Zeal.
22. Miscellaneous items like moss, dry grass, pegs, nails, bricks.

Part Two

Specific Crops

15

Fruit Trees

Most of the fruits are tree-borne, which need to be transplanted after being raised in the nursery. They are multiplied either by their own seeds or by the rootstock. Stem cuttings are also used for multiplication of trees/seedlings. Improved cultivar or the scion is budded or grafted over the stock when it is one-year old with a single stem of thickness of about 1 cm. Plants with tops of the improved or desired cultivar should be raised for economical quality fruit production. Detailed information about the nursery production of various fruits follows:

Sapota (*Achras zapota*)

Trees are tall, evergreen and may attain 12 m height with lush green foliage. The branches are initially upright and may droop later. Leaves are green, glossy and lanceolate resembling mango leaves. Flowers are solitary and axillary but sometimes may be clustered. Fruits are round to egg-shaped, 4-6 cm long and 3-5 cm across, brown coloured with rough skin. Pulp is sweet and light brown coloured. Seeds are dark brown to black, oblong but pointed on both ends and 2-3 seeds are present per fruit. Bearing starts 5 to 7 years after transplanting to the field.

Seeds are collected from tree ripe fruits. They can be picked easily from fruits and then washed in water and dried under shade.

Seeds are sown 2 to 3 cm deep in well-prepared seedbeds or in polybags. They germinate in about 6 to 8 weeks. Young seedlings when 25 to 40 cm tall or 6 months old are grafted onto known scions and allowed to grow for six months. They are transplanted along with their earth-balls to the well-prepared pits during rainy season.

Important cultivars are Kali Pattri, Chhatri, Dhola Diwani, Baramasi, Pala, Iyengar, Calcutta Special and Guthi.

Kiwi Fruit (*Actinidia deliciosa* Chev.)

It is a deciduous climber, perennial in nature and is best suited to mid-hills of the temperate region. The trunk is weak and twining and needs support so it is trained like the grape vines. Leaves are heart-shaped, 20 cm in diameter, alternate, simple, dentate with a long petiole. They are bright green on upper surface and slightly hairy on the dorsal side. Flowers are white, yellowish or pink in colour and appear in the spring season. Fruit is a berry, slightly hairy, earth coloured, egg-shaped, 6 × 4 × 3 cm, pulp is greenish-yellow, sweet and aromatic. A fruit may have thousands of seeds which are lined in the centre and embedded in the pulp, they are light brown and very small, often 2.2 mm.

Plants are multiplied by seeds and the stem cuttings. Seeds are collected from mature healthy fruits that are cut and kept in water for decaying the pulp. They are then washed in clean water and stored in airtight containers. Seeds are placed on well-prepared soil and covered by a thin layer of mixture of well-rotten farm yard manure and soil. Seeds are very small and hence do not need thick cover of soil. Seeds are sown in winter, and to keep moisture in the seedbed the bed is irrigated soon after sowing and later the irrigation may be applied as and when needed.

Softwood cuttings are planted soon after treating them with with 5000 ppm Indole Butyric Acid solution. They are best raised under mist.

Seedlings or the plants from the cuttings are grafted or budded onto suitable scions in early spring or late autumn and maintained in the nursery beds till they are 50 cm in height. One-year old trees are transplanted to well-prepared pits in the winter.

Abbott, Allison, Bruno, Hayward and Monty are recommended varieties.

Cashew Nut (*Anacardium occidentale*)

The trees are evergreen and grow in the coastal areas. They are susceptible to frost and are hardy towards drought. They can grow upto 1000 m amsl in subtropical conditions with sufficient moisture. Trees can grow upto a height of 12 m with a spread of 6-8 m. Canopy of the tree is round. Trunk is strong with branches spreading all over. Leaves are green, leathery, glabrous, 10-15 cm long and 5 to 10 cm wide with a thick petiole. Flowers are pale yellow in colour. Fruits are kidney-shaped, achene, 3 × 15 cm, greyish-brown with a hard cover (pericarp) embedded in extended pedicel and cashew apple is shiny, yellow to red in colour, pear-shaped with a soft but thick skin and juicy.

Seedlings are raised from seeds which are collected from tree ripe fruits. Seed is kidney-shaped with reddish-brown cover having 2 large white cotyledons and a small embryo. They germinate in 2 to 3 months, as their germination is both slow and poor. Seeds are sown *in situ* with a depth of 2 to 3 cm in rows and at a distance of 10 cm between the rows that are 25 to 30 cm apart. They can also be propagated by air layering, grafting or inarching. Vegetatively propa-

Fig. 32. Cashew nut (*Anacardium occidentale*).

gated plants are transplanted along with their earth-balls during the monsoon season.

Different states have recommended number of varieties.

Custard Apple (*Annona squamosa*)

Trees are deciduous in nature and attain a height of 6 to 8 m. Canopy is usually round to drooping. Best suited for subtropical areas where they are raised on rocky and shallow soil. Branching is strong but irregular. Leaves are green, lanceolate to oblong, leathery and acuminate at the apex. Flowers are greenish-yellow, borne on young branchlets, in clusters of 2, 3, or 4. Fruits are aggregate and berry. They are orange-shaped or heart-shaped, sweet and pleasantly flavoured. Seeds are dark brown, smooth, 20-70 in a single fruit, flat and 0.5-1.0 × 0.2 cm in size.

Seedlings are raised by seeds that are sown during November in polybags or in nursery beds in the beginning of monsoon. When they are 25 to 30 cm in height they are grafted or budded onto a good scion and later transplanted in the monsoon season.

Washington, Batanagar, Mammoth, Red Sitaphal, British Guinea, Local Selection, etc., are usually the preferred varieties.

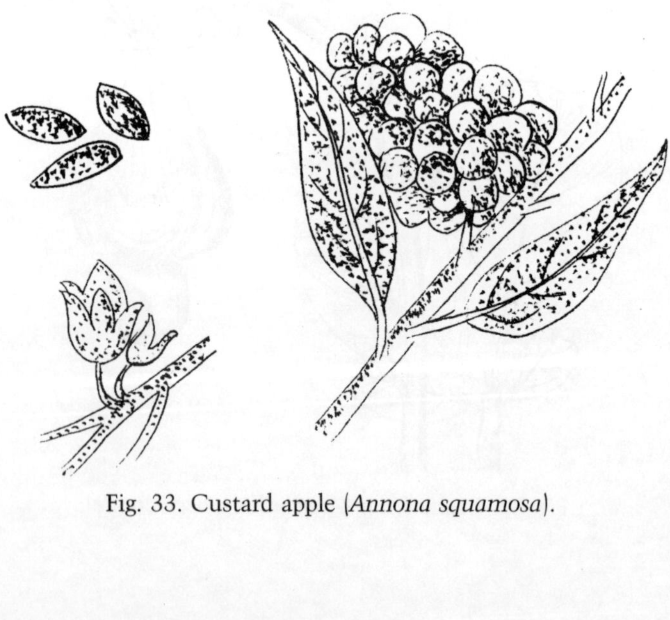

Fig. 33. Custard apple (*Annona squamosa*).

Papaya (*Carica papaya*)

It is an herbaceous tree with a short life span. Average size of tree is 3 to 4 m and may attain a height of 8 m with branches, but usually they are kept single stemmed. Dwarf trees are preferred as they are easily manageable and yield better fruits. Leaves are dark green growing in cluster like an umbrella and have long and hollow stalks. With the emergence of new leaves old leaves are shed and their scars remain on the trunk. Flowers are usually pale green and unisexual. For every ten female trees, one male tree is regarded sufficient to yield fruits. Fruits are yellow in colour with a thin skin, round to oval in shape. Pulp is yellow or reddish-yellow, sweet and is 2 to 3 cm in thickness below the outer skin. Seeds are round, brown to black coloured and placed in the central cavity of the fruit. The tree may start bearing after a year of transplantation.

Seeds can be gathered by cutting open the ripe fruit and then washing them in water. These are usually smaller than pea seed.

Seed sowing is done *in situ* or in polybags in March, monsoon or September. Usually 3 seeds are sown in one bag and the one giving vigorous seedling is retained. Transplanting is done during September to March.

Improved cultivars are Honeydew, Coorg, Ranchi, Washington, Pusa Delicious, Pusa Dwarf, Co-2, Pusa Giant, Local selections.

Citrus Fruits

These are small trees attaining a height of 3 to 15 m. Main cultivated species are lime (*Citrus aurantifolia*), lemon (*Citrus limon*), grape-fruit (*Citrus paradisi*), mandarin (*Citrus reticulata*), sweet orange (*Citrus sinensis*). Seeds are collected from ripe fruits of wild citrus trees, which vary from place to place. Generally, *Citrus jambhiri* rootstock is preferred. Rangpur Lime is also used. Some other rootstocks may be used.

Seeds are extracted from ripe fruits by cutting them and then picking out the seeds carefully and washing them in water. Seeds are cream coloured. Fresh seed should be sown. Seeds germinate in about 3 weeks. A single seed may give rise to many plants. Only one vigorous seedling is retained from one seed. For budding the seedlings, 25 to 30 cm in height are selected and budded onto suitable scions when the sap has started its movement in the stem. Transplanting is done with intact earth-balls around the roots.

Cultivated species are lemon, lime, mandarin, sweet orange that are of medium height and spread. Branches may be strong but spreading. Leaves are lush green in colour, glossy on the upper surface and hairy on the lower surface. Branches may have thorns. Fruits are usually round with green to orange skin, which is thick and oily. Seeds are placed in the pulp. Size and number of seeds per fruit are quite variable.

Lemon

Seedlings can be raised through stem cuttings, seeds or the rootstock. Budding and inarching is done in spring. Transplanting is done in monsoon.

Improved cultivars are Eureka, Lisbon, Baramasi, Nepali Oblong, Italian, Local selections, Pant Lemon.

Lime

Seedlings are raised from seeds. Pencil-thick seedlings are budded in early spring. Transplanting of one-year-old saplings is done in rainy season.

Improved cultivars are Coorg Lime, Vikram, Pramalini, Abhaypuri Lime, Local selection, and Meetha.

Mandarin

Seedlings are raised from the seeds of rootstocks best suited to the local areas. *C. jambhiri*, Rangpur Lime, Sour Orange, etc. can be used as rootstock. Budding is done during spring. Transplanting is done during rainy season.

Improved cultivars are Kinnow, Srinagar, Nurpur, Local, Coorg, Emperor (Kaula), Khasi, Butwel, and Satsuma.

Sweet Orange

Seedlings from the seeds of suitable rootstock plants are collected and sown within a week of collection. Budding is done during early spring. Shield or 'T' budding is most common. Planting is done in rainy season.

Improved cultivars are Mosambi, Red Blood, Jaffa, Pineapple, Hamlin, Valencia Late, and Sathgudi.

Coconut (*Cocos nucifera*)

It is a typical tropical crop, widely distributed in coastal regions of the tropics and subtropics where the trees can get at least 1500 mm well-distributed rainfall per annum and temperature between 26° and 32°C. Trees are tall upto 25 m, single stemmed, bearing green palm-like needles (leaves) which look like an umbrella. Fruits are borne in clusters below the leaf canopy. Fruits are nuts, oblong, 30 × 20 cm with an impermeable cover followed by a fibrous layer of 5-10 cm, and nut-like structure that is usually round having oily endosperm. The cover is green when fresh but turns brown on maturity. With time, the liquid of the nut dries up and an edible layer of endosperm develops.

Nuts containing liquid are collected from healthy, mature, high-yielding and regular bearing trees of 20-25 years age, from the winter crop. Well-prepared raised seedbed is made by digging at least 45 cm deep and then mixing ample well-rotten farm yard manure. These seedbeds are prepared close to the proposed site of plantations. Nuts are buried 8-10 cm deep in the soil by placing the nuts horizontally at a distance of 30 cm in rows that are 45 cm to 50 cm apart.

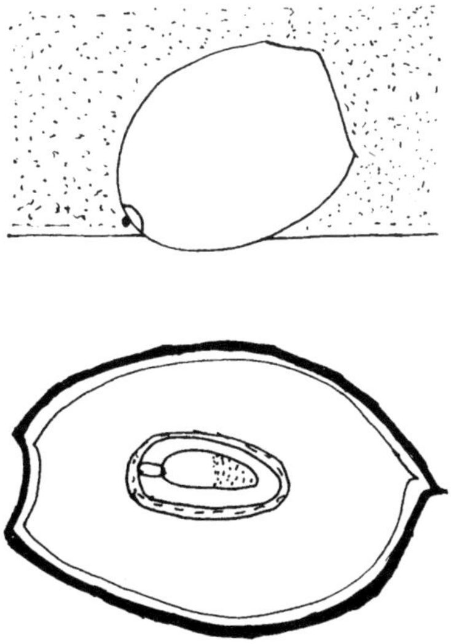

Fig. 34. Coconut (*Cocos nucifera*), nut and planting.

Germination starts after 2 months and is complete in about 3-4 months, and in six months the nuts produce about 3 leaves with sufficient roots. Ungerminated nuts are rejected at this stage while others are allowed to grow for one year. 6 to 12 months old seedling plants are transplanted and watered daily for about a fortnight.

Improved cultivars are *Tall*—East Coast Tall, Laccadive Andaman, Java Giant. *Dwarf*—Gangabondum, Chennangi, Chowghat Dwarf Orange, Malayan Dwarf Orange.

Persimmon (*Diospyors kaki*)

It is a deciduous tree suited to temperate region where the tree may attain a height as much as 13 m with a spread of 7 to 8 m. Canopy is round and tree has strong upright branches. Leaves are simple, thick, large, leathery and glossy green on the upper surface and light green on the lower surface. The fruit is round to oblong, conical, few seeded, fleshy, juicy, and skin may be light orange to bright red in colour. Flesh is yellow to orange, soft and stingy when immature and turn sweet when mature.

Seeds need stratification before sowing in late winter or early spring but they can also be sown before stratification during winter but they start germination only in the spring. Seed germination is rather slow. Seedlings are budded or grafted when 30 to 50 cm in height and later transplanted in winter.

Indian Gooseberry (*Emblica officinalis*)

Trees are evergreen of medium height and spread. Best suited for valley areas and drier areas as they can tolerate drought to a great extent. Trunk is strong with profuse branching. The branches droop to provide the tree an umbrella-shaped canopy. Leaflets are small, 1-2 cm long and 0.3 cm wide, and typically olive green in colour. Fruits are smooth-skined, green, fleshy, hard and tight, 4-5 × 4-5 cm. Each fruit has a round, hard, brown and ridged seed. On maturity, the seeds are extracted by removing the pulp and keeping them in water for two days. They are washed in clean water, dried under sun and then stored in airtight containers.

Seeds may be soaked in 500 ppm Gibberellic Acid solution before

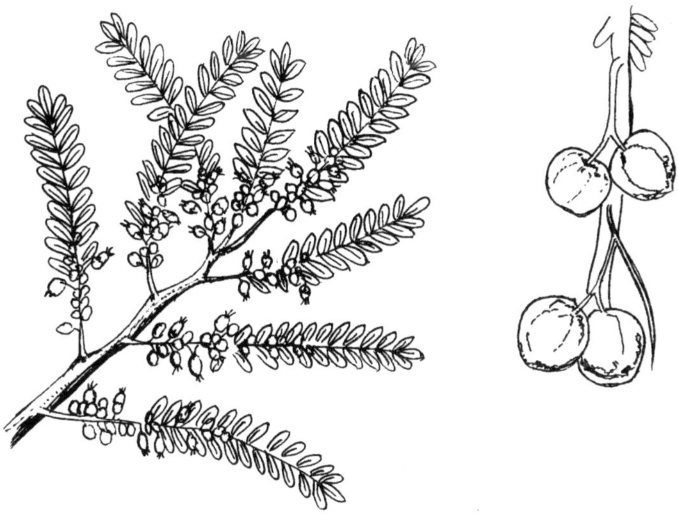

Fig. 35. Indian gooseberry (*Emblica officinalis*).

sowing to quicken the germination. Seedlings are raised either from rootstocks or seeds. Fresh seeds are sown 2 cm deep in well-prepared beds during monsoon.

Budded by Shield Bud method in June when seedlings are pencil-thick. Transplanting along with earth-balls is done in monsoon.

Improved cultivars are Banarasi, Chakaiya, White Streaked, Red-Tinged, Green-Tinged, Katha, Francis, Krishna, Kanchan.

Loquat (*Eriobotrya japonica*)

Trees are evergreen and found growing in the subtropical regions of the country. They are moderately resistant to drought and frost. Canopy of the tree is usually round; trees are 6-7 m high with spreading branches like umbrella. Leaves are 15 × 5 cm, green, leathery and slightly glossy on upper surface but having rust coloured tomentum on the lower surface. Flowers are white. Fruits conical to round, golden yellow in colour with a soft skin and may have two large brown seeds. Trees start bearing fruits 4 years after transplanting.

Seeds are extracted from tree ripe fruits by decaying them in water for 2-3 days and then washing with clean water and drying under shade.

Seeds are sown for raising seedlings. Air layering is also practiced. Budding or grafting of the seedlings is done during spring. Transplanting with earth-balls is done during monsoon season.

Improved cultivars are Golden Yellow, Tanaka, Fireball, Thames Pride, Matchless, California Advance, Pale Yellow.

Strawberry (*Fragaria ananassa*)

These are herbaceous plants that trail over the ground and send their roots from nodes into the soil. Leaves are green, large and soft with long stalks. Flowers are white in colour while fruits are sweet and scented, pink to reddish-pink and conical in shape. Fruit is an aggregate and 2-3 × 2 cm.

Seeds are many but do not germinate under normal conditions

Fig. 36. Strawberry (*Fragaria ananassa*).

so plants are easily propagated by vegetative means. They are propagated by runners before spring or autumn. Best planting time for hills is July-August while for plains it is September-October.

Improved cultivars are Teoga, Torrey, Cavelier, and Pusa Early Dwarf.

Walnut (*Juglans regia*)

Trees are deciduous in nature, which may grow to a height of 25 m, and trunk may be 1½ m in diameter. They are best under cool climate in mid-hills and higher hills where they can get chilling requirement for 2 to 3 months during winter. Trees start bearing after 5 years in case of vegetative propagated trees and 10 years for seedling grown trees. The bearing age of the tree may be more than 50 years under normal conditions and they may even bear upto 100 years of age. Canopy is round and branches are strong and well placed. Leaves are large, oblong to lanceolate, shiny green on upper surface. Flowers of brownish-green colour appear in clusters during spring season. Fruit is nut like a drupe with hard cover, 4 × 3 cm, and of brown colour having edible kernel of white to cream in colour.

Seeds are sown 3 cm deep in well-prepared beds in winter for raising stocks/seedlings. They take 30 days to germinate. Budding or grafting is done during July-August. Transplanting of 1 to 1½ year old trees is done during winter.

Important cultivars are Waterloo, Gobind, Franquette, Placentia, Eureka, Wilson, Thin Shelled.

Litchi (*Litchi chinensis*)

Trees are evergreen in nature and of moderate height (8-10 m) with more spreading and pendulous branching. They are best suited for subtropical areas where they can get enough humidity for their fruit development. Canopy is usually drooping and spreading about 7 to 10 m in diameter. Leaves are 12-18 cm × 3-5 cm, green and glossy. Flowers are white coloured. Fruits are round, borne in cluster, pericarp is woody and brown to reddish-brown in colour, and pulp is white and scented. Fruits are sweet to sub-acidic in taste. A white and scented juicy pulp followed by semi-hard skin covers single, brown, hard and bold seed.

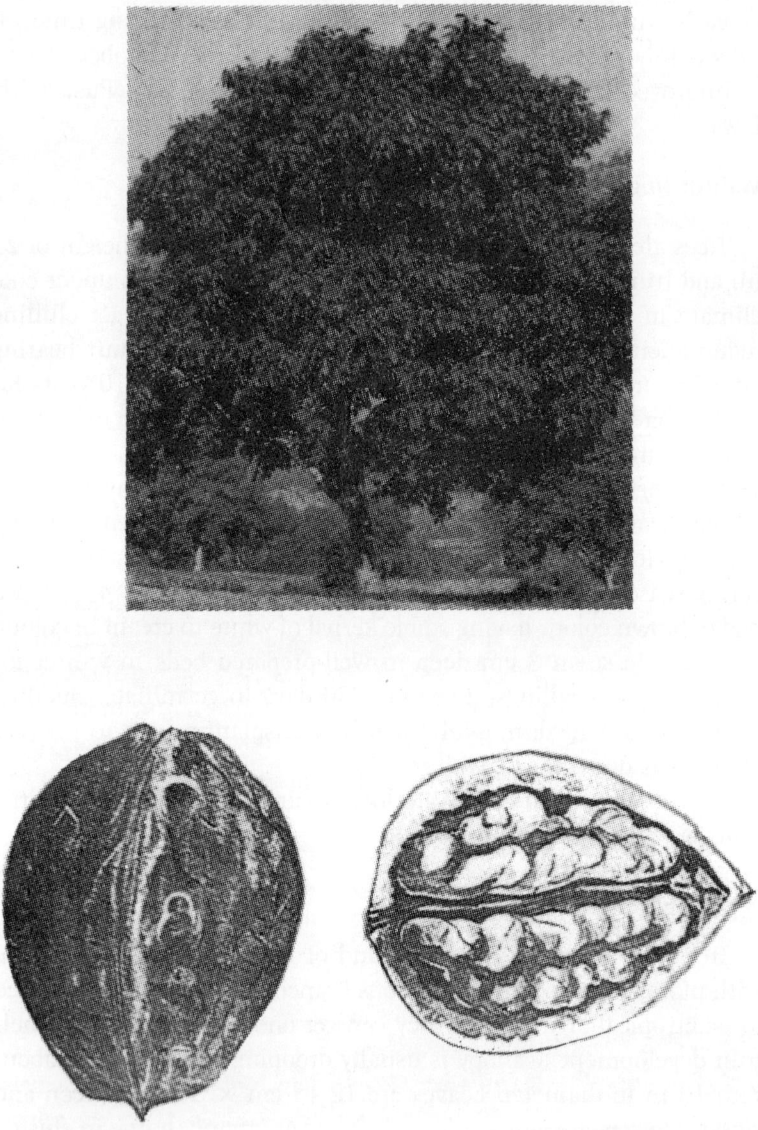

Fig. 37. Walnut (*Juglans regia*) tree and seed.

Fig. 38. Litchi (*Litchi chinensis*).

Seeds are collected from ripe fruits from which the pulp has been removed. Seeds have slow growth so vegetative propagation is commercially practiced. Air layering is done during monsoon. Generally the seedlings are raised under the litchi tree or the soil from the basin of litchi tree is spread in the nursery bed where the seeds are being planted for raising seedlings. One-year old seedlings are transplanted with earth-balls during monsoon.

Improved cultivars are Dehradun, Calcuttia, Muzzaffarabadi, Rose Scented, Seedless, Bedana, Derby, and Kaspa.

Apple (*Malus domestica*)

An important fruit crop of the temperate region is raised from lower hills to higher hills (above 1300 m amsl). Trees are deciduous in nature, round (8-10 m) with strong and upright branches. Leaves are 12-15 cm × 5-7 cm, leathery, green, toothed, glossy on upper surface while hairy on the lower surface. Flowers are borne in clusters of white with pink flush during spring. Fruits are pome, round to oblong in shape with different colours, usually green or yellow with a reddish blush on the skin but the flesh is off-white,

Fig. 39. Apple (*Malus domestica*).

sweet, juicy and sweet smelling. Seeds are placed in the core, 1 cm long and 0.3-0.5 cm wide, and 5-15 in number, brown, flat to swollen but pointed on one end.

Seeds are extracted by cutting the ripe fruit into pieces and then keeping it in water for 2-3 days to decay the pulp. Seeds are washed in clean water and dried under the sun for a day and then stored in airtight containers.

Seedlings or stocks may be raised from seeds of apple, crab apple or rootstocks. Bold and healthy seeds are selected for sowing. Seeds after stratification for 90 days are sown in the seedbeds. They germinate in 3 to 4 weeks. Unstratified seed will take long time to germinate. The seedlings when 5 to 10 cm in height are transplanted in nursery beds at a spacing of 25-30 × 25-30 cm for budding or grafting in spring season.

Rootstocks are also used for multiplication of plants as they yield trees of uniform size. There are rootstocks of known character as MM 108, M 26, M 9, etc. These rootstocks are resistant to Woolly Apple Aphid and the scions grafted over them yield fruits of uniform size and shape after 2 years of transplanting.

Budding or grafting is done either in late summer or early spring on pencil-thick single stemmed stocks. Transplanting of one-year old trees is done during winter.

Improved cultivars are Royal Delicious (Starking Delicious), Red Delicious, Rich-a-Red, Golden Delicious, Red Gold, Tydeman's Early Worcestor, and McIntosh. Yellow Newton, Ambri, Starkrimson Delicious, Red Spur, Well Spur, Oregon Spur, Red Chief, Tropical Beauty, Granny Smith, Lord Lambourne, Royal Gala, Scarlet Gala, Fuji, Benoni, Black-Ben-Davis, Ambred.

Mango (*Mangifera indica*)

Trees are evergreen in nature and of moderate height (10-20 m) and spread (6-8 m). They are best suited to valley areas and the areas adjoining the humid and fertile belt of Gangetic plains. Seedling trees may go as high as 20 m with a spread of 6-10 m but vegetative propagated trees are usually round (6-8 m). Branches are strong and mostly upright with lush green leaves that are large, often 20 × 5-7 cm, lanceolate, glossy on upper surface and slightly hairy on the dorsal side. Flowers are borne in panicles that are white to yellow-brown in colour and many in number. Fruit is drupe, green to golden yellow with reddish blush, juicy and with scented pulp. Fruit size may be 10-15 cm × 8-10 cm with or without fibre in the pulp. A single seed is present in each fruit. It may be flat or papery and the size ranges from 5-7 × 4-6 to 1.5-3 cm. Colour of the seed stone is white to off-white or whitish-yellow. Seed may be extracted by squeezing out the pulp and then washing in clean water.

Fresh seed (seed stone) is used for planting and the depth of

Fig. 40. Mango (*Mangifera indica*).

planting is usually 3 to 5 cm deep in the bed or the polybag. Seed-stones are generally sown *in situ* or in polybags. Three seed stones are planted in one pit. Seed germinates in 3 to 7 days and the germination is complete in a month's time. There can be two to three seedlings from a single seed but the vigorous one is retained and others are rejected. The seedlings when 5 to 10 cm in height are transplanted in nursery beds at a spacing of 25-30 × 25-30 cm for budding or grafting in spring season.

Budding or grafting is done either in early spring or during monsoon on pencil-thick single stemmed stocks. Transplanting of one-year old trees is done during monsoon.

Improved cultivars are Alphonso, Bombay Green, Chausa, Safaida, Langra, Dussehri, Swaran Rekha, Totapari, Banganpalli, Saraul, Ratual, Fajri, Kesar, Vanraj, Mallika, Ratna, Amarpalli, Kishenbhog, Rajapuri, Neelam, Bangalore, Piari, Jahangir and many others.

Banana (*Musa* spp.)

Plants are herbaceous in nature and are about 1½ to 3 m in height and dwarfs are 1½ m. They are best suited for all the areas in the country except the windy and the chilly areas. Not good for windy or frost pockets since their leaves shatter with wind and they are killed by the frost and as a result are not able to manufacture their food, so there may be no crop from the plants. Leaves are lush green, long, often 1 metre long and 15 cm wide with a well-marked mid-rib. They are mostly upright and their base is wrapped around the main stem and they form an umbrella over the trunk. Flowers are bisexual and the plants bear only once in their life. Fruits are known as fingers and the bunch of finger is known as hand. Fingers are borne once and hence the stock after bearing is removed.

Seeds are produced only under specific conditions and are valued for breeding purposes. Multiplied by suckers in monsoon season.

Improved cultivars are available for both dwarf and tall varieties. Basarai Dwarf, Harichhal, Robusta, Michel, Giant Governor, Rasthali, Amritsagar and Kothiar are few to name.

Fig. 41. Banana (*Musa* spp.).

Date Palm (*Phoenix dactylifera*)

An evergreen tree that grows best under specific warm conditions where the roots get high humidity and the top of the tree may get high temperature and full sunlight. The tree may go as high as 30 m with an umbrella-like canopy of green needle-like leaves. Leaves are simple, pinnate, 45 to 60 cm long, narrow, stiff, borne in pairs and upturned. Small flowers of yellow colour are borne in clusters of 6 to 20 in a spadix. Fruit is a berry with fleshy pericarp, which is sweet and edible, 1.5-2 × 3-5 cm, and cylindrical or oblong ellipsoid, yellow to brown in colour, flesh is semi-dry with a smooth, thin but slightly thick skin. Seed is cylindrical, about 1.5 cm long, hard, endospermic and has a groove and pointed on both ends.

Trees are multiplied both by seeds and suckers. Sucker propagation is best and easy. The trees raised through suckers yield fruits of uniform size and better quality. Suckers are grown in nursery bed for 12 to 18 months before being transplanted during the rainy season.

Barhee, Medjool, Thoory, Zahidi, Hillawi, Khadrawy are some of the common varieties.

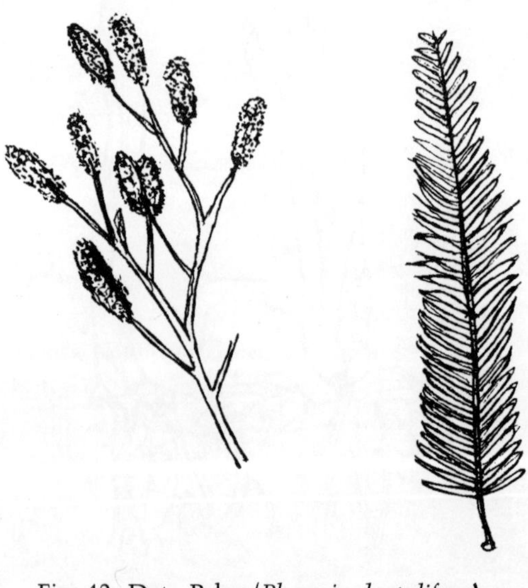

Fig. 42. Date Palm (*Phoenix dactylifera*).

Almond (*Prunus amygdalus*)

Trees are deciduous in nature and best suited for mid-hill areas of the lower Himalayas. They are of moderate height (8 m) and spread (4-6 m) with twisted branches. Leaves are lanceolate, olive green, 10 × 3 cm with thick petioles. Flowers are usually white. Fruits are nuts, yellowish-green in colour and drupe. Kernel is edible that has a thin brown covering. On maturity the kernel becomes seed that may be conical, bold and hard.

Seeds of bitter almond, apricot or peach are sown directly outdoor in well-prepared beds in early winter or after stratification for a month during spring. It is better to sow the seeds after stratification, as the germination of these seeds is uniform and early. Germination is complete in 3 to 4 weeks.

Seedlings of pencil thickness are budded or grafted in the coming spring or autumn season. One-year old seedlings are transplanted during winter.

Improved cultivars are Drake, IXL, Non-Pareil, Thin-Shelled, Merced, Ne-Plus Ultra, Peerless, Dhebar, Katha.

Fig. 43. Almond (*Prunus amygdalus*).

Apricot (*Prunus armeniaca*)

Moderately tall deciduous trees with strong but shabby branches. Leaves are thin, green, leathery, and ovate to round in shape. Flowers white or pink-white and appear in spring. Fruits are light yellow to golden yellow in colour, oblong, hairy or velvety, divided by a central groove. Seeds are round, brown, oblong and with a hard coat.

Seedlings are raised from wild apricot seeds. Seeds are collected from the tree ripe fruit and kept in water for 2 days to decay the pulp. The seeds are washed off the pulp and cleaned. They can be stored till the end of December. Seeds may be sown directly in the field during winter or stratified and then sown in early spring. Seeds start germinating during spring and complete their germination in

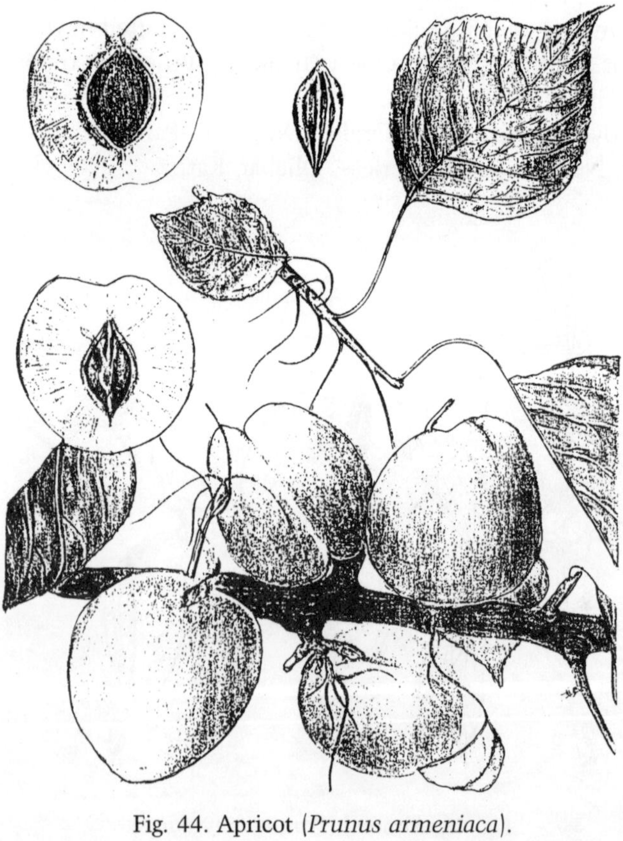

Fig. 44. Apricot (*Prunus armeniaca*).

3 weeks. Young seedlings are replanted in nursery beds at a spacing of 25 × 25 cm in lines. Seedlings when 30 to 45 cm tall are budded or grafted onto a suitable scion in spring or autumn to have a variety of desired characters. Transplanting is done during winter in well-prepared pits.

Improved cultivars are Kaisha, Royal, Safaida, Char Magaz, Shakarpara, Castle, Turkey, Quetta, Frogmore Early, Nugget, and Early Shipley.

Sweet Cherry (*Prunus avium*)

Trees are usually tall (6 to 8 m) like the mango trees but are smaller in size and have pyramid shape. They are deciduous in nature. Main trunk is straight that bears well-distributed upright branches. Leaves are 15 × 5 cm, green, glossy and double-toothed,

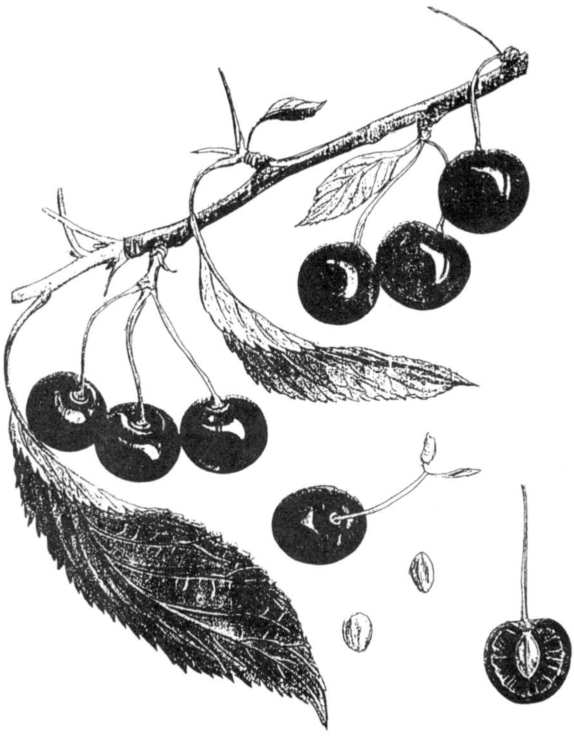

Fig. 45. Sweet cherry (*Prunus avium*).

lanceolate with hairy, lower surface. Flowers are white and scented. Fruits are round to heart-shaped, 1.5 × 1 cm, deep pink to deep red in colour with a thin glossy skin and are edible. The seed is a stone of light brown colour surrounded by a pulp layer of 1 cm thickness of light red to deep red colour.

Seeds are sown during spring after stratification. Rootstocks like Paja (*Prunus pudam*) or Colt F/12 can be used for raising seedlings. Seeds take 15 to 21 days to germinate. They are sown after winter in early spring. Stocks raised by rootstocks are preferred as they provide trees of uniform vigour.

Budding or grafting on one-year old stocks is done during early spring or late summer on pencil-thick stems. Transplanting of grafted seedlings is done during winter.

Improved cultivars are Black Heart, White Heart, Bing, Pobeda, Napoleon, Stella, Sue, Van, Lambert, Black Republican, Makhmali, Governor Wood, and Prolific.

Plum (*Prunus domestica*)

Fast growing, upright deciduous trees with elliptical leaves with serrated edges. Small white flowers are borne in clusters. Fruits are egg-shaped or globulous, yellow to crimson in colour with smooth skins. Pulp may be green, yellow or purple according to variety. Seed may be free or clinging. Seeds are round, ridged and brown in colour. These may be extracted by keeping the fruit in water for a week followed by washing in water.

Stocks of peach and plum are used. Seeds of peach, apricot and plum can be used. They are sown after stratification in winter. Seeds take about 30 days to germinate. Pencil-thick stocks usually 45 to 50 cm tall are grafted or budded in late summer or early spring. Transplanting is done during winter.

Improved cultivars are Santa Rosa, Formosa, Burbank, Methley, Satsuma, Wickson, Mariposa, Alubukhara, Titron, Amritsari, Beauty, Washington, Kala Alubukhara, Green Gage, Green, Damsen, and President.

Fig. 46. Plum (*Prunus domestica*).

Peach (*Prunus persica*)

Deciduous trees that grow upto a height of 6-8 m. Branching is shabby like guava or apricot. Leaves are glossy like apple but deep green in colour, lanceolate with toothed margins. Flowers pink in colour and small in size. Fruits are round to flat, drupes, having a dividing line on the skin. They are pale yellow to golden yellow coloured with red blush. Pulp is pale green to typically peach coloured. Seed is hard, single, brown, bold and is pointed on one side and ridged.

Seeds are used for raising seedlings. Seeds of apricot, plum and almond can also be used. They are sown either direct in early winter or after stratification in late winter in the field. Seeds germinate in spring in about 45 days after sowing. Budding and grafting is done during late autumn or early spring. One-year old plants are transplanted during winter.

Improved cultivars are J.H. Hale, July Elberta, Alexander, Flordasun, Sharbati, Alton, Kanto-5, Sun heaven, Shane-Punjab, Early White Giant, Shimizu Hakuto, and Flordared.

Fig. 47. Peach (*Prunus persica*).

Guava (*Psidium guajava*)

Trees are evergreen and may behave as deciduous under cold conditions. Trees are best suited to subtropical areas where they can tolerate drought to large extent but irrigation at the time of fruiting provides fruits of better size and shape. Trees are of moderate height

Fig. 48. Guava (*Psidium guajava*).

with irregular branching and sparse foliage of light green colour. Leaves are usually leathery, mildly scented, 12-15 × 5-7 cm with a long petiole of greenish-brown colour. Fruits are of greenish-yellow colour from outside but white to slightly cream coloured from inside. Sometimes the pulp is pinkish-red in colour. Pulp is sweet and hard when immature but becomes soft on ripening. Seeds are round, light brown in colour, small and embedded in flesh. Bearing starts after 3 to 5 years of transplanting.

Seeds are extracted by cutting the fruit into pieces and keeping in water for 2 to 3 days to get the pulp decay. By washing in clean water, the seeds are separated from the pulp and dried under shade.

Seeds are sown either after boiling in water for 8 minutes or soaking in water for 2 weeks. Seeds are usually sown 0.5 cm deep in well-prepared beds and later transplanted to another bed. Seedlings raised from seeds do not produce uniform seedlings so the plants are reproduced by vegetative propagation methods like budding or inarching. Transplanting of one-year old seedlings after grafting is done during monsoon.

Improved cultivars are Allahabadi Sufaida, Lucknow 49 (Sardar Guava), Nasik, Banarasi, Red Fleshed, Chittidar, and Dholka.

Pomegranate (*Punica granatum*)

Trees are generally evergreen but may behave as deciduous in temperate region due to severe cold in the area. Trees are not very tall but are mainly bushy with long and slender leaves of dark green colour. Flowers are very showy and have red calyx, which persist even with the fruit. Fruits are large, 6-10 × 6-10 cm, round, yellow to red in colour. Seeds are many with juicy pulp. The pulp of pink to red colour surrounds the seeds. Seeds or stem cuttings can be used for raising seedlings. Grafting and air layering can be done during early spring or late summer. Planting is done in rainy season but can also be done in June-July or in February-March.

Improved cultivars are Ganesh, Muscat Red, Kandhari, Bedana, Seedless, Dholka, Ruby, Papershell, and Jyoti.

Pear (*Pyrus communis*)

Trees are deciduous in nature and are best suited for temperate region but there are some varieties that can grow in plains but the quality of fruits produced is poor in the plains and these fruits are used for cooking and preserve making. Trees are usually 15 m high with a spread of 6 to 8 m. Leaves are green, ovate, toothed at margins and glossy. Flowers are white in colour. Fruits are round to typically pear-shaped, green to greenish-yellow in colour, pome, juicy with thin skin. Pulp is cream in colour and is grained. Seeds are placed in the core of the fruits, many in number (5-10), light brown in colour with pointed ends.

Seedlings may be raised from seeds, which have been stratified earlier as in case of apple. Seeds after stratification are sown in early spring and germination is complete in 4 to 5 weeks. Seeds, if sown during early winter do not germinate till the spring. Quince stock can be used for raising seedlings. Kainth (*Pyrus pashia* Linn.) is also a good stock. Top working of quince is also desirable. Grafting is done during late summer or early spring on stock of 1 cm diameter. Transplanting is done in winter.

Improved cultivars are Bartlett, Max Red Bartlett, Laxtons Superb, Flemish Beauty, Beurre Hardy, Favourite, Conference, Starking Delicious, Winter Nellis, Kieffer, China pear, Pathar Nakh, Clapp's Favourite, LeConte, and Babugosha.

Fig. 49. Pear (*Pyrus communis*).

Grape (*Vitis vinifera*)

Grapes can be raised from sea-coast to higher hills as the varieties suitable for all the regions are available but best quality fruits are available in dry areas with plenty of chill during winter. Fruits are borne on vines that are usually curled and weak and as such they need support at fruiting. Generally, they are trained on Kniffin or

Telephone system. Seeds can be collected from the berries but plants are multiplied by the stem cuttings.

Seedlings are raised by planting the stem cuttings collected during pruning in winter. Semi-hardwood cuttings can also be used. 30 to 40 cm tall seedlings are budded or grafted in late summer or early spring on pencil-thick stock. Transplanting in well-prepared pits is done after a year during winter in mid February or March or directly in the field in the end of December, i.e. prior to start of winter.

Improved cultivars are Thompson Seedless, Beauty Seedless, Anabe-Shahi, Delight, Perlette, Himrod, Black Prince, Pusa Delicious, Bangalore Blue, Kandhari, and Gulabi.

Jujube (*Zizyphus mauritiana*)

These are evergreen trees of 10-12 m height with strong branches having thorns here and there. Leaves are small, oval to oblong in shape, leathery and tomentose on the lower surface, green in colour. Fruits are greenish-yellow to brown in colour, round to oblong in shape and 2 to 4 cm long and 1 to 4 cm wide. Pulp of the fruit is sweet and 1 cm thick. Each fruit has one seed. Seed-coat is stony and non-endospermic. Usually on maturity the pulp dries up and the seeds are kept in water to wash off the pulp.

Seeds of the wild species of *Zizyphus* are used for raising the seedlings. They may be cracked or boiled in water to crack them to hasten the germination. Sowing is done in March. Seeds are sown 1 cm deep. Germination is complete in 3 to 8 weeks depending upon the nature of treatment. Seedlings may be budded or grafted to improve their nature. One-year old trees along with their earth-balls are transplanted during monsoon.

Improved cultivars are Umran, Gola, Sanaur, Banarasi, Prolific, Nagpur, Dhudhia, Mehrun, Nazuk, Seb, Jogia, Katha, Thornless, and Kaithali.

16

Forest and Avenue Trees

Initially all the trees earlier grew in the wild as the forest lands were uninhabited. On finding the utility of the trees, man domesticated them by bringing them closer to their habitats and thus many of the trees acquired some modifications due to adaptation and later became the parts of agro-forestry, social forestry and avenue or landscaping plans.

Most of the seeds of these trees are collected from the forests, roadsides or lawns and like places where they remain on the ground for a number of days under unfavourable conditions. Such seeds are likely to lose their viability very early and have low germination. To get seeds of good quality and high germination percentage, pods and other seed-bearing parts should be harvested or collected directly from the trees before they split open. Many a times these pods and seed-bearing parts are collected from the ground level but preference should be given to harvesting them from the trees. These pods and seed-bearing parts should be dried for 2-3 days in the sun by spreading them over a tarpaulin sheet or clean ground. The dried pods split open to release the seeds and seeds can be separated from the husk and other unwanted material by winnowing. Broken parts of the husk, and other unwanted material like the broken and immature seeds should be rejected. Store the clean seeds in airtight conditions for some period or use them for sowing as the case may be.

These seeds are sown either in the beginning of rainy season or the early winter. Seeds of evergreen trees are sown in the monsoon season while those of the deciduous trees are sown in the winter.

Use only the clean, disease-free and viable seeds. Seeds are usually sown in nursery beds. Parts for vegetative propagation are also planted in the beds. When the seedlings are 10 cm tall, they are transplanted to polybags or other beds where they are allowed to grow for 6 months or so. Size of the polybag will depend upon the duration of the plant to be retained in the bag. Bold seeds may be sown directly in the polybags. Still bigger seeds can be sown *in situ* in prepared pits. Generally, 2-3 seeds are sown per pit. They are taken good care of in the nursery by giving them all the necessary weeding, irrigation and other cultural and plant protection practices. Later on retain the vigorous and healthy plants.

The plants to be planted in the field or outdoor are uprooted when their main stem is 50-60 cm tall and they are pencil to thumb thick. For roadside planting, 1 m tall plants are preferred.

It is better to use the fresh seed after washing or keeping in water for 12 hours or so. In the following paragraphs the details of raising plants of some major forest and avenue trees are described.

Kikar (*Acacia arabica*)

These are evergreen trees that are moderately tall and may go as high as 15 m and are upright in nature. The canopy of the tree is umbrella-shaped. Trees are suitable for wasteland and marginal land

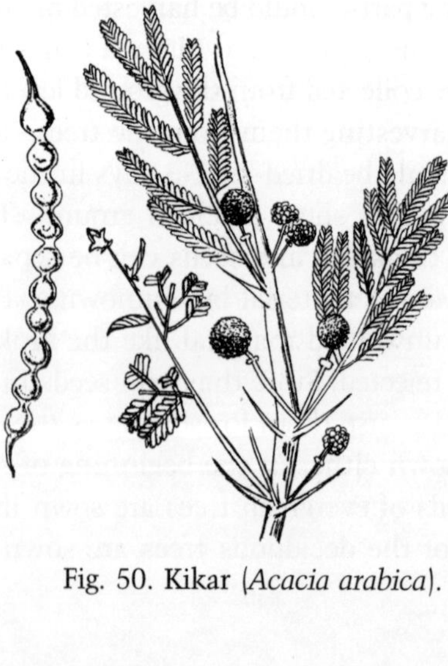

Fig. 50. Kikar (*Acacia arabica*).

development and for roadside plantation in the valley, foothills and plain areas of northwestern India, in dry to moist tropical areas. It yields fodder, fuel, timber and wood for furniture and domestic sue. Flowers are mostly yellow, borne in clusters. Pods are long, constricted and green when fresh but turn brown on maturity. Pods are used for medicinal purposes.

Seeds are borne in pods that are dried after beating them with sticks. Seeds are very small and are sown after soaking them in water for 24 hours. They are sown during spring and summer. Germination is complete in about a month. Planting is done during monsoon.

Khair (*Acacia catechu*)

It is a moderately-sized deciduous tree about 10 to 12 m tall. Tree has a feathery crown of green leaves. Trees are found in dry and moist tropical areas that yield katha which is used in a number of medicines. Other uses are for fodder and fuel and for soil conservation. It is a commercial tree as the plantation can be seen in many parts of the valleys in the north Indian region. Flowers of pale yellow

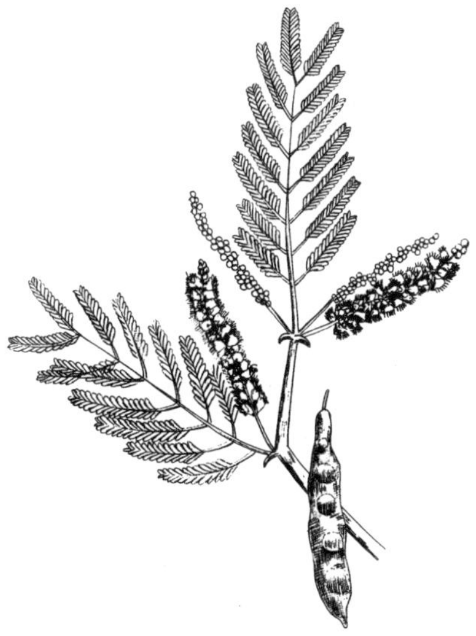

Fig. 51. Khair (*Acacia catechu*).

colour appear during May-June. Seeds of greenish colour appear in the pods that are flat, thin, brown and shining.

Seeds are 0.5 cm in diameter and are sown 1.5 cm deep during February-March after soaking them in hot water and then in water for 24 hours. Seeds germinate in about 30 days. Stump planting is also practiced. Transplanting is done during monsoon season.

Babool (*Acacia nilotica* sp. *indica*)

Trees are deciduous in nature, umbrella-like, 10 m tall and with a good canopy. They grow under dry tropical to subtropical climates on wastelands, roadsides and banks of fields. Wood is hard and used as timber, fuel, and leaves are used for fodder to sheep, goat and camel. Flowers are smelling and yellow. Pods are yellow to light brown to black in colour. Collect them early before their dehiscence so that only good seeds are collected.

Seeds are boiled for 5 minutes in water and then kept for 24 hours in water and sown during February-May. Seeds germinate in about 30 days. Planting is done during the rainy season.

Israeli Babool (*Acacia tortilis*)

Moderately tall but spreading trees grown on roadside or on wastelands for soil conservation, fencing, fuel and fodder. Leaves are green and compound with leaflets. White flowers are borne in bunches. Evergreen in nature and best suited for dry tropical areas. Seeds are borne in pods.

Seeds are treated either in boiling water for 10 to 30 minutes or immersed in 20% sulphuric acid for 1 hour and then washed in water, before sowing. Seeds are sown during March-April. Seeds germinate in about 60 days. Planting is done during July-August

Horse Chestnut (*Aesculus indica*)

Deciduous tree usually found in the temperate region growing as high as 30 m. They may live for more than 50 years. Trees are planted for commercial wood, as it is very strong. Nuts are used for manufacturing of insecticides. Canopy is round to oval but spreading. Leaves are large (10-15 cm long), petioled, green and compound. Flowers are borne during late spring or summer in white panicles, which develop into dark brown or blackish heart-shaped inedible fruits. These are nuts covered with a fuzzy surface, which contain the seeds. Shady tree is used for furniture, timber and fodder.

Seedlings are raised from seeds that are sown during October-November and they germinate during spring. Single stemmed plants are transplanted when they are 1½ years old in the next year during December.

Maharukh (*Ailanthus excelsa*)

It is a fast growing deciduous and shady tree of 20 m height with curved trunk and spreading branches. Soil conservation, fodder and wooden articles are its uses. Suitable in dry to moist tropical areas. Leaves are compound in 6 to 12 pairs, green and opposite. Flowers are of light yellow colour and appear during February-March. Fruits or pods are pink to pale red in colour and 4-6 cm long and 1.0-1.5 cm wide and flat but rounded on both ends. There is one seed in each pod.

Fig. 52. Maharukh (*Ailanthus excelsa*).

Fresh seeds are sown in polybags or in beds during June and then transferred to polybags during February. Germination gets completed in about 1½ months. Stump and stem cuttings are also used for their multiplication. Transplanting is done during July in the next year.

Black Siris (*Albizia chinensis*)

Trees are found in tropical moist to subtropical areas, mostly grown along the river sides and cultivated areas. Trees are deciduous in nature but may behave as evergreen in some pockets. Canopy is broad with a flat top. Leaves are compound in 5-20 pairs of pinnate end with leaflets of 6 to 10 cm length. Flowers are yellowish in colour and appear during early summer along with leaves. Pods are pale reddish-green when young and turn light brown on ripening during September to December. Pods are 8-15 × 1.2-2.0 cm, flat and hairy. Seeds are long, flat and greenish-brown in colour. Trees are used for timber, fodder and fuel. It is also a shade tree for tea gardens.

Seeds are kept in water for 48 hours before sowing. Seeds are sown during March-April. Seeds germinate in about 30 days. Planting is done during July-August.

Siris (*Albizia lebbeck*)

These trees are also deciduous in nature and 20-30 m tall, having umbrella-like canopy. Trees are suited to tropical climate. Shallow rooted and fix nitrogen from atmosphere in the soil. Leaves are feather-like and compound with 6-18 leaflets. Flowers are cream white to yellow, fragrant and on 5-8 cm long peduncles. They appear during April-May. Pods are light pale in colour which are collected during June. Trees are used for fuel, wood, fodder, green manure and soil conservation. Seeds are light brown, smooth, obovate to oblong, compressed and have hard seed-coats.

Seeds are kept in boiling water for 10 minutes and then in cold water for 24 hours and then sown 1.5 to 2 cm deep in spring. Seeds are sown during March. Seeds germinate in about 30 days. Transplanting of 30-50 cm tall plants with their earth-balls is done during July-August.

Fig. 53. Siris (*Albizia lebbeck*).

Safaid Siris (*Albizia procera*)

Suited for waterlogged areas in the tropical region but is found throughout the sub-Himalayan tract and the Andamans. Trees are used for fodder and fuel purposes. It is large deciduous tree with clean bole and light crown. Yellowish white flowers appear in large bunches during June to September. Pods are red and ripen from February to May.

Seeds are small and are kept in water for 48 hours before sowing during spring. Seeds are placed 20 cm apart in rows in the nursery beds. Germination gets completed within 30-40 days. Transplanting of 30-45 cm tall seedlings along with earth-balls is done during July-August. Stumps are also used for multiplication of tree.

Araucaria (*Araucaria* spp.)

Evergreen with horizontal branches is a landscape and ornamental tree that is grown at various elevations but moist and warm climate is most suitable. It can be grown in pots for many years as an indoor plant or a small tree. Leaves are needle-like but fleshy and 2 cm long. It is a unisexual plant so both male and female trees are needed to have seeds.

Propagation is by seeds. The seeds are sown during winters preferably under glasshouse conditions. Young seedlings need to be protected from extreme cold. Transplanting is done when plants are 30 to 50 cm tall in well-prepared pits.

Neem (*Azadirachara indica*)

Neem is both a medicinal and an avenue tree that is planted along the roadsides and near the wells. Though it is an evergreen tree but in cooler areas, it behaves as deciduous tree. Trees are raised for their leaves, seeds and wood. Leaves are used in medicinal preparations and bark as tonic. Seeds are used for extraction of oil being used as insecticide; oil cake as a fertilizer and cattle feed. Twigs are generally used in villages as toothbrush. Wood is a good timber. Trees are moderately large with a spread of 6 to 8 m and usually has a clean bole upto 3-4 m. Canopy is round to oval. Leaves are

Fig. 54. Neem tree and seeds.

compound, having 9-13 leaflets crowded near the end of each branch and green. Flowers are small, numerous and of white, yellow or cream coloured that appear during the spring season. Fruits are of yellow colour, sweet, pulpy and 2 × 1 cm. Seeds are bold, hard, round, black or purple in colour.

Tree ripe fruits are collected and dried to get the pulp dry and the seeds are sown fresh. Seeds may be sown *in situ* in polybags or in beds during the end of summer so they get moisture during monsoon. Depth of seeding is 1 cm. Germination gets completed within 14-20 days. Transplanting with their intact earth-balls is done during the next monsoon.

Semal (*Bombax cieba* syn. *B. malabaricum*)

Trees are deciduous, tall (10-15 m) and spreading with strong branches. Suited for moist tropical to subtropical regions upto 1000 m above mean sea level. Wood is used in the manufacture of matchbox, plywood and packing material. Cotton is used for pillow and mattresses while the seeds are used for extraction of oil used in cosmetic industry. Foliage is sparse but enough to provide good canopy. Leaves are green, leathery and compound. Flowers are red in colour and appear in clusters before the emergence of new leaves during the early spring and these last for a month. Though it occurs wild in the dry and moist areas is also used as avenue tree and for roadside plantation. Generally planted near paths as landscape trees.

Fig. 55. Semal (*Bombax cieba* syn. *B. malabaricum*).

Fruits are long pods that are collected prior to their splitting so that the seeds remain intact. Seeds are very small with cotton fuzz around them, which make them flown away by wind. Seeds may be separated from the cottony fuzz by rubbing them gently with sand or well-rotten farm yard manure. Seeds are sown in summer. Germination is complete in 3-4 weeks. Transplanting is done with the start of summer or monsoon.

Dhak/Palash (*Butea monosperma*)

Trees are deciduous in nature and medium to tall about 10 m height, spreading and deep rooted, they are seen in the mixed or dry forests of central and western India but are also common in the plains and upper regions in the Western Himalaya. Trees are mostly raised as avenue and landscaping trees. It is used as an ornamental tree in valley and moist subtropical areas. Leaves are used as fodder and for fuel purposes. Flower, seed and bark are used for medicinal purposes. Branches are crooked or irregular with compound leaves having 3 leaflets that are tomentose on the lower

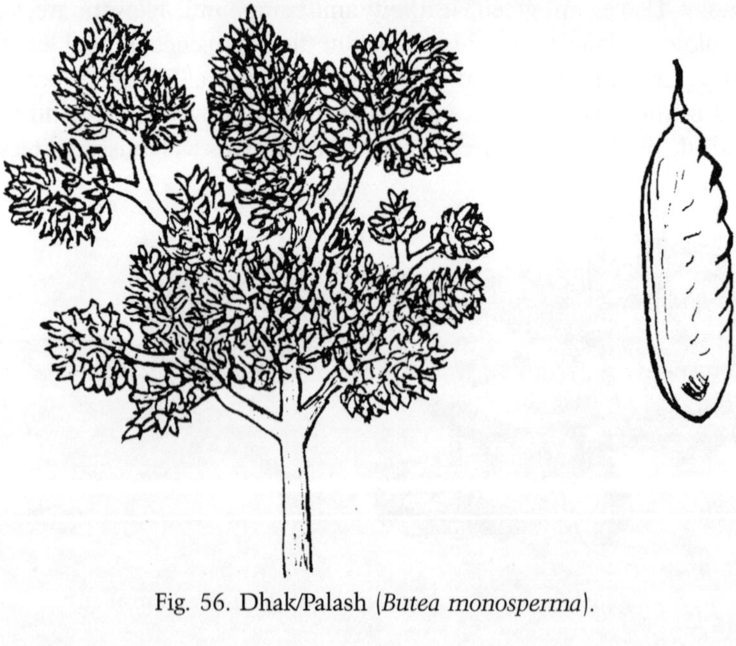

Fig. 56. Dhak/Palash (*Butea monosperma*).

surface. Flowers of deep red colour that hang appear during summer. Pods are oblong, hairy, 15 × 3 cm, cylindrical and black or dark brown in colour. Seeds are flat and 3-4 × 2.5 × 0.1 cm.

Seeds are sown fresh after soaking them in water for 2 days. They are sown during May-June. Germination gets completed within 2-3 weeks. 1 to 3 year old plants are transplanted during July-August.

Amaltas (*Cassia fistula*)

Trees are of medium to tall nature, deciduous and suited to moist tropical areas. They can fix the atmospheric nitrogen in the soil through their nodulated roots. Bark of the tree has medicinal properties and is also used for fuel. Good avenue tree due to its shade and yellow flowers in bunches. Leaves are compound in 3-8 pairs, pinnate and leathery. Flowers are large about 5 cm across that appear in long pendulous bunches of large, bright yellow colour during April-June. Pods are long, round (25 to 30 cm), and 2 cm thick and bright brown in colour. Seeds are contained in sweet pulp, which is brown and there are many seeds in a pod.

Seeds are round, flat, pale yellow to black in colour and are hard surrounded by sweet pulp when in the pod. On ripening seeds are separated on alkathene sheet where the pods are dried in the sun for 2 to 3 days. They dry and split open to release the seeds that are collected. Before sowing they are soaked in warm, rather boiling water for 5 minutes followed by soaking in water for 12 hours. They are sown in beds or specially prepared wooden trays during the months from November to March, shifted to polybags during February or July and then transplanted during March-April.

Casuarina (*Casuarina equisetifolia*)

The trees are with straight trunks, deciduous or evergreen and drought resistant. These are suitable for moist tropical (1600 m amsl) areas where they work as windbreak trees and fix atmospheric nitrogen in the soil for the tree. Bark is of medicinal value while pulp is used for manufacture of prefabricated wood. Trees are valued for their wood in the temperate region and can grow as high as 30 m. It is used for timber and for making quality furniture. Since branches are horizontal, main stem remains straight for the maximum length. Leaves are whorled, reduced to minute scales or teeth and broadly oblong. Fruit is a woody cone and short stalked. Seeds are greyish, 1 seeded samara and 1 cm in diameter.

Seeds are sown fresh during June-November after keeping them in cold water for 24 hours. Germination gets completed within 7 to 10 days. Planting in the field is done during December.

Deodar (*Cedrus deodara*)

A majestic, evergreen and a conifer tree of temperate region that may go as high as 60 m with a trunk diameter of 2 m. The crown is pyramid in shape. Main branches are horizontal but have pendulous terminal shoots. Leaves are long, needle-like, smooth, shining and green. Cones are 7-12 cm long with their heads round

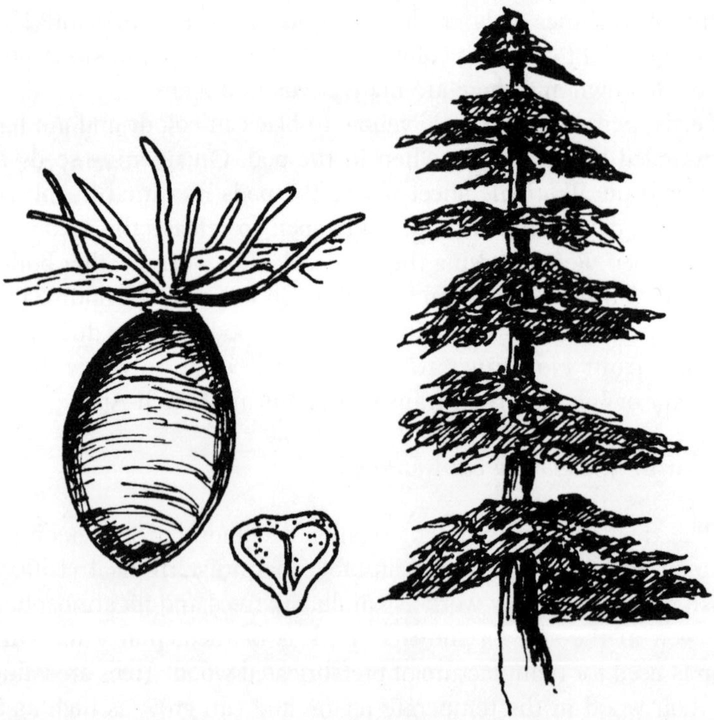

Fig. 57. Deodar (*Cedrus deodara*).

and brown in colour. The wood is generally used for the construction of temples and temple-related buildings in the hills as this tree is regarded as a tree of the Devta or god. Wood is also used for making valuable wooden articles. Cedar oil of commerce is extracted from this tree. Leaves are sharp, pointed and of deep green colour. Seeds are produced in cones that may be 8-10 × 5-7 cm of brown to dark brown colour.

Seeds from the cones are collected. Only ripe seeds are able to germinate. In higher hills, they are sown prior to snowfall during December while in other places, they may be sown during June-July. These are transplanted in nursery beds after a year and then allowed to grow there for another year. Outdoor planting is done of 2-3 years old plants.

Khirak (*Celtis australis*)

Good, tall (25 m) and spreading tree of temperate zone and best suited for fine and strong wood. Leaves are used for fodder. It can be grown from 800 to 2000 m above mean sea level. It is a deciduous tree with a thick trunk. Leaves are dark green, oval-lanceolate and sharply pointed with a short stalk and toothed margin, rough on the upper surface. Flowers appear in spring, small and are

Fig. 58. Khirak (*Celtis australis*).

greenish to pale yellow. Fruits are long stalked, ovoid, dark purple in colour and drupe in nature. Seeds are hard and wrinkled.

Trees are multiplied by seeds, suckers, cuttings and layers. Planting is done in winter with bare roots of the seedlings. Seeds are sown in polybags while other plant parts are transplanted in beds and then raised with care and later transplanted when 1 to 2 years old in the field.

Cupressus

These may be trees of medium height or bushes that are well trained. They are mostly erect, stiff; forming a narrow columnar head, attain the shape of a triangle or cone. Leaves are thick and mildly scented. Trees grow upto a height of 30-50 m when planted outdoor, but in pots they remain stunted. Evergreen with short but stiff and swollen small scale-like leaves. Wood is with fragrance and is used for furniture making. Generally grown as ornamental and landscaping tree.

Seeds are winged and sown during winter while the seedlings of 1-year age are transplanted during monsoon season.

Shisham (*Dalbergia sissoo*)

Trees are mostly deciduous in nature but behave as evergreen under valley areas. Most common tree found near the roadsides as avenue tree attaining a height of 25 m. Wood is valued for its quality of getting good polishing surface and strength. Leaves are green and edible. Trees do shed their leaves. Pods are 5 to 7 cm long and 1 cm across but flat and of light yellow colour with 3-7 seeds, which are flat and brown in colour. Freshly harvested seeds give high percentage of germination.

Seeds should be collected from the pods that have ripened on the tree. Seeds are small, papery and brown in colour that germinate without any treatment but germination can be speeded up if kept in water for 72 hours before sowing. Germination gets completed within 7-10 days, when sown during February-March or May-June. Plants can also be had from stem cuttings. Planting of 1-year old or still older plants is done during monsoon season.

Fig. 59. Shisham (*Dalbergia sissoo*).

Gulmohar (*Delonix regia* or *Poinciana regia*)

Also known as Flamboyant tree is a deciduous avenue tree that grows to a height of 12 m with strong and wide spreading branches. Though the tree is of tropical origin it can grow in valley areas with good success. Trunk is knotty and strong with greyish-brown bark. Leaves are green, compound bearing 20 to 30 tiny leaflets, long and leathery. Flowers may be from carmine to orange or yellow in colour that appear in clusters. The fruit or mature pod is long 30-35 cm and 2 cm in diameter, hard and brown on maturity. Trees are mostly planted for landscaping purposes along the roads or in center of a lawn as they are fast-growing avenue, ornamental or shade tree.

Propagated by seeds and cuttings. Seeds are oblong to round, yellowish marbled and many in a single pod. Seeds being hard-coated take long time to germinate while cuttings do sprout early. Seeds are soaked in hot water for 8-10 minutes before sowing. 2-3-years old plants, whether raised through seeds or by stem cuttings are transplanted during the monsoon.

Fig. 60. Gulmohar (*Delonix regia*).

Bamboo (*Dendrocalamus strictus*)

These are evergreen plants rather trees that go straight and are found in clumps near the water courses or lands that have some moisture for a long period. Plants go to a height of 30 m or so but they are mostly single-stemmed that have an impermeable thick skin which makes them most durable for use as poles. They are mostly found in moist valleys, tarai areas and like places. Internodes are long and the diameter may be 10 to 15 cm and the length of node from 20 to 60 cm depending upon the size of the tree. Leaves are narrow, lanceolate with prominent mid rib, finely pointed 5 to 10 cm long.

Seeds are equal to the size of wheat grain and are edible. They are soaked in water for 48 hours before sowing during April-June. Germination gets completed within 2-3 weeks. Plants can be propagated by vegetative means. Transplanting is done during June-July.

Eucalyptus (*Eucalyptus* sp.)

Trees are generally evergreen in nature but behave as deciduous under temperate climate where leaf fall is almost complete as old leaves are replaced by new leaves in a short span. Trees are found growing in almost every place because there are many species and hybrids available for different climatic and soil conditions. They are mostly planted along the roadsides and for development of waste-lands. Trees are usually single stemmed going as high as 30-45 m. Wood is strong, straight, smelling and used for timber, oil extraction and for match industry and prefabricated wood. Good as a roadside avenue tree. Leaves are olive green, 10 × 3-5 cm, aromatic, sparse, long petioled and pointed on both sides. Flowers are white, aromatic; almost invisible from a distance while fruits are woody, odd-shaped capsules and brown in colour.

Seeds are brown in colour, small in size and do not need any treatment. They are sown during February-March or October-November. They germinate in 1-2 weeks time. Transplanting of 30-50 cm tall plants is done during monsoon.

Fig. 61. Safaida (*Eucalyptus*) foliage, fruits (seeds).

Banyan (*Ficus benghalensis*)

It is also known as Bargad or Barh and is a huge tree that lasts for over 100 years. Hindus and Buddhists who worship the tree and believe that gods live in this tree regard the tree as a sacred tree. Trees are raised as avenue and shade trees. They are found planted near the temples and ponds and other such places where they are not damaged by animals and other living beings. Trees may be 20 to 30 m tall with a spread of about 10 m canopy of the tree which is usually round to oval. Leaves are green, large, leathery with prominent ribs, stalked obtuse, entire and thick. Fruit is a composite, 2 × 1 cm across, round, hairy and edible.

Seeds are dark brown, small and numerous in a fruit. Seeds can survive for a long period, passs through many odd conditions and they can germinate even after a year or so. Plants are multiplied by seeds.

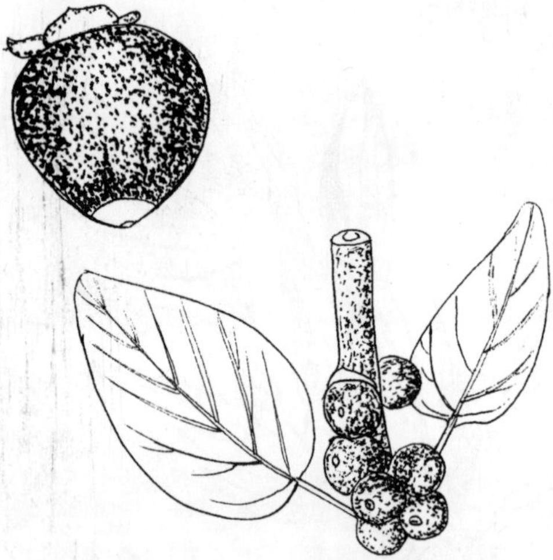

Fig. 62. Banyan (*Ficus benghalensis*).

Beul (*Grewia optiva*)

It is a deciduous tree that is valued for fodder of cattle, fuel to the owner and fibre for making ropes. Trees are suitable for sub-tropical areas and are planted along the sides of roads, on wastelands and marginal lands. Leaves are broad, large and appear during the spring. Fruits are fleshy drupe, olive green which later become blackish and have scattered hairs and ripe during October-December. These can be grown upto a height of 1000 m above mean sea level.

Seeds are hard-coated and are kept in boiling water for 12 hours and then sown 2 cm deep during March-April. Use fresh seeds. Germination gets completed within 3 weeks. Seedlings are transplanted when 50 to 60 cm tall during winter.

Jacaranda (*Jacaranda mimosifolia*)

Ornamental trees for moist tropical and subtropical areas are most ideal in tarai and valley areas where they can grow upto 10 m height. It is a deciduous tree with a strong and straight trunk. Canopy is oval. Leaves are compound with 40 to 100 green and oval-shaped leaflets and stalked. Flowers are borne during March-May in panicles, which are blue-mauve in colour. Fruits are capsules. Seeds are papery, brown and winged.

Plants are easily propagated by seeds. Propagation is also done by semi-hard wood or soft-wood cuttings but seed propagation being easy is much preferred.

Fig. 63. Jacaranda (*Jacaranda mimosifolia*)

Lagerstroemia spp.

Usually found in the forest of moist tropical region. Trees are deciduous in nature. Its wood is second to teak as it is used for industrial timber, poles, fuel, fodder, gum, tannin, soil conservation, boat-making and medicinal purposes. Trees are 8-10 m tall and are avenue or ornamental in nature. Leaves are bright green, large (15 × 18 cm). Flowers purple to mauve in colour and are borne in long panicles.

Seeds are light brown in colour and have stiff brittle wings, which make them possible to disperse to long distances. Seeds are sown during January to March and then transplanted in the next year during monsoon. Cuttings can also be used for propagation. They are planted in the beds and then transplanted when one-year old or 60 to 75 cm tall.

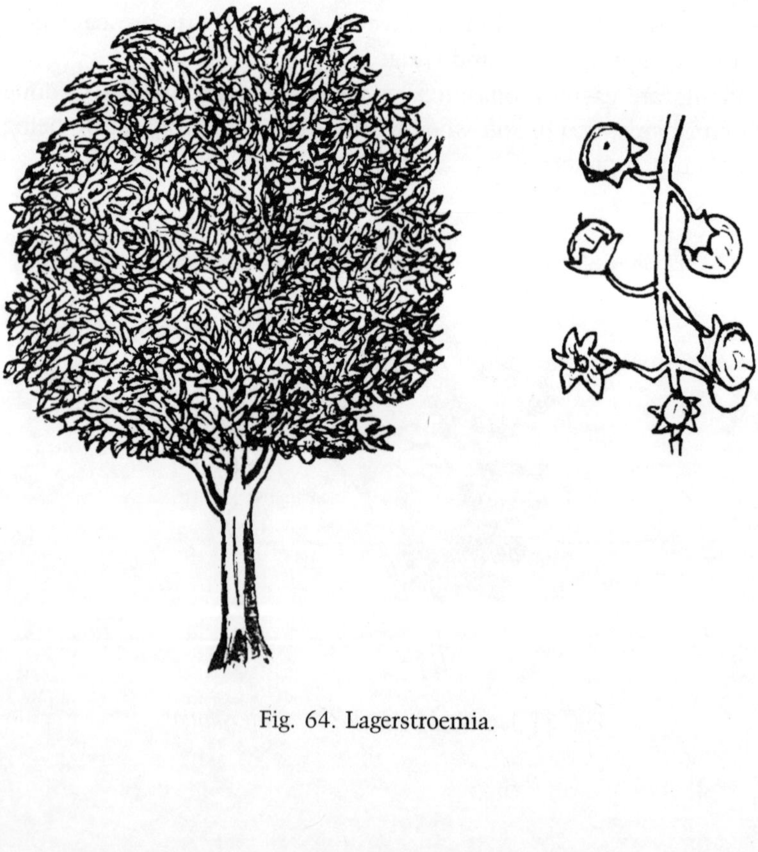

Fig. 64. Lagerstroemia.

Subabool (*Leucaena leucocephala*)

Trees are multipurpose; they provide fuel, fodder and timber. Suited for dry to moist tropical zones. Leaves are used as fodder. Trees serve the soil conservation purposes.

Seeds are tiny and need to be boiled in water for 10 minutes and kept for 12 hours before sowing which is done during February to May depending upon the altitude. Use fresh seeds. Germination gets completed within 3-4 weeks. Transplanting of one-year plants is done during July-August.

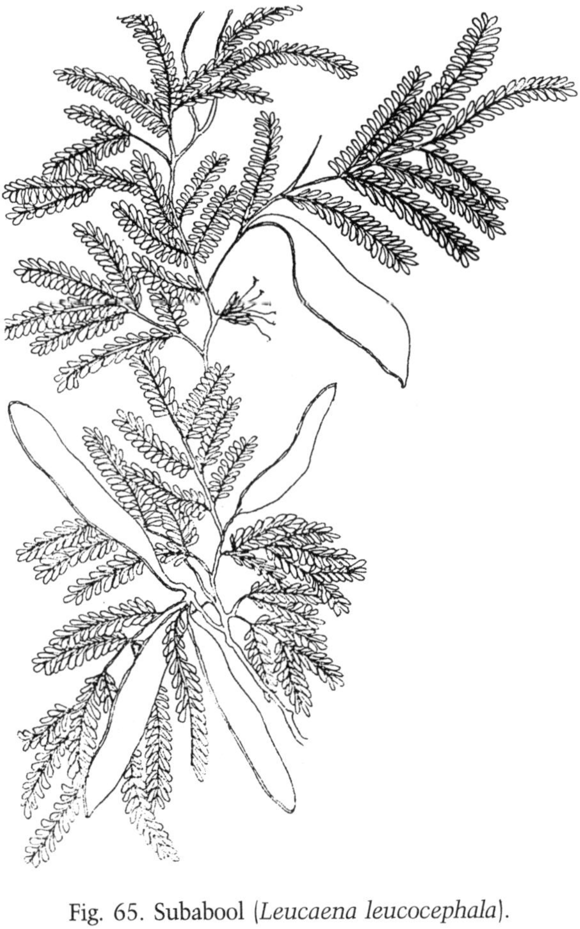

Fig. 65. Subabool (*Leucaena leucocephala*).

Mahua (*Madhuca indica*)

It is a tree of the deciduous forests of central, western and south-eastern parts of the country and extends north to the sub-Himalayan tract. Trees are big (15-20 m), round, shady with large and thick leaves. New leaves appear in clusters during summer. Fruits are berry, juicy, edible and are used for preparation of chutney, jelly, syrup, etc. Seeds are used for oil extraction that is used for making soap, candle and other articles. Wood is used for making many useful articles like boats, bridges, furniture, etc. Grows upto 1200 m above mean sea level. Leaf fall occurs during February-March. Flowers are light yellow in colour, small and sweet smelling.

Fig. 66. Mahua (*Madhuca indica*).

Seeds are light yellow or copper coloured, smooth and bright in colour. Fresh seeds are sown during June-August. Seeds do not need any treatment. Germination gets completed within 3 weeks. Planting of the seedlings is done in dry and moist tropics during July.

Bead Tree (*Melia azedarach*)

This tree is also known by the name of Bakain or Drake. They are deciduous in nature and are mainly grown for timber and fodder in moist tropical to subtropical areas. It is also grown as an avenue and landscape tree on the roadside and on the sides of fields. Trees have a spreading crown and reaches a height of 12-15 m. Branches are weak, easily breakable even with high winds. Leaves are pinnate with several pairs of ovate-acuminate leaves toothed at the margins. Flowers appear during summer and are scented. Fruits are yellow coloured and round. Seeds are round in shape with 1.3 to 1.8 cm diameter.

Seeds are kept soaked in cold water for a week before sowing during spring. Depth of seeding is 2 cm and seeds germinate within 2 months. Seeds germinate upto 80%. Plants can also be propagated by stem and root cuttings. These are planted in beds during winter and then transplanted when 1 m tall in the field.

Mulberry or Toot (*Morus alba, M. nigra*)

Fast growing, tall but spreading tree, raised for fodder, fruit, sports goods, fuel, timber, ornamental purposes and for rearing silkworms. Fruits are edible and are used for making syrup, jam, etc. Young shoots are used for making baskets. Found in moist tropical to subtropical regions and grows best near the water channels. Deciduous tree with 3-lobed green smooth leaves. Flowers are white and in catkins. Fruit is white to light yellow or brown to purple in colour and may be round or long and cylindrical.

Propagation is both by seed and cuttings but cuttings are much easier to grow during June-July and are transplanted after a year.

Chir (*Pinus roxburghii* syn. *P. longifolia*)

Trees are found on the outer ranges and in the main valleys of the Himalayas and on the ridges of the Shiwalik hills from 500 to 1500 m amsl. Trees are typically gregarious and tall (30-40 m) but less spreading, evergreen and valued for industrial timber, poles, gum, oil, tannin, ornamental and soil conservation uses. Best suited for subtropical regions. Leaves are needle-like that appear in clusters and are long and green. Seeds are borne in cones that take two years to ripen.

Mature cones are collected in summer, dried in the sun and seeds

Fig. 67. Chir (*Pinus roxburghii*) cone.

taken out. Seeds are stratified or kept under cool conditions in the open field. They are sown in early spring. 2-3 seeds are sown in each polybag, which has good soil mixture. Later, retain only one plant that is vigorous. One-year old saplings are planted in the field.

Himalayan Blue Pine (*Pinus wallichiana*)

It is also known as Kail. Trees are evergreen, pyramidal and are quite tall upto a height of 40 m or so. Best suited for temperate region and are valued better than *Pinus roxburghii*. Needle-like green leaves are 15-20 cm long, shining and slenderly borne in clusters of 5. Cones are ovoid, woody, long and pendulous.

2-3 seeds are sown in each polybag that has good soil mixture. Later, retain only one vigorous plant. One-year old saplings are planted in the field.

Chinar (*Platanus orientalis*)

One of the best ornamental trees of the temperate region largely grown in Kashmir valley but now is being raised in many other temperate regions of the country. The wood is used for small timber purposes while the tree has ornamental, avenue, medicinal and soil conservation uses. Trees are deciduous in nature as the new leaves

Fig. 68. Chinar (*Platanus orientalis*).

appear with the spring season and the old leaves drop during autumn. Trees are straight, cylindrical and trunk is covered with a white or silvery bark. Trees have a dense crown of top leaves which are big palmate-lobate. Flowers appear in spring or early summer and are long stalked. Seeds are small and hairy and easily dispersible.

Seeds are mixed with sand, loam soil and spreaded evenly over the surface of beds and then covered over and watered. Seeds are sown in May, their germination is slow and the seedlings of 50 to 75 cm height are transplanted in spring or monsoon. 2-3 years old cuttings are planted in beds for raising seedlings.

Poplar (*Populus ciliata*)

Trees are good for soil conservation and pulpwood. Wood is generally used for timber and making packing cases or boxes. They are found growing in subtropical and temperate regions. Different species of this tree are available. Being deciduous in nature, leaf shedding is very common which is not like avenue trees. Due to their fast growth, they are preferred for planting near the fence and roadsides. Trees are tall (15 m) with a spread of 4 to 5 m and the crown is usually oval but may become oblong. Leaves are pale green, stalked, ovate-lanceolate, 7-12 cm long and 5 to 8 cm wide. Fruits are capsule, ovoid and 0.5 cm across. Seeds are small and hairy.

Planting is by cuttings that are 20-30 cm long and have 1-2 cm diameter. These cuttings are planted at least 15-20 cm deep in the soil. Generally, 1½ to 2 m tall plants are transplanted during monsoon season.

Jand (*Prosopis cineraria*)

It is a deciduous, tall (18 m), thorny, less leafy and spreading tree. Yellow flowers appear after leaf fall. Used for fuel, fodder and making tools. Pods are collected during August and dried to get the seeds.

Seeds are fairly small and can remain viable for 2 years. Fresh seeds after being treated with boiling water for 10 minutes give better and early germination. Sowing is done in spring. Seeds may germinate in about 2 weeks.

Muscat or Wilayati Kikar (*Prosopis juliflora*)

It is a semi-green to evergreen tree with zigzag, staggering or pendulous canopy. It is a medium-sized tree of about 10 m height with nodulated and deep roots. Leaves are almost hairy, pinnate, 2-3 leaflets. Flowers appear during February and October, white, fragrant and in groups of 2-4. Seeds are small, round to flat and slightly bigger than *Prosopis cineraria.*

Seeds need to be soaked in water for 2 days after keeping them in boiled water for 15-30 minutes. They are sown from November to February. Germination is complete in a month's time. Planting is done during rainy season.

Oak (*Quercus incana* syn. *Q. leucotrichophora*)

It is a common oak tree found growing in the temperate region from 1200 to 2400 m amsl scattered on dry, grassy hillsides and adjoining areas. Trees are evergreen, medium to large-sized, often 10-12 m with an uneven spread of 6 to 8 m. Branching is upright

Fig. 69. Oak *(Quercus incana* syn. *Q. leucotrichophora).*

but spreading and canopy is oval to round. Leaves have dense white woolly hairs on the dorsal side, dark green and sharply toothed towards their tips. Nuts are ovoid, 1-1.5 cm across, half encircled by the involucral cup when mature, glabrous and brown.

Seeds are collected during January-February. They are dibbled in winter or early spring in the nursery beds. The rate of germination is high but slow and may take 1 to 4 months. Seedlings remain in the nursery beds for 3 years and then transplanted during the rainy season.

Bras (*Rhododendron arboreum*)

This is the common red coloured flower tree found in the hills of north India. Trees are tall (25 m) with spread of about 6 to 8 m and have weak stems that break easily. It is an evergreen tree with green somewhat coarse and toothed-margin leaves which have a pronounced mid-rib and are 5" × 2.5". Good avenue trees having red and showy flowers.

Trees can be reproduced by layering, grafting or by stem-cuttings

Fig. 70. Bras (*Rhododendron arboreum*).

after soaking them in IBA @ 500-1000 ppm for 3 hours or in IBA @ 2000 ppm by quick-dip method. Seeds are collected during autumn and then sown in spring. Fresh seeds are used. Seeds may be sown in nursery beds or polybags. Germination is poor but complete in about 4 weeks. Transplanting is done after 2 years when the seedlings have attained the height of about 1 m.

Robinia/Black Locust (*Robinia pseudoacaia*)

Black Locust is a deciduous tree that grows well in the temperate region upto 2400 m amsl. Tree is about 25 m tall with erect, often bifurcated trunk having furrowed bark that turns greyish-brown on maturity. Wood is used for poles and the tree can serve the purpose of soil conservation. Branches are spiny but provide round shape to the canopy. Leaves are yellowish-green, pinnate with 7-20 leaflets. Flowers are white in colour, scented and borne in raceme inflorescence. Fruits are leathery pods of red-brown colour with 4-10 seeds.

Seeds are kidney-shaped but small. Treat the seeds with hot water for 12 hours or cold water for 2 days. Soaking in concentrated or

Fig. 71. Robinia/Black Locust (*Robinia pseudoacaia*).

95 per cent sulphuric acid for 20-60 minutes followed by washing in clean water may increase the rate and speed of germination. Sow 1-2 seeds in each polybag during the spring. 25-30 cm long cuttings are planted during February and they are transplanted after slight root pruning after a year. Also propagated by suckers.

Willow (*Salix babylonica*)

Trees are deciduous in nature and are found in the temperate region in the subtropical areas. Trees are 10-15 m tall with spreading branches, which droop downwards to give the tree the shape of a dome or umbrella. Branches are slender and pendulous giving the tree a weeping look. Fast growing, suitable near the water site, and as a soil conservation tree.

Propagation is by cuttings that are collected and planted during monsoon. It is better to plant the cuttings in polybags and then shift to the field rather than planting *in situ*.

Sagwan/Teak (*Tectona grandis*)

It is a large deciduous tree with a slender, clean and straight trunk that can grow upto 60 m height. Wood is highly priced since it gives a very good finish and is strong and does not absorb water. Used for veneers and furniture. Trees are suited for hot and humid tropics. Leaves are ovate, 30 × 60 cm, green and tomentose. Flowers are bluish-white that appear during summer. Fruits are like plums, hard, drupe, spherical and brownish. Seeds are heavy and compact.

Insects damage seeds as they eat the seed and hence fresh seed after drying may be stored till sowing. Seeds have less germinating power and remain dormant for a long period. Treated seeds are sown in nursery beds during early spring. They are kept in water for 12 hours and then dried and it is repeated twice. Another popular way to get early germination of the seeds is to put them under a cover of well-rotten farm yard manure with enough moisture for 2 weeks.

The best method is of planting stumps during the monsoon. The plants raised by seeds or stump planting is done during the rainy season when the plants are 1 m tall.

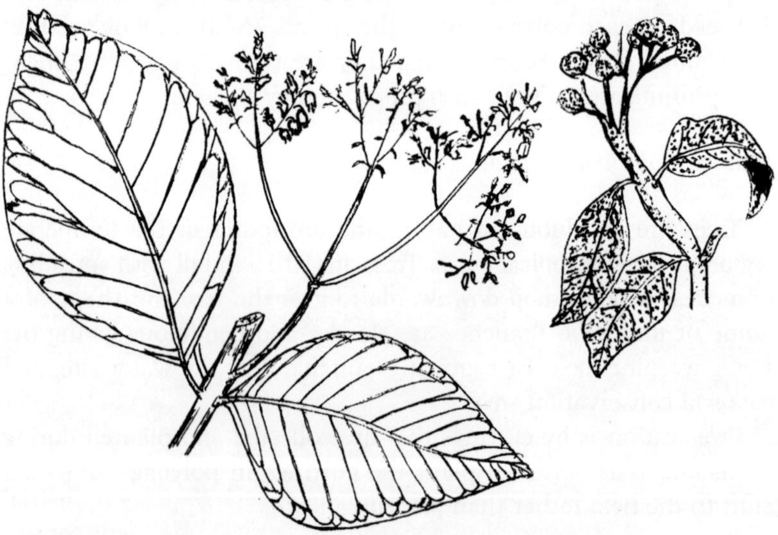

Fig. 72. Sagwan/Teak (*Tectona grandis*).

Arjun (*Terminalia arjuna*)

A large evergreen, shady tree, suitable for tropical areas the wood of which is used for industrial timber, small timber, poles, fuel, fodder, etc. Trees are also valued for tannin and grown for ornamental, landscaping, medicinal and soil conservation purposes. Trees are common throughout the greater part of the sub-Himalayan tract and central India. Leaves are oblong, leathery and green. Flowers are pale-yellowish-white. Seeds are bold and remain in the fruit, which are of tan colour.

Seeds or fruits are sown in such a way that half of them remain over the ground. They are sown in nursery beds during April-May. Seedlings are sensitive to frost, drought and dense overhead shade. One-year old seedlings are transplanted during June-July.

Bahera (*Terminalia bellirica*)

Trees are deciduous, tall and mostly grown in tarai and valley areas where they are valued for fuel and fodder. Fruits are used in Ayurvedic medicines and for tonic preparations. Leaves are green, pointed at their tips, clustered at the end of branches and are with small petioles. Flowers are pale green to greenish-white that appear during spring. Fruits are 2-3 cm long, ovoid, brownish and densely covered with hairs. There is one seed in each fruit.

Seeds are fairly large, brown to greenish-black in colour. Though they can germinate as such but to increase their speed of germination, they may be soaked in water for 24 hours before sowing. Seeds can also be treated with concentrated sulphuric acid for 10-12 minutes followed by washing in clean water. Use fresh seeds. Sowing is done during the spring. Seeds germinate in about 2 months. Transplanting of one-year old plants is done on the onset of rainy season.

Harad (*Terminalia chebula*)

Trees are of moist tropical zone and are valued for their industrial timber, small timber, poles, gum, tannin, ornamental, soil conservation and medicinal uses. These are deciduous in nature with round but spreading canopy. Leaves are 10-25 cm long, ovate, green and in almost pairs. Flowers are dull white in spikes at the ends of branches. Fruit is a drupe, 2-4 cm long and 1-1.5 cm in diameter.

Seeds are quite bold and hard like a nut and each may weigh about 7 g. They are kept in water for 2 days prior to sowing like Bahera. They are sown during February to May. Fresh seeds can be used. Germination is complete in about 2 months. Stumps can also be used for propagation. One-year old plants are transplanted during July.

Thuja (*Thuja occidentalis*)

A slow growing, evergreen tree which grows to 20 m height is suitable for all climates and is a good avenue tree. Trees can be trained and pruned to become a bush-like. Branches and shoots are erect. Leaves are green, aromatic and scale-like. Foliage is like fern. It can be grown in pots for number of years. Fruits are brown and ovoid and have many seeds.

Propagation is by seeds and air layering.

Tun/Toon (*Toona ciliata* Syn. *Cedrela toona*)

Large deciduous tree with a spreading crown that yields good timber, fodder and house construction timber. It is a good avenue tree of valley areas in the sub-Himalayan tract. Trees are large in size with a spreading crown. Leaves are compound with 10-20 leaflets, green with prominent mid-rib and other veins. Flowers are white, small and honey-scented that appear along with new leaves during April-May. Fruits are oblong and capsule. Seeds are minute and winged.

Seeds are collected from dry fruits that are beaten with sticks and then separated from the husk and other unwanted material. Seeds cannot be stored for more than a year. Fresh seed is sown during May-June. Germination is complete in about 2-3 weeks. Transplanting of 2-years old seedlings along with their earth-balls is done during monsoon.

17

Other Tree Crops

Tea (*Camellia sinensis*)

It is an evergreen shrub or a bush that is grown in the valleys and the like areas. Shrubs require fairly high humidity and annual rainfall of at least 150-200 cm. They grow best on well-drained acid soils free of excess lime and with a pH between 4.5 and 6. Plants also need shade but it should not be dense. Plants may attain the height of 1 m with a spread of about 1 m. Branching is profuse with good foliage. Tender leaves along with buds are collected when mature for manufacturing tea.

Plants are multiplied by seeds that are sown in well-prepared seedbeds. Seeds are collected from ripe fruits when they are dark green and tinged purple. Collected seeds are placed in water to scum off the immature seeds and other unwanted material. They are dried under shade and sown soon. Seeds should not touch each other in the bed. Depth of seeding is almost 1 cm. Seedlings are grafted with suitable scions of good and uniform crop. When the seedlings are about 40 cm in height they are transplanted along with their earth-balls in the field.

Coffee (*Coffea arabica* and *C. canephora*)

Coffee is a short-day tropical plant requiring a hot climate with rainfall of over 150 cm, well-distributed throughout the year for healthy growth and constant productivity. Plants are sensitive to frost. They may attain a height of 2 m or so depending upon the species and the conditions required for their growth. Spread of the tree is about 1 m. Leaves are large, green and slightly leathery. Seeds of the plant are used for coffee powder.

Fully ripe fruits are collected from the trees by hand. They ripen during September-October. Fruits are pulped and beans are placed in water for a short while so that the immature seeds come to the top. Sinking seeds are collected for sowing. They should not be exposed to unwanted and unfavourable conditions for a long period as they lose viability very soon. Seeds are sown in nursery beds or containers like baskets and then shifted to field when they are 9 to 12 months old.

Oil Palm (*Elaeis guineensis*)

These are erect growing trees, about 8-10 m height and are tropical in nature. Fruits are used for jaggery making and for brewing into Neera and other drinks. Shoots and leaves are used for basketry. They need abundant rainfall for their proper growth. They grow best on terrains where they may get permeable soil rich in organic matter. Fruits are borne in bunches. Ripe fruit is orange-red with parts at the base of fruit that is light yellow in colour. They are collected from the tree and the spikes are separated and fertile fruits separated from infertile. Fertile fruits are left in water for 5 to 6 days for fermentation and later the pulp is washed and the seeds are separated carefully by washing them in water.

Seeds are first sown in nursery beds or special type of germinator as the seeds take long time to germinate. They are planted in the field along with their earth-balls after a year.

Rubber (*Hevea brasiliensis*)

It is an evergreen tree that grows to a height of 18 to 30 m. They grow best in lowland areas requiring rainfall of atleast 190 mm per year. Trees begin to produce fruits after 5-6 years and come into full seed production within 5 to 10 years. Fruit is a capsule.

Seed capsules are opened by hand, removed and stored. Fresh

seeds are used for sowing, as the seed viability is low. Seed is first sown in seedbeds, shaded from sun and well-watered. Later, the seedlings are transplanted.

Cocoa (*Theobroma cacao*)

The trees are bushes or small trees and are best for tropical areas where they get annual rainfall of at least 150 cm and temperature never below 16^0 C. Trees start bearing at 4 to 5 years of age and may continue to bear 50 years or more. Fruit and seed require six months to mature, attaining maximum size.

Ripe pods are picked and broken open by pressure so that seed beans come out. It is better to cut the pods that are full ripe from the tree with a sharp-edged knife. Seed beans removed from pod with mucilage and can be sown direct after or without removal of mucilage by washing off or rubbing off with wood ashes. It is better to use the fresh seed that is sown in seedbeds or direct in the field. Seed is sown in such a way that its hilum is downward and there is shade on the seedbed. In field 2-3 seeds are planted per hole. Seedlings are transplanted after 4 to 5 months in the field.

18

Oil Crops

These crops are grown for their seeds that are used for extraction of oil. The oil is used for commerce and domestic purposes. They may have some other uses also. Some of these crops are given here.

Groundnut (*Arachis hypogaea*)

It is an herbaceous legume, intermediate in response to day length and is drought hardy but frost sensitive. Plants grow upright about 30 to 60 cm with spread of 40-50 cm. Moderately strong stem with green foliage. Fruits are borne in pods that go underground and hence their colour becomes cream to off-white.

When foliage turns light yellow in colour, it indicates that the pods are ripe and the plants should be lifted along with their roots with care. Pods may be opened with hand or with slight beating with sticks so that seeds should not get damaged. Sow seeds by dibbling or line sowing method, 2 cm deep in well-prepared field. They germinate soon and the plants are visible after 7 to 10 days of sowing.

Sarson (*Brassica* spp.)

Commonly grown species are *Brassica napus, B. campestris* and *B. juncea* for oil extraction. These are herbaceous plants that are usually 75 to 100 cm tall with a spread of about 50-76 cm. Main stem is straight and branched. Leaves are green and fleshy used for vegetable and cattle fodder. Fruits are pods that shatter easily. Ripening of pods is uniform which are harvested and threshed to get the seeds separated. Seeds are cleaned and stored in an airtight container for next sowing.

Seeds are brown to dark brown in colour, round, bold and sown by line sowing or by broadcast method and are then covered over by a layer of soil. Germination of seeds is completed in 10 days.

Safflower (*Cathamus tinctorius*)

It is an herbaceous annual plant attaining a height of 30 to 120 cm depending on the variety and moisture conditions of the soil and around the plant. Well adapted to hot deserts and warm dry regions with at least 50 cm annual rainfall. Crop is ready when seed-heads are dry. They may be picked or harvested and seeds are separated. As the seed has spines, careful handling is needed. Seed is winnowed to remove trash and other unwanted material after threshing.

Seeds are sown 5 cm deep in rows that are 90 to 100 cm apart. The germination starts soon but the complete germination may take place within 2 weeks.

Soyabean (*Glycine soya*)

It is an annual herbaceous plant, leguminous in nature, short-day plant and grows to a height of 60 to 160 cm.

Crop is harvested when the pods are fully mature and seeds are hard. At this time, leaves turn yellow and drop. Plants are harvested and threshed after drying them for few days in open so that pods may crack or open easily by slight pressure on them. Seeds are winnowed to get them separated from inert material and husk of the pods and leaves.

Seeds are sown in rows by keeping the depth of about 3 to 5 cm in well-prepared soil. Seeds germinate soon.

Sunflower (*Helianthus annuus*)

It is a plant of the tropical region that has found good place in the subtropics also. Plants attain a height of 1.5 to 2.5 m and spread to 50 cm under good conditions and are sun-loving. Main stem is strong and have few branches. Leaves are coarse, green and slightly leathery. Flowers are composite with yellow petals and brown central portion.

When flowers start shrivelling and the leaves show drying and yellowing, heads are removed with shears or knives. Later, they are dried, threshed and seeds are separated from the total material and finally, stored in an airtight containers for next season.

Seeds are sown in lines, the distance between the lines depends upon on the size of plants. The depth of sowing is less than a cm. They germinate easily on getting suitable conditions.

Linseed (*Linum usitatissimum*)

It is an annual long-day plant that is 40 to 70 cm tall and highly branched, producing a large number of seeds.

Seeds are borne in balls. When the plant starts showing the signs of maturity, i.e. the leaves turn yellow and seed-balls rattle, the plants are harvested. The pods are collected and harvested with care. Seeds are sown half a cm deep in lines or by broadcast method and are covered with a layer of earth. They germinate soon.

Castor (*Ricinus communis*)

Plants grow well under subtropical and tropical conditions where it behaves as a perennial. Even in temperate region, they are cultivated. Plant height varies from 1 to 10 m depending upon the variety and conditions of their growth. Main stem is strong, green to brown in colour with many side branches and green foliage. Leaves are large, green and spreading. Fruits are capsular and hence seeds are contained in the capsules. They are harvested during the month of November. After drying them under sun, they are threshed and cleaned.

Seeds are planted 2 cm deep in well-prepared field but they are likely to be damaged soon with ample moisture. Careful planting is done in lines that are 90 × 90 cm apart. Germination is completed within 3 weeks.

Sesame (*Sesamum indicum*)

It is a short-day annual plant that grows to a height of 60 to 100 cm and is grown in temperate to subtropical regions for oil extraction. It is a highly-branched plant with sparse foliage of light green colour. Fruits are capsules. They mature after 3 months of planting.

Capsules are hand cut, dried and then threshed. Seeds are sown directly in the field at a spacing of 40 × 50 cm. Depth of seeding is usually half a cm.

19

Fibre Crops

Hemp (*Cannabis sativa*)

It is an annual long-day plant that grows upto a height of 90 cm to 3 m in temperate region and 4.5 m in the tropics.

Seed matures when leaf bracts surrounding fruits are half-dried and curled back (then seeds mature on middle branches). The seeds first mature on lower branches and than on the top. Seeds shatter easily, hence plants should be cut in the early morning when there is slight dampness. Dry them for 3 to 7 days, thresh in the usual manner and clean the seeds by winnowing.

Seeds are sown 1.2 cm deep in seedbed with fine tilt with spacing of 30 to 40 cm between lines and 90 to 100 cm between plants.

Jute (*Corchorus olitorius* and *C. capsularis*)

These are short-day annuals that grow to a height of 2-3 m best under tropical conditions with an annual rainfall of 150 cm.

Seeds are ready for harvest during October-November and at this time the pods turn brown. The plants are cured, stacked in bundles and later threshed. Seeds are dried after harvesting.

The seeds are evenly broadcasted and covered by a layer of soil and later watered.

Cotton (*Gossypium hirusutum*)

An annual short-day plant that grows upto 1.5 m in height in tropics, as this crop is suited to warm climate. Main stem is brownish-green and leaves are green, large and spreading. Fruits are balls that contain cotton fibre and seeds.

When fruit-balls start opening, these are collected by hand and kept for drying. Lint has to be separated from the seeds by mechanical means and then the seeds are freed from lint. Seeds are sown 1 to 2 cm deep by line sowing method. Germination starts after 7 to 10 days and is completed within 2 weeks.

Flax (*Linum usitissimum*)

It is an annual long-day plant that requires abundant moisture and cool weather during the growing season and so is restricted to cool temperate regions with moist cloudy weather during the early growing period. Plant height is 75 to 120 cm with spread of about 30 cm.

For seed collection, crop is harvested when one third to one half of seed-balls are brown or yellowish in colour with fully developed brown seeds. At this stage stems are yellow. Special de-seeders are used for threshing and seeds are separated from the ball chaff by winnowing machines.

Seeds should not be sown deeper than 1.3-2.5 cm. It is better to sow the seeds in lines rather than broadcasting.

20

Drug Crops

Dill (*Anethum graveolens*)

Dill is an annual or biennial and long-day plant. Usually grows as an annual crop, producing seeds in one season if planted early in warm soil. It grows well under much cooler conditions.

For seed collection, harvesting is done when few seeds get riped as they shatter readily. They are harvested in the early morning and then kept for drying and later threshed carefully. Seeds are sown *in situ* with a spacing of 20-30 cm apart in rows.

Wormseed (*Artemesia maritima*)

It is a much branched, perennial and aromatic shrub that grows to a height of 1 m. Leaves are 2-5 cm long, whitish in colour and divided into numerous fine, linear segments. Flower heads are small and in short spikes. These are common in the sub-Himalayan tract between 2000 and 3000 m altitudes.

Seeds lose their viability very rapidly. They are sown during November in nursery beds and than the seedlings of 30 to 40 days old are transplanted at a distance of 10 × 15 cm.

Indian Barberry (*Berberis* spp.)

It is a large, erect and thorny shrub with whitish or pale grey branches. Leaves are sharp-toothed and green with fine veins.

Flowers are yellow in colour and in short bunch. Fruits are void, bluish-purple with few seeds. Shrubs are common in forest in the Himalayan region between 2000 and 3000 m altitude. They are also seen in Nilgiri Hills in south India.

Plants are propagated by seeds, cutting of young shoots or by layering.

Senna (*Cassia* spp.)

It is an erect, low growing, highly branched shrub that grows 60 to 100 cm in height. Plants require bright sunshine with occasional rainfall. The crop is ready in about 120 days.

Generally, first leaf crop is harvested during June-July and then plants are left in the field to give further crop of leaves, bear flowers and set seeds. Seed pods when almost dry are removed from the plant, dried under sun, threshed and seeds are cleaned.

Seed-coat is tough and needs abrasion to induce germination, therefore, seeds are mixed with sand and grounded gently in a mortar. Seeds are sown in lines 30 cm apart either by dibbling or behind a plough.

American Wormseed (*Chenopodium ambrosoides*)

An annual plant that grows to a height of 30 to 120 cm depending on the soil, climate and other conditions for growth. It is being cultivated upto 1500 m amsl where temperatures are not too low.

Seeds are harvested when mature and black, usually during September. The crop is cut with sickles, about 10 cm above the ground level. It is dried under the sun and then threshed and winnowed to get rid of broken husk and other unwanted material.

Seeds are first sown in the nursery and when the seedlings are 10-12 cm high are transplanted to field in rows 90 cm apart with plant spacing of 25 cm.

Pyrethrum (*Chrysanthemum cinerariaefolium*)

It is perennial (5 to 7 years) long-day plant but suits well to short-day conditions in the tropics provided that rainfall and mean temperatures are favourable.

Seed-heads are ready for harvesting when flower corollas can be removed easily from fruits and small portion of stalk below flower receptacle becomes yellow-brown. Flowers are plucked by hand, dried in the sun, threshed with wooden sticks and the seeds after cleaning are stored in airtight containers under dry and cool conditions.

Seeds are first sown in seedbeds and then seedlings when 10-12 cm high are transplanted to field. The spacing in the field is 75 × 75 cm.

Quinine (*Cinchona* spp.)

These are perennial trees that are evergreen in nature. They are medium-sized to large and are grown upto 2700 m amsl with annual rainfall of at least 140 cm.

Trees start flowering after 3-4 years. Seeds are borne in capsules that are collected by hand from trees, using bamboo ladders. They should be collected before splitting from bottom towards upward releasing seeds. The seeds are stored in dark room and then opened by hand or gently cracking.

Seeds are short-lived and hence fresh seed should be sown in the seedbeds, partially covered to exclude rain but allows some sun for good air circulation. Seeds are very small and are spread over the seedbed and then covered with a layer of fine soil. When plants get 7.5 cm high, they are transplanted to nursery beds at 15-25 cm apart and after three months they need re-spacing. Seedlings of 25-35 cm height are ready for transplanting in the field.

Datura (*Datura stramonium*)

Plants are found in temperate Himalayas upto 2500 m and in hilly regions of central and southern India. It is a bushy plant that grows upto 1 m in height. Leaves are large (15 cm), ovate, unevenly toothed and dull green in colour. Flowers are large, sweet-scented and white while fruits are ovoid, deeply divided into four segments and are covered with prickles.

Seeds are black and sown in nursery for raising seedlings.

Foxglove (*Digitalis purpurea*)

The plant is cultivated in the hills of north India and in some portions of Nilgiri Hills. It is a biennial to perennial plant that grows upto the height of 1.2 m. Leaves in the lower portion are with stocks while at the upper part are short stalked or almost without stalks and they tend to decrease in size from bottom to top. Flowers are 5-8 cm long, white or purple with ciliate lobes. Fruits are ovoid.

Plants are multiplied by their seeds that are sown in nursery beds and the seedlings of 40 to 50 days age are transplanted in well prepared field.

Tobacco (*Nicotina tobacum* and *N. rustica*)

Both these plants are used for medicinal purposes. *N. tobacum* is herbaceous and cylindrical plant that reaches to a height of 3 m while the *N. rustica* is small and less woody plant.

Seeds are borne in capsules. When the capsules become brown and dry, they are collected. The ripening is uneven and so the harvesting has to be at regular intervals. Capsules are dried and transferred to trays and then capsules are crushed with hand and later the seeds are cleaned carefully as the seeds are very small.

Seeds are first sown in nursery beds by spreading the seeds after mixing it with sand for even distribution. It is covered by a fine layer of soil mixed with well-rotten farm yard manure. Seeds start germinating within 3 days and complete it within two weeks. When seedlings are 15-20 cm high with 4 to 6 leaves they are transplanted in the field.

Chiryata (*Swertia chirayata*)

The plant occurs in the temperate region under the Himalayan track between 1200 and 3000 m from Kashmir to Assam. It is an annual herb about 1.5 m in height and is highly branched. Leaves are borne in pairs, long about 10 cm but without stalk and pointed at the tips. Flowers are pale green and tinged with purple colour. Fruits are 6 mm or more long and ovoid.

Plants are multiplied by seeds.

21

Vegetable Crops

This group of plants is diverse in their requirements for soil, nutritional and other needs but in general, they are annuals when raised for fresh vegetable consumption as they remain in the field for about one season of about 3 months. For seed production, they flower in the next season i.e., after winter. Seeds are either sown in the nursery or directly in the field. In nursery, they can be sown in beds or in polybags. Cucurbits are generally sown in polybags and then planted in pits in the open. Some of them are multiplied through their vegetative parts like tubers and buds.

Methods of commercial multiplication of some important vegetables are as follows:

Onion (*Allium cepa*)

For seed production, it is a biennial crop but for vegetable purposes, the bulb maturation takes place in the same season. Plants adapt to various types of soils and climate but cannot tolerate frost and drought. Bulbs of pink colour are used as vegetable. Even green leaves and small bulbs are used in preparation of many vegetables.

Seeds are brownish-black in colour and are sown 0.4 to 0.6 cm deep in lines on flat beds. Germination starts after 4 days and gets completed within 7-10 days. Seedlings are ready for transplanting in 4-5 weeks; they are transplanted at a distance of 15 × 20 cm in the field.

Improved varieties are Pusa Red, Nasik Red, N-53, Red Globe, White Globe, Prize Taker, Patna Red, Rampur Red.

Celery (*Apium graveolens*)

It is a biennial long-day plant but flowers under wide range of day lengths provided the temperature is favourable for flower initiation. In the first year rosette of leaves are produced, while in the second, plant elongates to a height of 60 to 90 cm and is highly branched. Fresh green leaves are used for salad and other preparations.

Seeds after soaking overnight in water are sown in beds and take 18-25 days to germinate. The plants are uprooted for transplanting when 8-10 cm tall which take 60 to 75 days. Off-type seedlings are rejected. Planting distance in the open field is 30-45 cm × 30-45 cm.

Improved varieties are Golden Self-Blanching, Standard Bearer, Pascal, Simpson, Utah.

Asparagus (*Asparagus officianalis*)

It is a perennial crop that may go on producing good crop for 20 years or so if maintained properly. Best suited to temperate climate but can be grown where nights are cool and plants can complete their dormancy. Spears are used as vegetable, particularly for soup preparation. Fresh stems are crispy and are edible.

Plants are multiplied by seeds or rhizomes. Seeds are soaked in warm water for 60 to 80 hours to induce early and uniform germination. Water should be changed daily. They germinate in 3 to 4 weeks.

One-year old rhizomes or crowns are much preferred for transplanting.

Improved varieties are Prefection and UC-72.

Beet Root (*Beta vulgaris*)

It is a root vegetable which is used in the first year and produces rosette of leaves in the second year. The plant elongates to a height of 60 to 90 cm and is much branched. Generally, the swollen root is of red colour and is used in salad.

Turnip (*Brassica campestris* subvar. *rapa*)

Herbaceous biennial long-day plants that are best adapted to cool or moderate climate where rainfall averages between 700 and 1000 mm per annum. In the first season, there is a swollen root which is used as vegetable while the seed formation takes place in the other season.

Seeds are bold, reddish, brown and slightly swollen. They are sown directly in the field at a spacing of 15 × 15 cm and later thinned to 30 × 30 cm.

Purple Top White, Globe, Snowball, Pusa Swarnima, Pusa Chandrima are recommended varieties.

Cauliflower (*Brassica oleracea* var. *botrytis*)

Cauliflower is raised as annual crop for heads that are used as vegetable but seed crop takes one more year and hence are biennials. Seed stalks develop in the second year.

Seeds are sown in lines at a depth of 0.5 cm and about 3-5 cm apart on flat beds. Generally, the seeds start their germination after 3-5 days and complete within 7-10 days. They are uprooted when the plants are one month old, have 4-5 good leaves and their height is usually 10 to 12 cm. Planting distance in outdoor is 45-60 × 30-45 cm.

Improved varieties are Snowball, Pusa Katiki, Pusa Dipali, Improved Japanese, Early Kunwari, K-1, Early Patna, Pusa Himjyoti.

Cabbage (*Brassica oleracea* var. *capitata*)

It is a day neutral plant that is biennial when raised for seed crop. Plants produce head in the first year while seed formation takes place in the second year. Compact mass of leaves which is in the form of head is used for vegetable and salad purposes.

Seeds are sown 0.5 cm deep and 4-5 cm apart in lines in well-prepared seedbeds. Germination starts after 5 days and gets completed within 10 days. Plants are ready for transplanting within 4-5 weeks when they have 4 leaves and are 10 to 12 cm in height. Planting distance in the field is 45-60 × 30-45 cm.

Improved varieties are Pride of India, Golden Acre, Drum Head, and Copenhagen.

Brussel's Sprout (*Brassica oleracea* var. *gemmifera*)

Plants are biennial and day neutral with an erect stem of 60 to 75 cm height. Plants are hardy and can withstand freezing but need cool weather to initiate flower stalks. Heads are usually much smaller in size than the cabbage but are greenish-pink to purple in colour and are used for cooking as a vegetable.

Seeds are sown 0.5 cm deep in beds and the plants are ready for transplanting when 10-15 cm tall. Direct planting of seed in the well-prepared beds in the field is also practiced but nursery raised plants are considered better. Transplanting distance is 75 × 60 cm.

Improved varieties are Express, Z. Cross.

Broccoli (*Brassica oleracea* var. *italica*)

These are also known as Sprouting Broccoli. Plants are biennial day neutral as they normally take two seasons to produce seeds. Seed stalks develop in the second year. The sprouted flowering stalks are used for cooking as vegetable.

Seeds are very small, sown 0.2 to 0.5 cm deep in nursery beds or in polybags. They germinate in 5-10 days. Seedlings are uprooted when 15 cm tall and having 2 leaves. Planting distance in the field is 30-45 cm × 30-45 cm.

Improved varieties are Italian Green, Cleopatra, Green Duke.

Sweet Pepper (*Capsicum annum*)

These are annual plants that are raised for their fruits that are not bitter but sweet and are also known as Bell Pepper as the shape of the fruit resembles the bell. They are best suited for cold climate and they cannot tolerate frost and extreme cold, i.e. freezing.

Seeds are small, cream coloured and flat. They are sown 0.5 cm deep and 3 cm apart in lines on flat beds. Seeds start germination in about 5 days but complete germination in 10 days. Plants are ready for transplanting in about a month. Planting distance is 60 × 45 cm.

Improved varieties are California Wonder, Yellow Wonder, Bharat, Arka Mohini.

Chillies or Hot Pepper (*Capsicum fruitescens*)

Capsicum fruitescens is the main species grown in most of the areas. It is a warm season crop that is sensitive to frost. Low temperature and high humidity can cause abscission of buds and flowers and development of small fruits.

Seeds are usually flat, pale in colour, light in weight and sown 0.4 cm deep in lines. Seeds start germination after 5 days and complete it in about 10 days. Plants are ready for transplanting in about a month's time. At this time they have 4-6 leaves. Planting distance is 45 × 45 cm.

Improved varieties are Hot Portugal, Sweet Banana, Hungarian Wax, Pachad Yellow, Punjab Red, Faizabadi, Darbhanga, Golden Queen, Spanish, Nalapadu, Indore, Jwala, Bhagyalaxmi, Apama.

Melon (*Cucumus melo*)

It is also known as Musk melon or Sweet melon. Plants are day neutral and annual with trailing vines that are 1.2 to 3.6 m long. Plants are best adapted to warm climate but require somewhat higher temperature during the fruit maturation stage. Plants need frost-free growing period of 3 months. Fruits are mostly cream to yellow in colour with a pulp of about 2 to 3 cm thickness which is sweet in taste, slightly sweet-scented and are lined with seeds.

Seeds are cream to off-white in colour, flat but pointed on one side and round on the other side. They are usually 0.4-0.5 × 0.2-0.4 cm with a smooth surface. Depth of seeding is 0.5 to 1 cm in lines that may be 1 m apart. Seeds are sown directly in the field and the spacing retained for developing plants is 75-100 × 75-100 cm.

Pumpkin (*Cucurbita moschata*)

It is a crop of the tropical region but is grown successfully in the subtropical and temperate regions where the danger of frost is low. Plants can tolerate dry conditions to some extent. Plants are weak stemmed and need support and hence trail along the ground or on roofs of huts. They are annual with large velvety, broad-ovate to nearly circular-ovate green leaves. Fruits are large, often weighing 10 kg, greenish-yellow to brownish-yellow with the pulp of yellow colour and are lined below the outer hard skin. The pulp layer may be 4 to 6 cm in thickness. Seeds are lined with fibres on the pulp. Seeds are flat, bold, cream coloured and oblong with a pointed end.

2-3 seeds are sown in each polybag or pit. Depth of seeding is 1 cm. Seeds start germination after 3 days and complete it in 10 days. Only one good plant is retained per pit. Planting time and distance vary from place to place.

Improved varieties are many and vary from place to place.

Globe Artichoke (*Cynara scolymus*)

It is a perennial plant that grows best under temperate region. Edible portion is the immature bud known as heart that is round and of head-shape; in fact it is the receptacle, scale or buds of blossom buds. Artichoke is herbaceous and bushy, usually 1.5 m tall and of 1 m diameter. Stem is green, round, solid and branched. Leaves are green, thistle-like and flat.

Plants are raised by the seeds but the vegetatively propagated plants are uniform in size and produce buds of good quality. They are planted 10 cm deep in rows that are 2 to 3 m apart by keeping a distance of 1 to 1.5 m between two plants.

Improved varieties are Purple Globe.

Carrots (*Daucus carota*)

It is another root crop that is used as vegetable as the roots are rich in carotene and are tapering. Plant height is 40-50 cm as the leaves are over the ground while stem is like a disc and the roots are swollen and unbranched.

Seeds are with a fuzz and hence separated before sowing by mixing or rubbing them with sand or soil. The seeds are yellowish brown and light. They may be dibbled or spread in the field that has enough moisture and then covered with a layer of soil for easy germination. Seeds germinate in about 10 days and later the plants are thinned to 30 × 30 cm so that the root size is developed.

Early Nantes and Chanteny are improved varieties.

Lady's Finger/Okra (*Hibiscus esculentus*)

It is a tall erect annual plant that reaches to a height of 1.8 m but usually they are about 1 m in height. Plants are sensitive to frost but grow best in the regions with long growing season. Fruits are like fingers, long, tapering, ridged and usually green when fresh but on maturity they turn brown.

Seeds are bold, round, yellowish-green and light. They are directly sown in the field by dibbling method or sown in lines behind a plough. Germination of seeds is very slow rather poor, hence the spacing at the time of sowing is kept 5 to 10 cm and later plants are thinned and retained at a distance of 50-60 cm apart in rows.

Improved varieties are Pusa Sawani, Long Green, Harbhajan and P-7.

Lettuce (*Lactuca sativa*)

It is an annual long-day plant. Plants require long, warm growing season and low rainfall at harvest time. Compact heads of green colour are preferred as vegetable and for salad purposes.

Seeds are sown 0.5 to 1.0 cm deep in rows. Germination is over in a week's time. When seedlings have 4 leaves, they are thinned and transplanted. Planting distance in the field is 45 × 30 cm.

Improved varieties are Simpson, Black Seeded, Alamo-1.

Tomato (*Lycopersicon lycopersicum*)

It is long-day annual plant that grows under varied agro-climatic conditions. It is a warm season crop, intolerant to frost and high temperatures as high temperature does not favour fruiting. Fruits are of various sizes but usually of round to oblong shape and their colour is yellowish-red at the time of harvest that turns red to typical tomato. Half ripe and ripe fruits are used as vegetable.

Seeds are yellowish-green, flat, round and small. Sowing of seeds is done 0.5 to 1 cm deep and 3 cm apart in lines on flat beds. Germination is complete in about 10 days. Seedlings are uprooted when 8-10 cm tall, having 4 leaves and are usually 4 weeks old. Planting distance in the field is 60-75 × 45-60 cm. For bushy varieties the distance may be reduced, while for long and spreading varieties, it may be 75 × 75 cm.

Improved varieties are Solan Gola, Yashwant, Marathan, Roma, Rupali, Chhuara, Naveen, Money Maker, Arka Saurabh, Skew, Marglobe, Pusa Ruby, Sioux, Fire Ball.

French Beans (*Phaseolous vulgaris*)

These are the most common beans that are grown for vegetable purpose. Plants being leguminous fix the atmospheric nitrogen in the soil. These are weak stemmed plants and need support. Dwarf varieties are common. Beans as fresh and as seeds are used as vegetable in different ways.

Plants are multiplied by their seeds that are usually dibbled, 2 to 3 cm deep at a spacing of 50 cm from plant to plant and 75 cm from row to row in well-prepared field. In some cases, the seed is broadcasted in well-prepared field and later are covered with the soil as plank is run over the soil. They germinate within 10 days.

Improved varieties are Premier, Contender, Kentucky Wonder, SVM-1, Pusa Parvati, Lakshmi (P-7), V.L. Dwarf 1.

Peas (*Pisum sativum*)

Peas are leguminous crop that fixes the atmospheric nitrogen in the soil through their nodulated roots that have the ability to fix the nitrogen. Plants are with weak stem and hence need support. The fruits are pods that are green when fresh or immature. Length of pod may be 6 to 10 cm with a width of about 1.5 cm. The number of seeds in each pod may be 5 to 12.

Seeds are yellowish-white, round and 0.3 cm across. They are sown directly in the field by dibbling or by broadcasting. Depth of seeding may be 1 cm in lines. Seeds complete their germination within 10 days.

Improved varieties are Lincoln, Bonville, Boach Selection and Kinnauri.

Radish (*Raphanus sativa*)

It is an annual or biennial long-day plant that grows upto 15 to 25 cm height depending on the variety. Both leaves and roots are used as vegetable. The roots may be tapering or round but they should not be branched and should be white without wood. Sometimes the roots may be as long as 60 cm. Best suited to cool moderate climate especially in the vegetative stage.

Seeds are sown directly in the field like turnip, the depth of seeding may be 1 cm and the spacing between lines is 45-50 cm and between the plants is 30-45 cm.

Improved varieties are Japanese White, Chinese Pink, Pusa Himani and White Icicle.

Brinjal or Eggplant (*Solanum melongena*)

These are compact bushy plants growing upto 45 to 75 cm height with spreading branches. They can be raised under almost all types of climates except very harsh, as these cannot tolerate frost. Fruits are purple coloured with their shape ranging from oval to long with a slight bend. Their size is also variable, ranging 6-15 cm × 6 to 10 cm. Inner mass is of white colour. Seeds are placed in the pulp. Seeds are sown 0.5 cm deep in nursery beds, start germination after 7 days and complete within 10 days. They are ready for transplanting when 10 cm tall or having 4-6 leaves. Planting distance in the field is 60-75 × 60 cm.

Improved varieties are Pusa Purple Long, PH-4, Dwarf Pusa, Kranti, H-8, Black Beauty, Pusa Purple Round, Cluster White, Gudyattam.

Potato (*Solanum tuberosum*)

It is a tuber crop that is grown at almost every elevation from sea-coast to higher altitude in the hills, as there are many varieties that are suitable for various regions. Seed-potato production is best under temperate climate due to lack of attack of insects and pests. Since, it is a stem tuber, its colour is usually whitish-yellow and the size varies from variety to variety. Tubers are round to egg-shaped but there are some varieties that yield tubers of undesirable size and shape.

Under normal conditions, plants do not produce seeds and hence are multiplied by tubers. Tubers may be cut into pieces to have at least 2 to 3 eyes or buds on them or they may be sown as such. Small tubers are sown as such while large tubers are cut into pieces. Tubers are sown *in situ* in lines in well-prepared beds or ridges by keeping the depth of seeding from 2 to 4 cm.

Improved varieties are Kufri Kundan, Kufri Chandrima, etc.

Spinach (*Spinacia oleracea*)

It is a herb as leaves of this plant are used as vegetable in many ways. It is a rich source of Vitamin C and iron. It is an annual plant that can be grown under almost all conditions. Leaves are green, broad, flat and petioled, often 10 cm long and 8 cm wide with wavy margins.

Seeds are compressed, small with grey to brown fuzz. Seeds are usually sown *in situ*. They are broadcasted over well-prepared soil and then covered with planking. The depth of seeding is mostly 0.5 cm.

Improved varieties are Banerjee Giant, Long Standing and Virginia Savoy.

22

Ornamental Plants

These plants are planted for the sake of beautification of an area or in the house and outside the house. Some of them are grown commercially as they are used as cut flowers and as fresh flowers. According to their growing season they may be seasonal i.e., summer or rainy season, annual or perennial, bushy, shrubby, bulbous, tuberous, twining, etc. The methods of their multiplication are discussed under this chapter.

Summer and Rainy Season Annuals

These plants are multiplied by their seeds which are sown in the nursery beds. The depth of seeding depends upon the size of the seed. Almost all these plants have small seeds, they are spread over the surface of soil or the pot-mixture and then covered with a layer of well-rotten farm yard manure or compost or sand so that the emergence of plume becomes easy. Sowing of seed is done on raised seedbeds. After sowing, gentle irrigation with a fountain is given. They complete their germination within 10 days and are ready for uprooting and transplanting in 3-4 weeks. The seedlings are washed in water before planting in well-prepared beds.

Acroclinum: Popularly known as Paper Flower and also Ever Lasting flower. Plants are 40-70 cm high. Rose coloured flowers are produced profusely. For drying, fully opened flowers are plucked.

Ageratum: Plants grow upto 15-60 cm and produce flowers of blue, pink and white colour. They are very suitable for rock garden. Flowers remain fresh for long time.

Seeds complete their germination within 21 days.

Amaranthus: Plants are tall (90-120 cm) and very ornamental due to colourful (red, yellow, bronze and green) foliage. Grown in rainy season as mixed planting.

Germination of the seeds is complete within 21 days.

Anchusa: It is highly suitable for pot. Plant attains a height of 45 cm. Flowers are bright blue and produce clusters.

Seeds germinate within 2 to 3 weeks.

Antirrhinum: Popularly called as Snap Dragon or Dog Flower. Plant height varies from 30 cm to over 90 cm. Magnificent flowers are produced on long spikes in variety of colours.

Germination of seeds starts after 3 days and completes within 14 days.

Arctotis: Commonly called African Daisy. Plants are suitable for pots, beds and herbaceous border. Plants grow tall. Flowers are 4-5 cm of white colour having lilac centres. Flowers close in the night and reopen in the morning.

Seeds are sown in nursery beds where they complete their germination within 2 to 3 weeks and later transplanted on raised beds.

Aster: Dwarf (15 cm) and tall (90 cm) varieties are available. Flower size also varies from button-like to large size. Wide range of flower colours from white to scarlet are seen.

Though the seeds germinate aftcr 5 days of sowing they complete it within 21 days.

Hardy perennials may be propagated by lifting clumps in fall and dividing into rooted sections while discarding the older parts.

Balsam: Very showy annual that may be 25 to 75 cm high. Leaves are simple with serrated margins. Flowers are single or double in pure or variegated colours. The dwarf variety Tom Thumb is bushy and compact.

Brachycome: Plants are dwarf and grow upto 15-18 cm height. Flowers are small, 2.5 cm across, abundantly produced, white, blue and light pink in colour. Most suitable for pots, beds and rock gardens.

Calendula: Plants are hardy, medium in height (20-50 cm). Leaves are long. Flowers are single, semi-double and double, yellow and orange in colour and 5-7 cm across.

Seeds are hand-picked before they shatter. Seed collection is at regular intervals. Seeds complete their germination within 21 days.

California poppy: Plants grow upto 30-40 cm in height. Flowers are open, cup-shaped, single, semi-double and yellow to crimson in colour.

Cockscomb: Very popular garden flower with leaves simple and have variation, light red or crimson coloured. Flowers deep blue to crimson in colour. Dwarf to tall and suitable for pot culture.

Annual Chrysanthemum: Plants grow upto 100-120 cm height; leaves are deeply cut, of shining green colour. Numerous single, semi-double and double flowers are borne on plants.

Seeds are sown in seedbeds and they complete their germination within 35 days.

Gaillardia: It is grown throughout the year. Plants are medium to tall in size and bushy (30-45 cm). Flowers are borne profusely in many colours.

Though seeds start their germination soon after sowing they take upto 21 days to complete their germination.

Gomphrena: Plants medium or dwarf. Round flowers about 2 cm across, white to rose coloured. There is profuse flowering during the months of September-November.

Kochia: Commonly called as Summer Cypress or Burning Bush. It is very popular due to its uniform ovoid, conical or globular shape, 90-120 cm in height and 30-40 cm in spread. Plants do not produce colourful flowers.

Portulaca: It is known as Sun Plant or Rose Moss. The flowers open in morning and closes by afternoon, most ideal for pots and hanging baskets. Plants are dwarf and have trailing growth. Flowers 3 cm across and white to blue in colour.

Sunflower: Hardy, vigorous and produce magnificient flowers. In tall varieties (150-300 cm), flowers rotate with the sun movement.

Zinnia: Common flower in gardens during summer season. Flowering continues upto September-October. Plants are 25-120 cm in height. Flower size is from 2.5 to 12 cm. Flowers have variety of colours, are single, semi-double and double.

Foliage Plants

Aglaonema sinensis: Large-leaved plants. There are many species in shades of green and white with cream or silvery markings.

Propagation is by division of the basal shoots and also from terminal or node cuttings of the stem.

Alocasia: The plants of this genus have beautiful showy foliage. The plants are rhizomatus or tuberous rooted. These plants love moist and shady places.

Propagation is from one bud node cutting of stem, tubers or rhizomes.

Aluminum plant (Pilea cadierei): Green quilted leaves marked with patches of silvery sheen. Does well in filtered sunlight.

Propagated by herbaceous cuttings.

Asparagus: A group of beautiful plants, which have leathery leaves like needles of shining green colour. Can adapt to bright or semi-shade conditions but away from direct sun.

Plants are multiplied by seeds and vegetative means. Seeds are sown in nursery beds and later transplanted. Crowns of roots are used for planting.

Aspidistra: Popular indoor plant, leaves are oblong, lanceolate, 40-50 cm long and quite broad and leathery. In var. Variegata the leaves are ornamentally and alternatively striped green and white.

Propagation by division.

Begonia rex: Leaves have pink, red lavender, silver or grey markings. Tolerates wide range of temperature from 40°F to 90°F. Likes humid air.

Propagated by seeds or cuttings.

Chlorophytum: An ornamental quick-growing rosette type succulent plant, leaves are 30 cm long, strap shape, green in colour with yellow central longitudinal bands.

New plant starts from the base of the old plant.

Coleus: A perennial (sometimes annual) and herbaceous plant very commonly grown in the garden for its colourful foliage. The plants grow upto a height of 30-50 cm. Plants are grown as pot plants and window boxes.

Propagation by tip cuttings of slips from leaf axils.

Cordyline: Evergreen shrubs or trees are prized for their richly coloured foliage. These are excellent pot plants.

Plants are propagated by division of suckers. The old stems are cut into bits each containing one node or joint and placed horizontally in moist sand. Terminal cuttings also root.

Crotons: Crotons are popular ornamental shrubs with colourful attractively-shaped leaves. Grown as ornamental hedge, best suited under warm and moist climate and cannot withstand frost.

Propagation by seeds or cuttings.

Indian Rubber Plant (Ficus elastica): A good house plant but grows wild as a tree upto 30 m height. The leaves are showy, large, leathery, oblong in shape and deep green in colour.

Propagation by air layering or by cuttings.

Peperomia: Small, succulent, herbaceous, mostly perennial plant with ornamental foliage often frettly marked. Plants are suitable for hanging baskets and for table decoration.

The plants are raised from seeds but more conveniently from short stem cuttings or one-node stem cuttings.

Philodendron: Mostly shrubby creeping plant or stemless herb of great ornamental value for the foliage which is leathery, heart to egg-shaped.

Seeds germinate readily if sown soon after they ripe. They are best propagated by stem cuttings, rooting sections of main stem and by air layering.

Syzgonium: Quick growing, ornamental foliage climber, suitable for pots and trellises. The plants are quite hardy.

Propagation is easy from cuttings. The plants root from the nodes whenever it touches ground.

Tradiscantia: Low growing herb, trailing or of creeping habit, some having beautiful variegated foliage. They are good for covering rockeries.

Propagation is very easy by cuttings.

Shrubs

Acalypha: Group of shrubs bearing colourful leaves and is used for hedge and colourful shrubbery. These are quick growing and can grow in any soil.

Propagated by cuttings.

Acuba japonica: A bushy tall shrub (2-4 m), best suited for most shady situations.

Propagated by half ripened green wood cuttings or freshly harvested seeds.

Azalea: Azalea can be grown only at high elevations. It does not like lime soils. Deciduous or evergreen shrub may grow upto 3 m. White flowers.

Though propagation by seeds is possible they are best by cuttings.

Beloperone: A small shrub, which rarely grows beyond 90 cm, orderly arranged branches are very showy.

Propagation from cuttings and by air layering.

Bougainvillea: Most popular ornamental shrub is widely grown in gardens and borders. Shrubs bloom during September to December and again from February to June. Leaves are green, broad with pointed tips and strong stalks. Flowers are papery, of white, orange or red purple colour.

Multiplication of plants is by hard-wood cuttings that are collected during winter and are planted soon, and by air layering in the month of July-August and February-March.

Bottle brush or (Callistem): Small tree, 3 m tall and of weeping habit. Flowers are borne in spikes 5-10 cm long. Flowers appear during February to November. It is especially suited for plantation near the ponds and roadside or on borders.

Propagated from seeds or by layers.

Buddleia: It is a deciduous but attractive shrub with long perfect lanceolate leaves which are silvery grey borne on upright stems. Flowering is profuse in long dense panicles, composed of small flowers, pink to mauve colour and flowers during summer.

Propagated from seeds, cuttings and by layers.

Camellia: Camellia is good for planting singly or in groups in parks and gardens. Shrub or small tree sometimes grows upto 3 to 5 m in height. Leaves oval, large, shiny and deep green. Flowering season is between April and June. Flowers may be single or double and of pink, red or white colour.

Propagated from seeds, cuttings, bud cuttings or layers.

Chinese Lantern: Good shrub for medium and high elevations and attains a height of 1-1.5 m. Propagated from seeds and by cuttings. The flowers are like Hibiscus.

Duranta: A large 2.5 to 3 m tall, woody shrub with axillary spines. Small, bright green leaves, blue flowers appear in abundance. Most suitable shrub as hedge and also for topiary.

Propagated by cuttings or seeds.

Euonymus: Shrub or small tree of 1-3 m height is grown for green foliage and red coloured fruits and autumn colouring. These are mostly grown in temperate region.

Propagated by cuttings.

Hibiscus: A group of flowering perennial shrubs having many species and numerous hybrids. They bloom on current season's wood, so prune in the winters for vigorous new growth. Most popular and widely grown shrub grows upto 1-2 m tall. Plants have numerous branches.

Plants are propagated by stem cuttings.

Hydrangea: These are deciduous shrubs or small trees (60-150 cm tall) grown successfully in medium and high altitudes. Leaves are green, leathery and oval with pointed tips. The flowers appear from June to September and are borne in large (20-30 cm) round heads of white, pink and blue.

Shrub is propagated through cuttings.

Night Blooming Jasmine (*Cestrim nocturnum*): A quick-growing bushy shrub. Mostly grown for scented flowers. Creamy-yellow or greenish-yellow, small tubular flowers are produced in clusters, highly fragrant during night.

Hardy plant and is propagated by cuttings.

Bulbous Plants

Agapanthus (Blue African Lily): A plant with long (50 cm), graceful evergreen leaves. Pale blue or white tunnel-shaped, 5 cm long and borne in umbles of 10-30 flowers. Planting is done in spring for flowering during July-September.

Propagated by bulbs and seeds.

Anemone: Plants are 10 to 20 cm tall with ferny leaves. Colour of flower may be white, red-violet, pink and blue and they are daisy like. Do best on the high hills. The planting time is October in plains and autumn or spring in the hills.

Propagated by seeds and tubers. Tubers are planted 4-5 cm deep in well-prepared beds.

Caladium: A popularly grown plant valued for its highly ornamental foliage with heart-shaped leaves of different colours like white, pink, red and green and 30 cm across.

Propagated from seeds or tuberous rhizomes. Plant tubers with their pointed end towards the upper side after the frost danger is over.

Canna: Plants 45 to 180 cm tall are grown in beds especially amidst lawns. Hardy, beautiful plants bearing flowers of different shades. Flower clusters appear above substantial clumps of broad green or rich purple bronze leaves on upright plants.

Cannas are propagated by division of rhizomes planted horizontally, 2-3 cm deep with the tips pointing up.

Cyclamen: This is herbaceous low growing plant grown in high hills. Leaves are green with a purple tinge, broad, oval and long

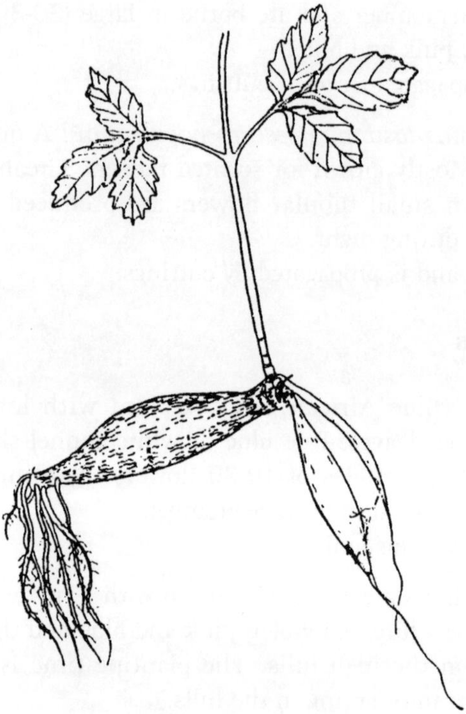

Fig. 73. Dahlia

Fig. 74. Begonia

stalked. Flowers are very large and the colour may vary from white, pink, purple to red. Generally cultivated in pots.

Propagated by seeds and corms. Corms are planted 1 cm deep by keeping the pointed end upside in early spring.

Dahlia: Most gorgeously coloured flowers, very popular in the gardens. Plant height varies from 30 to 130 cm. Flowers range from single to double and small to very large in size.

Dahlias are propagated from seeds, cuttings and tubers. Tubers are planted directly in the field (Fig. 73).

Freesia: The freesias have tubular and funnel-shaped flowers in various colours. Suitable for growing in pots, pans and beds.

Propagated by seeds or corms. Seedlings take about two years to come into flowering.

Tuberous rooted Begonia: These are exceedingly beautiful plants that can be grown in high hills. Flowers are very beautiful, resembling to rose in variety of colours but are more sensitive. Plants are generally 45 cm tall.

Plants are raised from tubers, which have pink buds and are planted with the concave side up. Avoid deep planting as they are covered with a layer of well-rotten compost or pot mixture for their easy take up (Fig. 74).

23

Cereal Crops

Mostly cereal crops are raised through seeds that a farmer produces himself in his own field but some precautions are kept in mind to keep the seed pure, healthy and of good quality. Multiplication of some important cereal crops are described here.

Oats (*Avena sativa*), Buckwheat (*Fagopyrum esculentum, F. tartaricum*), Barley (*Hordeum vulgare*), Rice (*Oryza sativa*), Millets (*Panicum* spp.), Rye (*Secale cereale*), Sorghum (*Sorghum vulgare*), Wheat (*Triticum aestivum*) and Maize (*Zea mays*) are most common cereals used in different forms throughout the world. They are part of the staple food of many people, particularly, the vegetarians. Different types of food preparations are made out of these cereals.

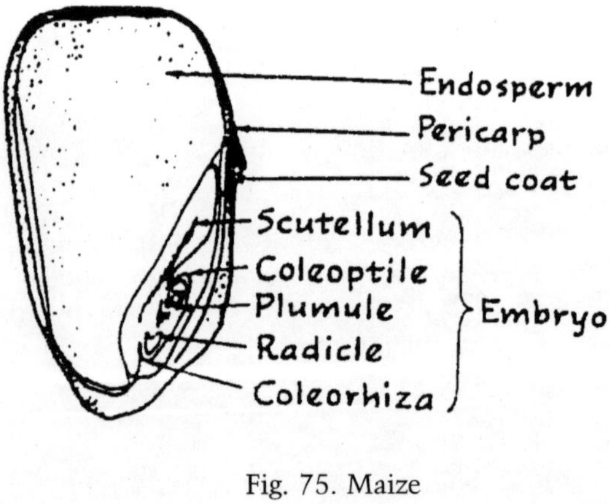

Fig. 75. Maize

Best suited for temperate region as well as for subtropical areas. Plants are usually 60 to 90 cm tall but some like sorghum and maize are 2 m tall and all are herbaceous and annual. Leaves are long, straight, upright and with pointed tips. Leaves are green and coarse in nature.

They are multiplied through the seeds that are collected from the plant ripe seeds and threshed without injuring the seeds. The seeds can be stored for 1-2 years but generally, the seed of last year's crop is used for sowing. Seeds are sown directly in the field by line sowing or dibbling method. In case of rice, the seeds are first sown in nursery beds and later transplanted in well-prepared fields that have water standing in them.

24

Miscellaneous Crops

Pigeon Pea (*Cajanus cajan*)

It is a short-day plant, which is perennial and grows 1.5 to 1.8 m with the roots going as deep as 1.8 m or more. The crop is suitable for moist tropics and more arid regions of the subtropics and tropics. Normal crop is there for 2-3 years.

Flowering is erratic and may continue for 2 months, as such the pods that have ripened are picked by hand at regular intervals. Bulk of the crop can be cut and put in bundles which are dried and threshed like cereals.

Seeds are sown in lines at spacing of 90 × 150 cm in lines when grown pure.

Chickpea (*Cicer arietinum*)

It is a herbaceous plant of legume family and grows upto 50 to 60 cm height with a spread of 40-50 cm. It is grown as mixed crop with wheat on less fertile soils where the crop is raised as rain-fed while in most areas where irrigation is available, it is raised as a pure crop. Seeds are borne in pods. There are two seeds in each pod. Ripe pods are threshed and seeds are separated from husk and kept for next year sowing.

Seeds are sown in lines by keeping 50 × 50 cm spacing. The depth of seeding is 1-2 cm. The germination gets completed within two weeks.

Lentils (*Lens culinaris*)

It is a much branched, herbaceous, long-day annual plant with weak stems growing upto 30 to 60 cm height with a spread of 30 cm or more. Mainly grown in subtropical regions.

The crop is ready within 90-100 days after sowing and the plants are cut down along with pods and placed in stacks for drying and later threshed to separate the seeds from the husk and straw.

Seeds are grey-brown, round and small. They are sown in lines about 1 cm deep and the germination gets completed within 2 weeks.

Cowpea (*Vigna* spp.)

Plants are annual, short-day and trail along the ground and need support. Plants are sensitive to frost.

Crop is harvested when all pods are brown and their seeds are ripe. They are dried under the sun and later threshed.

Seeds are quite bold and can be stored for two years under cool and dark conditions. They are sown 2 to 3 cm deep in lines. Seed germination is quick and gets completed within 10 days.

Index